ENGLISH PHILOLOGY AND STYLISTICS

Part of the fascination of Jane Austen's English is the way in which it differs, in slight and sometimes barely definable, but nevertheless unmistakable ways from our own. More of our pleasure in Jane Austen than we at first realize, perhaps comes from the charm of the language.

K. C. PHILLIPPS, *Jane Austen's English*

ENGLISH PHILOLOGY AND STYLISTICS

A Festschrift for Professor Toshiro Tanaka

EDITED BY
OSAMU IMAHAYASHI
AND
HIROJI FUKUMOTO

KEISUISHA
Hiroshima, Japan
2004

First printed in December, 2004
Published by
Keisuisha Co., Ltd.
1-4 Komachi, Naka-ku, Hiroshima 730-0041
JAPAN
ISBN4-87440-860-5

Professor Tanaka the Philologist

This festschrift was published with compliments to Professor Toshiro Tanaka, Emeritus Professor at Hiroshima University, who retired from Hiroshima University in March 2003. We would like to express our appreciation of his good and resolute character. He was born in Tottori Prefecture in 1939. After he graduated from Kurayoshi Higashi Senior High School, he entered Hiroshima University. He majored in English Language and Literature, the Faculty of Letters. Under the influence of Professor Michio Masui, D.Litt., he continued his study at the Graduate School of Letters, Hiroshima University. He was much interested in the language of English literature and especially published excellent articles concerning the language of late Modern English literature.

He studied the language of Mayhew's *London Labour and the London Poor*, in which he investigated the characteristics of the contemporary colloquial English, collecting slangs and jargons of London dialects and indicating how the word forms and syntax deviated from the norm. Then he compared the Kentish dialect of Joe Gargery in Dickens's *Great Expectations* with the language of the lower classes in London, which was described in Mayhew's *London Labour and the London Poor* and Dickens's other works. He continuously published articles dealing with the regional and social dialects in the language of English literature. The titles and dates of his papers are as follows: "The Language of Mayhew's *London Labour and the London Poor*" (1965, 1968), "Regional Dialect of Abel Magwich" (1973), "Substandard Vocabulary in *Oliver Twist*" (1974), "Substandard Grammar of *Oliver Twist*" (1975), "'Authography' in *The Yellowplush Papers*" (1977), "Cockney Consonants -With Special Reference to *The Yellowplush Papers*" (1982), and "The Language of Costermongers" (1983).

Keeping abreast of his interest in the substandard aspect of the language of English literature, he considered the sentence structure and the vocabulary of Jane Austen's works. His publications are "Free Indirect Speech in Jane Austen: With special reference to *Mansfield Park*" (1982), "The Constructions with Verbals in Jane Austen's English" (1992), "'Too Wordy' for Jane Austen" (1993), and "Double Negation in Jane Austen" (1994). His explanatory notes on *Mansfield Park* (1981-84), published by Kansai University Press, have been greatly admired by the Jane Austen scholars.

He has been actively engaged in editing and revising English dictionaries such as Taishukan's *Dictionary of English Linguistics* (1983) and Kenkyusha's *New English Japanese Dictionary* (2001). He served as Councilor of the English Literary Society of Japan (1992-95), President of Chugoku-Shikoku Branch of the English Literary Society of Japan (1998-2003), Councilor of the Modern Language Association of Japan (1994-), and President of the English Research Association of Hiroshima (1993-).

Then he presided over the Future Visionary Project Committee as chairperson, the Faculty of Letters, Hiroshima University. He was elected as Councilor (1995-99) and Dean (1999-2001) of the Faculty of Letters, Hiroshima University. Thus he has been not only a great philologist but also a capable and competent administrator at Hiroshima University. Last, but not least, it is noteworthy that he supervised a large number of postgraduate students, who contributed to the present festschrift volume. We would like to express our sincere gratitude to all the distinguished contributors for their generous contributions to this collection of essays.

Akiyuki Jimura

Hiroshima, 2004

Acknowledgements

We are particularly obliged to Professor Toshiro Tanaka who has guided us into the untrodden forests of "English" and "the Language" through literary texts from Geoffrey Chaucer to Charles Dickens. We are also indebted to the members of the English Research Association of Hiroshima for contributing this collection of essays. We are so grateful to Keisuisha Co. Ltd., Hiroshima for giving us an excellent opportunity to publish this festschrift.

Editors

List of Contributors

AKIYUKI JIMURA
Professor at Hiroshima University

YOSHIHIRO SHINODA
Professor at Hiroshima Women's University

MASAHIKO KANNO
Professor Emeritus at Aichi University of Education

YOSHIYUKI NAKAO
Professor at Hiroshima University

HIDESHI OHNO
Associated Professor at Kurashiki University of Sciences and Arts

HIROYUKI MATSUMOTO
Professor at Toyota Institute of Technology

NAOKI HIRAYAMA
Postgraduate Student at Hiroshima University

KAZUKO MATSUURA
Lecturer at Okayama University of Science

MASARU KOSAKO
Professor at Okayama University

SHIGENOBU FUAMI
Professor at Ohtani Women's University

HIROJI FUKUMOTO
Associated Professor at Tottori University

AKEMI SASAKI
Postgraduate Student at Hiroshima University

SEIICHI IKADATSU
Professor at Tottori University

EIKO TATSUMOTO
Postgraduate Student at Hiroshima University

MIYUKI NISHIO
Lecturer at Kibi International University

OSAMU IMAHAYASHI
Associated Professor at Kibi International University

SAOKO TOMITA
Lecturer at Fukuoka University

KEN NAKAGAWA
Professor at Yasuda Women's University

ETSUKO YOSHIDA
Associated Professor at Mie University

HIROYUKI SAKAUCHI
Lecturer at Kure National College of Technology

Contents

A Case of Lexical Convergence specially referring to the relations between words and their etymological meanings with the appendix of the "D" Entries in "A Glossary of the *Cursor Mundi*"

Yoshihiro Shinoda

1. The texts of the *Cursor Mundi*

(1) Richard Morris ed. EETS seven vols. OS. 57, 59, 62, 66, 68, 99, 101 (1874-93)
(2) J.A.W. Bennett and G.V. Smithers eds., *Early Middle English Verse and Prose* with *a Glossary* by Norman Davis, 2nd ed. Oxford at The Clarendon Press, 1968. Pp. 184-195.
(3) Sarah M. Horrall and et al. eds., *The Southern Version of Cursor Mundi*. The University of Ottawa Press. Vol. I, 1978.Vol. II, 1960. Vol. III, 1985. Vol. IV, 1986. Vol.V, 2000. (21347-23898; General Introduction) in hand of Laurence Eldrege at Oxford and Anne L. Klinck at Unviersity of New Brunswick). *The Glossary* is in charge of Professor A.L. Klinck.

2. The date and the provenance of the source manuscripts

(1) Datc: 1275-1325
(2) Provenance: Northumberland (Otto Strandberg). Cf. Durham (Sarah M. Horrall)
(3) Manuscripts:
  (a) Cotton Vespasian A. iii. (British Library): West Riding, Yorkshire
  (b) Göttingen theol.107: West Riding, Yorkshire
  (c) Fairfax 14: Lancaster
  (d) Trinity College Cambridge r.3.8: Lichfield

The occurrence of *stang* is remarkable. The word is a regional dialect word only found in Ripon. MED. sv. *stang* (a) first quotation from (1379-80) *Mem. Ripon* in *Sur. Soc*. 81, second quotation from (a1325) *Cursor* 15440. *Ibid*. 24029. *Ibid*. (Frf.) 21144. From the fact that it is found only in Ripon it may be suggested that the place where the *Cursor Mundi* was produced will be in the neighbourhood of Ripon or thereabout.

3. *Inglis tong* as a most popular speech

þis ilk bok is es translate
In to Inglis tong to rede
For the loue of inglis lede,
Inglis lede of Ingland
For the commun at understand.
Frankis rimes here I redd,
Communlik in ilka sted,
Mast es it wroght for frankis man:
Quat is for him na frankis can?
Of Ingland the nacion,
Es Inglis man þar in commun
þe speche þat man wit mast may spede,
Mast þar-wit to speke war nede; (232-44)

This passage suggests the way in which bilingualism was made use of among the people in the northern dialect area. Undeniably French still remained prevalent. It was a language commonly relied upon whenever people needed to understand highly sophisticated concepts either literary or non-literary. What is noteworthy in this passage, however, is that this is the evidence which historically first refers to the rising necessity of English as a native tongue toward assuming the social function which French had taken on the side of those people who were ignorant of French. Some explanation will be required about this linguistic condition. We do not say that the two linguistic communities were differentiated. We would rather say that as English and French were closer to each other, the former in particular became more influenced from the latter. Through this interactions, the speakers of English felt the pride and confidence that they should hold English and attempt to accommodate borrowed concepts into their own. The occupational terms will be a good indication of the interactions, because one of the most popular vocabulary originally borrowed from French was occupational terms. French words in high rank are *baron*, *commandur*, *gouernur*, *aduocate*, whereas the words such as *gardiner*, *iogolour*, *marchand*, *porter*, and *harlot* commonly used or understood in parallel with the native words such as *burwimmen*, *handwoman*, *chapman*, *potter*, *keper*, *wright* in the daily scene. Words of Old Norse were found in the illegal scene. We have Old Norse words: *okerer*, *vtelau*, *scald*, *suain*, *thrall*, *hore*. The following diagram shows how the occupational terms could be distributed according to the social scale.

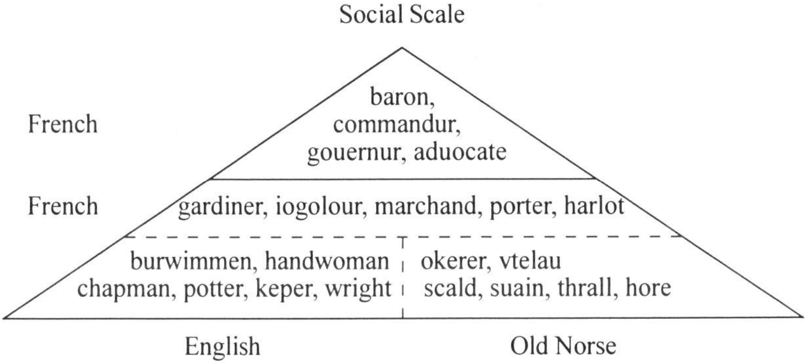

4. A Case of Lexical Convergence

It may be expected that linguistic interactions will cause the convergence in the lexical level. This problem is vitally important to deal with in making a glossary in the *Cursor Mundi*. The objective of this paper here is to show how the convergence takes place in certain words of our text. In prior to the case of convergence, we have to deal with cases of uncertainty first. For the convenience sake, the cases of uncertainty will be divided into (1) a case of errors (2) a case of uncertainty, and (3) a case of submergence.

(1) A Case of Errors

We may expect that erroneous forms could have occurred in the original source language. The comparison of the extant manuscripts of the *Cursor Mundi* makes it easy to recognize the erroneous forms. There are 78 erroneous forms in the text. They are:

> *þe* for *be* (27442), *best* for *bes* (23201), *hirth* for *birth* (3428), *bogh* for *dogh* (27656), *ald* for *cald* (20972), *chance* for *change* (16451), *thar* for *char* (4657), *clahtyng* for *clathyng* (4655), *knyue* for *clyue* (1856), *craf* for *craft* (22163, 27568), *dampaid* for *dampnid* (20888), *dai* for *dar* (23807), *dei* for *drei* (28655), *drif* for *drift* (9932), *dight* for *dright* (18532), *entens* for *entents* (365), *eien* for *eren* (19452), *ouer* for *euer* (3982), *fald* for *fall* (9467), *feis* for *feirs* (27250), *ferekin* for *felekin* (21), *firir* for *firin* (995), *gert* for *gret* (18524), *grund-wald* for *grund-wal* (9990), *hald* for *hale* (26340), *ne* for *he* (16964), *heiis* for *heries* (26026), *heit* for *hert* (9976), *here* for *hert* (19013), *il* for *it* (22439), *kiddli* for *kindli* (2370), *kinthe* for *knithe* (4515), *land* for *laued* (22001), *lauer* for *lauerd* (2644), *lauueding* for *lauerding* (2970), *leth* for *lech* (26322), *heft* for *left* (9462),

henthid for *lenthid* (21099), *liue* for *lift* (2568), *hight* for *light* (22392), *libyng* for *likyng* (28080), *litted* for *little* (18236), *mikes* for *mikel* (26113), *mistring* for *mistrowing* (4841), *nym* for *myn* (28702), *mai* for *nai* (24670), *nars* for *nais* (989), *nett* for *nete* (4597), *neus* for *treus* (26768), *noghti* for *noght* (4343), *noght* for *north* (22330), *þou* for *nou* (3589), *ouengart* for *ongart*/ *overgart* (478), *priuete* for *pouerte* (19058), *purchad* for *purchased* (29308), *Qua* for *Quat* (23853), *quar* for *quat* (2804), *reuthnes* for *rethnes* (24843), *roued* for *roned* (28110), *sa* for *sai* (18426), *sco* for *scop* (15483), *striueyng* for *scriueyng* (28122), *felli* for *selli* (12535), *sertles* for *settles* (13938), *snaip* for *snarp* (7753), *soght* for *soft* (3796), *songyng* for *sognyng* (28123), *vnserenes* for *vnferenes* (8174), *vp-pais* for *vn-pais* (21970), *wat* for *war* (1613), *wa* for *was* (24448), *wel* for *weld* (3108), *wend* for *werd* (27769), *werd* for *werld* (3108), *wil* for wit (3115), *wirche* for *wrecche* (4707).

(2) A Case of Uncertainty

There are cases which we can not recognize as erroneous because words themselves have their varieties of spelling forms. Such variant forms may also have been caused through the transmission of the copied texts. Charles C.V. Ross and Sarah M. Horrall postulate the stems of the transmitted texts of the *Cursor Mundi*.

(a) Charles C.V. Ross (b) Sarah M. Horrall

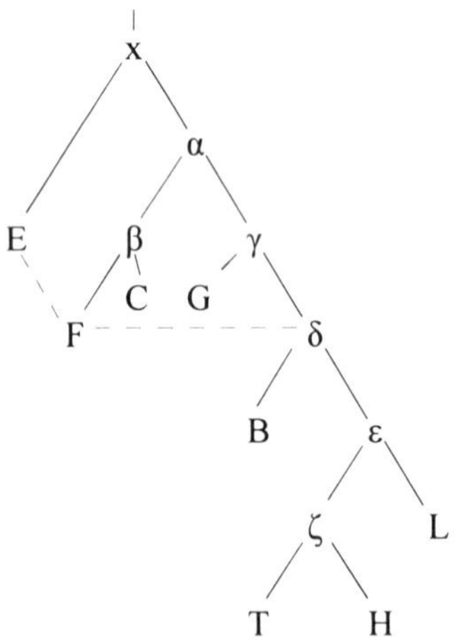

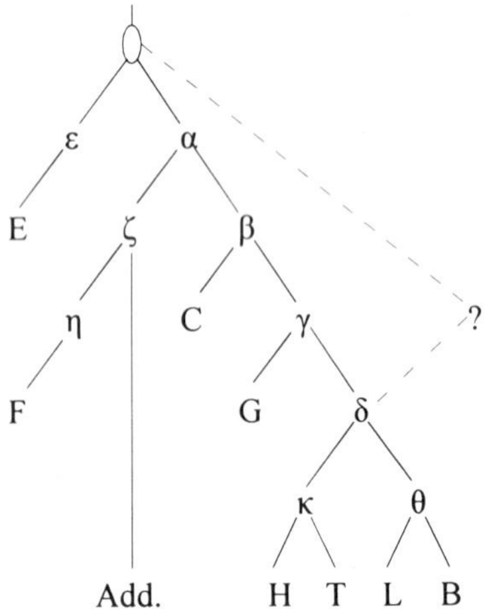

Charles C.V. Ross argues in his Oxford B.Litt thesis published in 1971 that MSS.Cotton and Fairfax differentiate from MSS. Götingen and Trinity in the source line, whereas Sarah M. Horrall insists that MS. Fairfax differentiates from MSS. Cotton, Göttingen, and Trinity at the earlier stages of the text transmission. MS. Fairfax takes the unique position in the stem in her tree system. We have the word *turnsum* as a typical example.

This word occurs once in a while in the text. It is in the line 26350.

> Wrei and *turnsum*, propre, stedfast,
> Ernext, willi, buxum, sothfast (26350-51)
> F: wreiande *tomsome* propre stedfast

MS. Cotton reads *turnsum*, while Fairfax reads *tomsome*. If the two manuscripts are closely related and have the same copy text line, we could understand that the author of the Fairfax MS. could rewrite the earlier *turnsum* into the correct form *tomsome*. On the contrary, according to Sarah M.Horrall's stem, MS.Cotton's *turnsum* could be regarded as a word form existing for itself at least at the time when the author attempted to compose the manuscript, because the two manuscripts does not share a close text line. It is very interesting to see that OED and MED. treat this word differently. OED infers that *turnsum* is an error for *tomsome* originally intended to mean "leisurely, free from hast". OED sv. *toomsome*. MED. recognizes *turnsum* as a word and infers that its intended meaning is "? Easy to convert, receptive to persuasion".

(3) A Case of Submergence

The case of submergence should be different from that of convergence. For example we have the word *dede*. In the Northern dialect the voiceless fricative /θ/ changed into the voiced sound /d/. The word *deþ* "death"and the word *ded* "deed" have the same written form. Accordingly the submergence easily takes place in such a written form *dede* as in

> Mi fete, mi hend, o blod er red
> Wit-outen right thol I *þis ded*. (20075-76)

Either of the two different words "death" and "deed" will be prominent or subdued in this written form *þis ded*. We can not say whether this linguistic phenomenon is intentional or unintentional. All we have to say is that the submergence will be unavoidable because of the dialectal conditions.

We also have the verb *band* (24361),which occurs in the following passage:

> Sua luue vs sammen *band*.
> þe luue þat mar mai lei
> þe dome vs did to-gedir drei (24361-4)
> F: squa loue vs sammen *bande*.
> G: Sua luue vs samen *band*!

The verb *band* may either be in the pret.3rd.pers.singular or in the subjunctive present. There is not enough evidence to approve the existence of the verb *band* directly derived from the noun *band*. According to the OED the verb derivative appears first in late 15th century. OED sv. *band* v.1[a. F. *bander*]. MED. shows that the verb *bonden* only occurs in 1500 (a.1460) Towneley Pl. Though the recorded evidence may not support the existence of the verb *band* in early 14th century, the optative makes sense in this context.
(4) A Case of Convergence
We have a following example.

> Wodd and wall al dun sal drau
> O demester þat dred-ful au. (22543-44: emphasis added)
> Cf. Edinburgh MS.: derful.

The noun phrase demester þat dread-ful au is built upon the two different words directly linked without any other element. It seems that the synonymous combination of the different word origins will be realized to strengthen the meaning which the noun phrase implies. But the word *au* ,ON. *agi* means "restraint, constraint" in the original sense. Dreadful restraint (constraint) may have originally been meant. If so, *al dun sal drau* will be paraphrased as "all shall hold back themselves, or all shall subdue themselves."

Then in the noun phrase mentioned above the two different senses are compressed, that is (1) the OE. sense: the dreadful look of the judge and (2) the ON. sense: the instantaneous reaction caused by restraint on the side of *wood and wall* as if they were personified. The OE. and ON. senses will be converged in the word *au*. *Au* in the ON sense is not so rarely used. The *Cursor Mundi* uses it in the adverbial phrase. *Vnder þair au* is "under their control."

> Vr flexs, þis werld, and þe warlau,
> We ar bunden *vnder þair au*.(23746-7)

The following is another example.

> Sun and mone had tint þair light
> þat al þis werld es turnd to night,
> *þat soru to see was ful gret au*. (1771-3)

The *au* occurs 36 times in the *Cursor Mundi*. "Reverence" is the main sense of this word. It very often takes the impersonal construction: *þam stode of him ful mikel au* (7474), *þai þat of him standes au* (22452), *Of he, drightin, stod þe nan au* (7945), *All behouis him standes au* (24995), *of him me standes au* (18050), *Him sal of stand sa mikel au* (22393), *þat al thing of standes au* (22713). They all describes God's creativity or the predestination which he ordains us human beings. The personal construction occurs only three times. They are: *It semes o godd has he nan au* (13806), *ye ber him right nan au* (12096) and *þat helt þam fra almens au* (6988).

The *au* in either OE. sense or ON. sense takes the phrasal construction. Thus, we have *wit gift or au*(22175), *wit-vten au* (16000), (19478), (19427), *a stret of au* (22691), *wit thret and au* (27304), *for dred and au* (19267), *under romes au* (22243), *bunden vnder þair au* (23748), *wit mikel au* (18168).

Lexical convergence is one of the serious linguistic phenomena wherever at least any two language coexists and interacts with each other for a certain length of time. Two words of equivalent semantic import are put in opposing conflicts until either of them will remain, casting away its opponent. It will accommodate the opponent's sense into its own domain in the way toward the diversified signification.

Appendix: The "D" Entries in "A Glossary of the *Cursor Mundi*" (EETS Texts, lines 1-29547)

This complete list of the "D"entries in "A Glossary of the *Cursor Mundi*" is compiled from the collection of the cards which contain all the forms of the words and their own senses attached with the full sentences in the texts of the *Cursor Mundi* Cotton Vespasian A. iii.(British Library) edited by Richard Morris for EETS parts 1-5. Though there are errors and mistakes in the texts, we hope that the comparison with the other texts of the same work as well as referring to the Ottawa Group's work will be a good guide to make us notice where they may take place. To be honest, we had to rely upon Richard Morris's edited texts because the description in the cards started more than two decades ago when we had no other textual editions of *Cursor Mundi* yet.

The concept of *A Glossary* is mainly based upon the suggestions of Professor Douglas Gray (Lady Margaret Hall, Oxford). Under Entry every word and form will be treated to specify its grammatical distinctions. In the case of nouns singular forms and plural forms are distinguished. In the case of verbs the inflections of infinitive, tense, case and number are specified. Frequency of occurrence is also a necessary component under Entry. Any word and its variant forms shown in bold type occurs with the numerical indication of frequency in brackets; the numerical indication otherwise shown is the line number where the word or form in question takes place in the text. Close to the entry are shown the senses. The senses given here are based upon the OED definitions. They are organized in the way commoner or principal meanings should be brought in prior to strange or isolating ones which can be observed only in the given contexts. The examples shown in line numbers are chosen to illuminate the senses required in the context where they occur in the text. Etymology is given, though in the simple way, to allow the tracing of any word and its meaning into earlier stages of the language. The main sources are OED and *Oxford Etymological Dictionary*.

Dai *n. sg.* (339), **day** (32); *pl.* **dais** (92), **daies** (2), **days** (2), **dayes** (2); sg. **dau** (11), **daus** pl. (7), **dauus** (1) day 21877, the time during which anything happens 4082, 6943, 29081, judgement day 27362, used in a exclamatory sentence 4381, *to bring, do of dau* kill 2932, 14533, 19477, 4168. [OE. *dæʒ*]
Dai-gang n. (1), **dai-ganges** pl. (1) a day's journey 11742, 5842.
Dainte n. (1) delightfulness; sumptuousness. 3655. [OF. *deintié*]
Dale n. (12), **dales** pl. (1) a valley 405, 1251, 13464, 18630, 22532, 22565. [OE. *dæl*]
Dame n. (13) title of a lady or woman of rank. 23719, etc. [OF. *dame*]
Damisel n. (1) young unmarried lady 3835. [OF. *dameisele*]
Damp vb. (1) pronounce adverse judgement 13756; **dampaid** (error) pt. condemned particular penalty or fate 20888; **dampned** pp. (4) doomed to eternal punishment in the world to come, condemned to hell 59, 14488, 16814, 18298. [OF. *dampner*]
Dampnacion n. (2) condemnation 16455, **dampnacioun** (1) 12775, **dampnaciun** (1) the act of condemning 14491. [OF. *damnation*]
Dan n. (1) title of a distinguished person 13291. [OF. *dan*]
Danais adj. Danish 24796. [OE. *denisć*]
Danis n. gen. (2) of a Dane 21975. [ON. *Danir*]
Dantand pr. p. (1) intimidating 21343. [OF: *danter*]
Dare vb. (1) be in dismay, tremble with fear 25444. [OE. *darian*]
Darworthi adj. (1), **derworthi** (1) worthy. esteemed 4731. [ME. formation from *dearworth*]
Dathait interj. (1) curse upon 5867. [OF. *dahet*]
Debonerli adv. (1) in a deboair manner, meekly, gently, graciously 23872. [OF: *debonaire + -ly*]
Deceueid pp. (2), **deceuid** (1) tricked 3172. [OF. *deceveir*]
Ded adj. (126), **dede** (13), as noun **ded** (9), **dede** (1) dead. Forms **ded** 2289, 3452, 4152, 4602, 4717, 5920, 6938, 7771, 8536, 8605, 12028, 12039, 14234, 14255, 15473, 17394, 18562, 18646, 19258, 20235, 21054, 21071, 23313, 24598, 24982, 26559, etc.; **dede** 2990, 11506, 11874, 17374, 17991, 18028, 18598, 20357, 27856, 28329, 28661, 29411; adj. as n. 8687, 12261, 18107, 18187, 18545, 20883, 21652, 22153, 24515, 25074, 29354. [OE. *déad*]
Ded n. (144), **dede** (22), **deid** (2), **did** (1) death 23123; dying 835; *dome o dede* dreadful doom 22971; *to ded* to the uttermost 13070; danger, peril, hurt 26193. [OE. *déaþ*, ON. *dauðr.*]
Dedeigne n. (1) scorn, contempt 11309. [OF. *desdeign, -dagn*]
Dedis n. pl. (35), **dedes** (18) deeds (often contrasted with words) 43, 8323. [OE. *dǽd*]
Dedli adj. (19), **dedly** (4) mortal 10919. [OE. *deadlic*]
Dedman n. (4), **dedmen** pl. (1) a deadman 11504, 12500.
Defaut n. (9), **defaute** (1) absence or want 1718, 26638, 4601, 4760, 20702, 13354; phr. *for defaut of* 26638, *haue defaut of* 1718, 20702; failure in duty, care, etc. 26241. [OF. *defaute*]
Defend vb. inf. (6), **defend** pp. (1) keep safe from assault 12965, 21802, 26979; prohibited, forbidden 21764. [OF. *defendre*]
Deghteres n. pl. (1) daughters 9623.

Dei inf. vb. (73), **de** (1), **dee** (1); 3rd. pl. **dees** (1), **deis** (2); pt. **deed** (4), **deid** (13), **deied** (7), pr. p. **deiand** (1) die 660, 768, 4703, 4831, 13320, 17153, 18593, 25055, 25850; *dei o duble ded* die a condemned death 660, *deid thoru hunger* starved to death 4703. [ON. *deyja*]

Deken n. gen. (1), **dekens** pl. (1) high officers 19482, applied to the Levites 7009. [L. *diacōnus*]

Delaiance n. (1) delaying 26134. [OF. *delaince, delayance*]

Delaid pp. (1) postponed 25192. [OF. *delaier, delayer*]

Dele n. (13), **del** (2) portion or section 23796; a quantity or amount 13493; adverbial uses *a dele* 23332; *ilk a dele* 26671 [OE. *dǽl*]

Dele vb. inf. (20), **del** (3), **deles** 3rd. pl. (3), **delt** pt. (19), **delt** pp. (24) divide 2262, 4033, 8739, 10384, 13497, 22927, 29542; bestow, render 22411; concern oneself with 1983; engage with in conflict 4301; associate with 12249; treat 26299; negotiate or treat with 28410; apportion 21289. [OE. *dǽlan*]

Delices n. pl. (1) sensual pleasure 23285 [OF. *delice*]

Delite n. (5), pl. **delites** (1) pleasure, joy, intense pleasure 21933, 23627; object of delight 27967. [OF. *delit*]

Delue vb. inf. (6), **delf** (2), pt. **delfd** (1), **delued** (2), pp. **deluen** (4), **doluen** (11) dig 4676, 21360, 21530; bury 8000, 14212, 16541; allit. phr. *ded and doluen* 24978, 14212. [OE. *delfan*]

Deme vb. inf. (38), **demes** vb. 3rd. sg. (1), imperat. (1), **demed** pt. (5), **dempt** pt. (6), **demyd** pt. (1), **demed** pp. (4), **dempt** pp. (18) rule as a judge 7016; decree or ordain 21445, 22530; form the opinion 26814; doom or condemn 14515, 23000, 25735; judge, give a sentence on 28178; fig. pass adverse judgement upon 28148. [OE. *deman*]

Demester n. sg. (8), **demestere** (1), **demesters** pl. (1) a judge 22712, 29225. [See OED *deemster*]

Demmyng vbl. n. (1) damming 1908. [OE. *demman*]

Dempster n. (5), **demmepster** (1) a judge 5670, 9737, 22537. [See **demester**]

Den n. (4), **denn** (1) cavern, habitation of a wild beast 24421, 4185, 27287. [OE. *dęnn*]

Denunced pp. (1) proclaimed, declared 29251. [OF. *denoncier, -noncer*]

Depe adj. (8), **dipe** (2) deep. 9899, 24071.

Depe adv. (8), **dipe** (1) deeply 494, 21531; fig. profoundly, earnestly 8269, 23447. [OE. *díope, déope*]

Depeli adv. (1) seriously, solemnly 10697.

Derai n. (1) violence, injury 23346. [OF. *desrei, desrai*]

Dere adj. (90), **der** (8) dear, beloved 560, 4219, 20162, 24183; adj. as noun (1) dear one 13086. [OE. *déore*]

Dere adv. (9), **der** (2) at a high price 1146, 13061, 20230.

Dere n. (2) a beast 3602 [OE. *dior, deor*]

Dere flesse n. (1) venison 3603.

Dere vb. inf. (4), **der** (1), vb. 3rd. sg. **ders** (2) hurt, harm, injure 692, 7731, 10014, 12061, 20224, 23469, 23670. [OE. *derian*]

Dereli adj. (1) dear 3700 [nonce formation from *dear + -ly*]

Derf adj. (5) bold, audacious, wicked 27749, 25451; adj. as noun 12936. [ON. *djarfr*]

Derfli adj. (1), **derfly** (1) terrible, grievous 1143, 7182. [See OED *derfly*]

Derfnes n. (1) trouble, hardship 3996.

Derling n. (3) **derlinges** pl. (1) a beloved person 24568. [OE. *deorling*]

Dern adj. (9), **derne** (1) charged with hidden matters 6509; alliter. phr. *ful dern and dere* 6509, *dern and hidd* 22739.

Dern n. (5) secrecy, concealment 8447, 17607, 21250, 2935; regularly in phr. *in dern* secretly. [OE. *derne*]

Derner n. (1), **dirner** (1) lintel of a door 2935. [etymology unknown]

Dernhede n. (1) secret, privity 18454.

Derth n. (1) famine 4700.

Derworthli adv. (6), **darworthli** (2) worthily, honourably, preciously 13669, 15010, 19470. [*dearworth* + *-ly*]
Des n. (2) A raised table in a hall 12560, 29335. [OF. *deis*]
Descend vb. inf. (5) come or go down, fall 10884, 22499. [F. *descendre*]
Deserit vb. inf. (1), **diserit** (1) disinherit 5358, 5508. [OF. *disheriter*]
Desire vb. (1), **desird** pt. (1), **desired** (1), **desirred** (1), **desird** pp. (1); wish 788, (pp. as adj.) desirous 28505; constr. with inf. *desired it to haue in weild* 788, phr. *desird o* longing for 28505. [OF. *desirer*]
Despite n. (12), **despit** (6), **despijt** (1), **despitte** (1) contempt, scorn, disdain 2037, 10394, 12085, 18232, 21913; phr. *haue despite o* 2037. [OF. *despit*]
Desseli adv. (3), **desselic** (1) continuously 19033, 26881, 11406. [etymology unknown]
Destru inf. (3), **destrui** (1), imper. **Destru** (1), **destrued** pp. (1) undo, demolish 9670, 22133, 22348, 25239. [OF. *destruire*]
Detours pl. (1), **detturs** (1), **deturs** (1) debtors 25110, 25300, 25399. [OF. *dettor, -ur, -our*]
Dett n. (14), **dete** (2), **dette** (2), **dede** (1); **dettes** pl. (2) obligation 6469, 7642, 18734, 25109; *wit dede* as is due or right 23886, 26167. [OF. *dete, dette*]
Deu n. (3), **dew** (2) dew 3760, 17682, 18112, 22464. [OE. *déaw*]
Deueli adv. (1) devilishly 14392. [OE. *déofollic*]
Deuer n. (1) duty, business, appointed task 21901; phr. *do þair deuer* do their business. [OF. *deveir*]
Deuis vb. (2), **deuise** (1), **deuised** pt. (1) describe 8979, 9895. [OF. *deviser*]
Deuise n. (1) will, pleasure 11576.
Deuocion n. (2) devotion 29077. [OF. *devocion, -ciun, -tiun*]
Deuote pp. (1) given to divine worship 29109. [OF. *devot*]
Diademe n. (1) royal or imperial diginity, worthiness 22357. [OF. *dyademe*]
Dight inf. vb. (23), **dightid** pt. (1), **diȝt** pt (1), **dight** pp. (20), **diȝt** pp. (1). appoint, ordain 25721; compose 12388, 26731; deal with, handle 21447; dispose, remove 11854; amend, put to right 19755; arrange 3364; make ready, prepare 24944; dress, decorate, adorn 24552. [OE. *dihtan*]
Dignite n. (4) worthiness, nobility, excellence 330, 22249, 27170; phr. *þe dignite o rome Imparre* 22249, *man of dignite* 27170. [OF. *dignete*]
Dil vb. inf. (3), **dill** (3), **dild** pt (1) keep secret, conceal 4271, 9292. [ON. *dylja*]
Dill adj. (2), **dil** (1) sluggish, slow, stupid, dull 17225, 23622, 27238; phr. *yong man idel, ald man dill.* [early form of *dull*]
Dim adj. (6) dark, gloomy 23, 16762, 18071, 24418; of eyesight, not seeing clearly 3570. [OE. *dim*]
Dime vb. inf. (1) grow dark 23695.
Din n. (2) a loud noise 6606, 23253. [ON. *duna*, OE. *dyne*]
Dind vb. pt. (1) sounded, resounded 1770; pr. p. **diming** (1) dinning 18630. [OE. *dynnan, dynian*]
Dinere n. (1) dinner, formal meal 3508. [OF. *diner*]
Dint n. (17), **dintes** pl. (4) stroke, blow 6108, 12184, 20990, 21682, 23237, 23239, 27732. [OE. *dynt*]
Dint pp. (1) struck, knocked 4302. [ME. *dynten*]
Dische n. (3), **diss** (1) dish 26368, 13159. [OE. *disc*]
Disciple n. (5), pl. **disciplis** (34), **discipleis** (1), **disciples** (2), **discipls** (1), **disciplus** (1) follower or the followers of Jesus Christ 21032, 24260. [L. *discipulus*]
Disciplin n. (1), **discipline** (1) mortification of the flesh by penance 23289, 29087. [OF. *discipline*]
Discord inf. (1) quarrel 23640. [OF. *descorder*]
Discord n. (4) discord, variance 22223,

24594, 27604; phr. *discord and strijf* variance, disagreement 22223. [OF. *descord, descort*]
Discouerd pp. (1) revealed, disclosed 28293. [OF. *descovir, descourvrir*]
Discreue vb. inf. (1) write down, inscribe 12245. [OF. *descrivre*]
Discumfit pp. (1) defeated, overthrown completely 7799; constr. with *discumfit wit þair fas*. [OF. *desconfit*]
Discurer n. (1) informer 27469. [OF. *descourvreur*]
Dishonur n. (1) vb. phr. *do dishonour to* impair the honour 27201. [OF. *deshonor*]
Dispraise vb. inf. (1) blame, censure. 27585; opposite to *upraise* as in "we agh ilk man upraise, And in vr hert vrself dispraise". [OF. *despreisier*]
Disput n. (1) debate, disagreement 20793.
Disputed pt. (2), **desputand** pr. p. (1) discussed, debated, holding disputation; constr. with *disputed wit* (a man). [OF. *desputer*]
Disputisun n. (1) disputation. [OF. *desputeisun*]
Dissenciun n. (2) destress, strain 22221. [F. *dissension*]
Distresse n. (1) strain, stress, pressure. 28360; phr. *vte of distresse* free from stress. [OF. *destrece*]
Disur n. (1) 27932. A story-teller, a jester. [OF. *disour*]
Ditt vb. inf. (4), **ditte** vb. (2), **ditted** pt. (1) shut, stop the course of 6726, 11942, 12019, 17284, 17438, 19452, 24003. [OE. *dyttan*]
Diuers adj. (3), **diuerse** (1) different, diverse 11054, 21808, 21277, 22098. [OF. divers]
Diuersli adv. (1) differently, diversely 21807.
Do I. Forms. **do** inf. (298), **don** (8), **done** (1); **do** ind. pres. (15), subj. (39), imper. (75), aux. (4); **dos** ind. pres. 3rd . sg. (84), 3rd. pl. (13), imper. 2nd. sg. (5), 2nd. pl. (12), interrogat. 2nd. sg. (9), 2nd. pl. (13); **dose** ind. pres. 3rd. pl. (2), imper. 2nd. sg. (1); **did** ind. pt. (372), subj. (6), aux. (5); **didd** ind. pt. (2); **dide** ind. pt. (10); **didest** ind. pt. (1); **ded** ind. pt. (1); **dede** (1); **doand** pr. p. (5); **dun** pp. (1); **don** pp. (233); **done** pp. (4). II. Functions 1. vb. intr. **do** (28), **did** (8) 2. vb. trans. **do** (184), **did** (145), **didd** (1), **dide** (2), **didest** (1) 3. vb. caus. **do** (123), **did** (169), **dide** (5) 4. vb. aux. **do** (14), **did** (5) 5. vb. substit. **do** (20), **did** (6), **didd** (1), **dide** (3). III. Senses 1. put, place 618, 21705, 2. refl. set oneself, proceed, go 14566, 3. render, administer, pay, extend, exhibit 24058, 4. show, bring to pass 257, 17288, 23840, 5. commit 26798, 6. perform duly 11306, 28251, 7. accomplish, complete, finish, bring to a conclusion 20319, 8. put forth, exert 14480, 9. make or cause a person to do 3071, 28803, 10. in the imperative positive, expressing entreaty 4893, 12049, 11. *do with*, deal with, have to do with 27220, 12. *do awai* put away, dismiss, remove 2679, 13. *do in* put in 2915, 11411, 28430, 14. *do wai* leave off, let alone, cease 12047, 17518, 18967, 19671, 15. *do of* put out of, deprive of, rid of 13243, 16. *do with* ill treat (?) 2786, 17. *do again* put back 4478, 18. *do males* do wrong 2794, 19. *do well* prosper, thrive 13492, 20. *do (a person) at vnderstand* inform 24894, 21. *do up* raise 17320, 22. *do boute* be of service, do good 4734. *doand* being done 26812. [OE. *don*]
Doer n. gen. (1) actor's 27678.
Doght vb. pt (2), **dught** (2) was of use or profit to, availed 10771, 16204, 16538, 23771; impers. constr. 10771, 16204. [OE. *duȝan*]
Dome n. (57), **dom** (24) judgement, decision 21700, 22406. [OE. *dom*]
Donfall n. (1), **dunfall** (1) down fall 280, 11365.
Donheild n. (2), **dunheild** (2), **doun heild** (1) decline 3112, 3822, 5468, 6431, 8134. phr. *at dun heild*, in decline 3822.
Dorward n. (1) door-keeper 29368. [OE.

duru + OE. *weard*]
Dozein n. (1) **dozen** 11407. [OF. *dozeine*]
Draght n. (2) burden 21266. [OE. *draht*]
Dragun n. (1), pl. **dragons** (5), **draguns** (1) dragon 23227. [OF. *dragon*]
Drau I. Forms **drau** inf. (31), **draw** (5), **drawe** (1); vb. **drau** (7), **draues** (1), **draus** (12), **drawes** (1), **draws** (1); **drau** subj. (1); pt. **draue** (1), **drogh** (32), **drou** (23); pr. p. **drauand** (1); pp. **draun** (19), **drawen** (1). II. Senses 1. pull 4387, 2. bear, endure 9398, 3. turn aside to 14651, 4. breathe 531, 5. conract 23089, fig. 28294, 6. assemble 15911, 7. extract 16869, 8. take water from a well 23481, 9. obtain 18795, 10. stretch 12406, 11. fig. extend 791, 12. compose, write 222, 28869, 13. refl. move oneself, come, go, 7412, 14. move, come, go 2914, 22543, 15. resort to 45. [OE. *draȝan*]
Dreching vbl. n. (2), **drightin** (1) delay 14197, 16390, 27792. [OE. *dreccean*]
Dred I. Forms inf. **dred** (18), **drede** (9), **dride** (1); vb. **dred** (13), **dredde** (1), **dredes** (6), **dredis** (5), **dredeþ** (1); imperat. **dredes** (2); pt. **dred** (22), **dredd** (2), **drede** (1); pp. **dred** (6), **dredd** (1). II. Senses 1. feel fear, regard with awe 7223, 23773, 2. fear greatly 13231, 28173, 3. refl. be afraid 3665, 13231, 16626. Constr. 1. with noun obj. 11956, 15673, 2. with to inf. 7613, 3. with refl. obj. (and to inf.), 3665, 6142, 10117, 20611, 4. with noun cl., 12438, 28173. [OE. *an-*, *ondredan*]
Dred adj. (3), **drad** (2) terrified 3469, 4047, 18950. [aphetic form of ME. *adrad*]
Dredand adj. (pr. p.) (4), **dridand** (1) being fearful 10679; *god dridand* in awe of god 10226.
Dredful adj. (2) inspiring dread, awe-inspring 18831. Cf. Ed. MS. *derful* (? hurtful)
Drednes n. (11), **dridnes** (1) dread, terror 11161, 11624, 11636, 23035.
Drei inf. (30), vb. **drei** (1), pt. **dreied**, (2), pp. **droun** (1). Senses (1) endure, undergo, suffer, bear 1300, 2248, 10917, 13844, 20966, 23497, 24216, (2) do, perform 496, 26434. [OE. *droȝan*]
Drei n. phr. **on-, o- drei** (3) at a distance 5511, 21859, 27281. [OE. *dreȝe*]
Dremreder n. (1) interpreter of dreams 4502. [OE. *dréam*]
Dremer n. (1) one who dreams 4111. [OE. *dryman*]
Drep vb. inf. (1) strike, kill, overcome 3602. [OE. *drepan*]
Dreri adj. (11), **dreurye** (1). Senses (1) bloody 7828, 22462, (2) cruel, grievous 214, 1085, 22221, (3) sad, doleful, 17986. [OE. *dreoriȝ*]
Drerili adv. (3) in a dreary manner 22188, 14371.
Dri adj. (12) dry 381, 383, 13241328, 3563, 4156, 4581, 8279, 12025, 16868, 20747, 24492. Phr. *dri and cald*. [OE. dryȝe]
Dri inf. (1), pres. 3rd. pl. **dries** (1), pt. **dried** (1). Senses 1. become waterless 310, 2. fig. fade away 12027. [OE. *drygean*]
Dri n. (1) dryness 16664. [OE. *dryȝe*]
Drift n. (1), error **drif** (1) shower of snow or rain 22462, 9932. [OFris. *drift*, Mdu. *drift*]
Drightin n. (167), **dright** (38), **drighten** (1), **drightim** (1), **drightun** (1), **drithin** (1), error **dight** (1) lord, ruler, chief; Lord, God 5365, 5776, 6564, 6983, 11339, 11439, 13418, 13510, 13619, 15240, 16725, 18398, 21465, 22965, etc.; 6454, 6639, 7087, 8110, 8395, 9995, 11000, 11030, 17618, 18487, 18532 (error for **dright**), 19234, 19938, 21788, 22585, 22977, 23052, etc. [OE. *dryhten*, *drihten*]
Dril vb. inf. (1), **drill** (1) delay, put off 16390, 23715. [etymology unknown]
Drinc n. (17), **drink** (11) a drink 3021, 3293, 3809, 4941, 5702 , 14413, 15253, 19219, etc.; 1718, 16807, 2105724398, 28457, 28461, 29027, 29036, 29075. [OE. *drinc*]
Drinc vb. inf. (22), **drink** (3), imperat. **drinc** (1), **drinckes** (1), vb. **drinkes** (1), pt. **dranc** (15), **drank** (1), pp. **dronken** (1) drink 3071, 27023. Constr. with *of*

(the supply). [OE. *drincan*]
Dring n. (4) a free tenant in ancient Northumbria 15414, 16022, 22051, 22353. [OE. *dreng*, ON. *drengr*]
Driten inf. as n. (1) defecation. 22398. MED. sv. driten vb. to defecate, inf. as n. defecation or excrement. 22398. [ON. *drita*, MDu. *driten.*]
Driue inf. (12), **drijfe** (1), vb. **driue** (1), **driues** (2), pt. **draf** (10), **draif** (1), pp. **driuen** (11). Senses 1. drive on 887, 26865, 2. cause to fall upon19335, 3. throw or cast 9100, 20953, 26047, 4. incite powerfully 4318, 25864, 26262, 5. force into a state or condition 24575, 26330, 26725, 28151, 6. conduct, perform, 26467, 7. endure, suffer 27421. [OE. *drífan*]
Drope n. (4) drop 39, 49, 51, 16814, 21459. [OE. *dropa*]
Droppes vb. pres. 3rd. sg. (1) decays 3572. [OE. *droppian*]
Droue adj. (1) disturbed 13769. [eME. *droven*]
Droue inf. (2), pres. 2nd. sg. **droues** (1), pres. 3rd. sg. **droues** (1), pt **droued** (1) trouble, disturb 11974, 18188, 24418, 27741, 28223. [eME. *droven*]
Drouing vbl. n. (1) troubling 22384.
Drught n. (3) dryness 4699, 4701, 6365. [OE. *druȝaȝ*]
Drun inf. (6), **droun** (1), **drune** (1), pt. **drund** (3), pr. p. **drunand** (1), pp. **drund** (2). Senses 1. drown 1848, 1652, 22566, 24867, 2. overwhelm 18361, 3. flood 11899. [OE. drunian]
Drunken inf. (1), pt. **drunkend** (1). become sunk in the sea 1236, 24862. [ON. *drunka*]
Drunken pp. (7) intoxicated 2021, 18968; adj. as n. 27894. [OE. *druncnian*]
Drunkenhede n. (3), **drunkenhedd** (1) drunkenness 27876, 27883, 28459, 28748.
Drunkennes n. (3), **drunkenness** (1) drunkenness 7229, 27899, 28569.
Drunkensum adj. (1) addicted to drunkenness 26188.
Druppand pr. p. (2), **drupand** (1), **droupand** (1), comparat. **droupander** (1) dejected, dispirited 4457, 12051, 12625, 16064; 4460. [ON. *drupa*]
Druri n. (3) sexual love 21372, 23786, 24668. [OF. *druerie*]
Duale n. (4) error, deceit 12841, 14197, 17708, 26323. [OE. *dweola*]
Dub inf. (1) dress, clothe, array 28014. [origin unknown]
Dubbing vbl. n. (1) attire, dress. 28032.
Duble adj. (5), **dubul** (2) double, twofold 660, 905, 1528. [OF. *duble*, *doble*]
Dubles vb. 3rd. sg. (1), **dublid** pt. (2), **dubled** pt. (1), **dubled** pp. (1) make double 17032, 24039, 24369. [OF. *dubler*]
Duell n. (3) delay, stop 2831, 12992, 25864; phr. *witvten duell* immediately. [from vb.]
Duell vb. 1 inf. (2), pp. **dueld** (2) lead into error, mislead 17708, 19526, 24941, 28031. [OE. *dwellan*]
Duell vb. 2. Forms inf. **duell** (31), **dwell** imperat.; imperat. **duell** (2), **duells** (1); pres. 3rd sg. **duelles** (1), **duells** (1), 3rd. pl. **duelles** (1); pt. **duelld** (5), **duelled** (5), **duelt** (1); pr. p. **duelland** (11). Senses 1. remain 14534, 14536, 24826, 2. enter into 468. [OE. *dwellan*]
Dughti adj. (33), **doghti** (1), **doghty** (1), **dughtiest** superl. (1) able, worthy, virtuous, brave 1947, 2112, 2752, 3555, 12662, 17557, 22353, 2765927692. [OE. *dyhtiȝ*]
Dughtihede n. (6), **doghtyhede** (1) valour 8482954, 10166, 10349, 10628, 12705, 28940. [OE. *dyhtiȝ* + *hede*]
Dughtili adv. (2), **dughtilik** (1) valiantly, stoutly 3673, 9900. [OE. dyhtiȝ + -ly]
Dughtines n. (1) valour, stoutness 9758. [OE. *dyhtiȝ* + *-ness*]
Duk n. (3), **duke** (1) leader, ruler. 17979, 18046, 18229, 18271,; always in phr. *duk o ded.* (*deeþ*) [F. *duc*]
Duked pp. (2) plunged into the water 23142, 23203. [MDu. *duken*]
Dule n. (2), **dole** (1), **doil** (1), **doile** (1) grief, sorrow 13040, 23975, 24216. [OF.

doel]
Dumb adj. (12) dumb 14420, 18463, 22521, 24308 (adj. as n.). [OE. dumb]
Dump inf. (1) cast down, plunge down 22643. [Norse origin]
Dun adv. (124), **doun** (12), **doune** (1), **don** (24), **dune** (3) down. Forms **dun** 4173, 8807, 10115, 10711, 11444, 11895, 12430, 14345, 16247, 16705, 18319, 18834, 19663, 19847, 21066, 23203, etc.; **doun** 3, 12, 30, 71, 76, 81, 131, 680, 3822, 16762, 16762, 16762, 16814, 16814, 16814, 16814, 17957, 20187, 20531, 20896; **doune** 11686; **don** 63, 1782, 1835, 1847, 1883, 2810, 3126, 4714, 4929, 5895, 8125, 8357, 8813, 8894, 10589, 10737, 11784, 12044, 12278, 15675, 15757, 20912, 26047; **dune** 473. phr. *vp and dun* here and there, far and wide 1883, 10737; up and down 2238.
Dunfalling (1) downfall 17734.
Dun n. (2), **don** (1), **dune** (1) hill; allit. phr. *don and dale* 17573, *dale and dun* 22532, 22565. [OE. *dun*]
Dune adj. (1) dark, gloomy 22510. [of Celtic origin]
Dunjon n. (1) dungeon 9926. [OF. *donjon*]
Dunward adv. (4) fig. downwards 1943. [aphetic form of OE. *adunweard*]
Dur inf. (1) **dar** (14) vb. 3586, 23807; **dare** (2) vb. 25444; **dere** (1) 18453; **durst** pt. (23) dare, be so bold as 1820, 2928, 6330, 7872, 12997, 15884, 19202, 19325, 21512. [OE. *durran*]
Durken inf. (1) grow dark 24414, **durk** vb. (1) 25444 allit. phr. *durk and dare.* [f. adj. *dark*]
Dust n. (2) small piece of decayed soil; fig. worthless thing 23786. [OE. *dust*]
Dute inf. (2), **doute** (1); vb. **dut** (1), **dutes** (1); imperat. **dut** (1); pt. **duted** (4), **dout** (1), **doted** (2); pp. **duted** (2). Senses 1. be in doubt, be undecided 12571, 21090 (error for **douted**); 2. mistrust 22811, 26359; 3. dread, be afraid 10841, 15171. [OF. *duter*, *doter*, *douter*]
Dute n. (1) duty, submission 29387. [AF. *duete*]
Dute n. (34), **doute** (10), **dut** (2), **dout** (1) fear, dread 1908, 12635, 24993; respect, reverence 11187. [OF. *dute*]

References

Anderson, T. and K. I. Sandred eds. (1978) *The Vikings*. Proceedings of the Symposium of the Faculty of Arts of Uppsala University. Uppsala.

Ball, C.J.E. (1985) "Homonymy and Polysemy in Old English: A Problem for Lexicographers," *Problems of Old English Lexicography: Studies in Memory of Angus Cameron*, ed.by Alfred Bammesberger. Regensburg: Pustet, pp. 39-46.

Barth, C. (1903) *Der Wortschatz des Cursor Mundi* ein Beitrage zur Kenntnis der mittelenglischen Dialekte. Konigsberg.

Bennett, J.A.W. and G. V. Smithers eds. (1968) *Early Middle English Verse and Prose* with *A Glossary* by Norman Davis. Oxford: The Clarendon Press.

Bense, J.F. (1939) *A Dictionary of the Low-Dutch Element in the English Vocabulary*. The Hague: Martius Nijhoff.

Cleasby, R. and G. Vigfusson (rev.) (1957^2, rpt. 1986) *An Icelandic-English Dictionary*. Oxford: The Clarendon Press.

Craigie, W. A. et al. eds. (1937-) *A Dictionary of the Older Scottish Tongue: From the twelfth century to the end of the seventeenth.* University of Chicago Press and Oxford University Press.

Eldredge, L. M. and A. L. Klinck eds. (2000) *The Southern Version of* Cursor Mundi. Volume V Lines 21845-23898. University of Toronto Press.
Fisiak, J. (1965) *Morphemic Structure of Chaucer's English*. Alabama: University of Alabama Press.
Jones, C. (1972) *An Introduction to Middle English*. New York: Holt, Rinehart and Winston.
Kaiser, R. (1937) *Zur Geographie des mittelenglischen Wortschatzes*. Leipzig: Mayer & Muller.
Klinck, A. L. (2000) *Glossary to The Southern Version of* Cursor Mundi. University of Toronto Press.
Kurath, H. et al. eds. (1956-2001) *Middle English Dictionary*. Michigan.
Lyons, J. (1968) *Introduction to Theoretical Linguistics*. Cambridge: Cambridge University Press.
McIntosh, A. et. al. (1986) *A Linguistic Atlas of Late Medieval English* Vol.1-4. Aberdeen: Aberdeen University Press.
Mugglestone, L. ed. (2000) *Lexicography and the OED: Pioneers in the Untrodden Forest*. Oxford: Oxford University Press.
Murray, J.A.H. et al. eds. (1933, rpt. 1961) *Oxford English Dictionary on Historical Principles*. Oxford: The Clarendon Press.
Ross, C. V. C. (1971) *An Edition of Part of the Edinburgh Fragment of the* Cursor Mundi. Oxford.
Thompson, J. J. (1998) *The Cursor Mundi: Poem, Texts and Contexts*. Medium Aevum Monographs. New Series XIX. Oxford: The Society for the Study of Medieval Languages and Literature. Oxford.
Zoëga, G. T. (1926) *A Concise Dictionary of Old Icelandic*. Oxford: The Clarendon Press.

A Note on Gower's Narrative Art

MASAHIKO KANNO

Genius, priest of Venus, tells the 'Tale of Florent' (I, 1407-1882)[1] as one of the *exempla* of 'obedience in love' (1401). The lover is required to obey his lady as is codified in the *De Arte Honeste Amandi* of Andreas Capellanus.[2] The specific source that Gower used has not been found. There are, however, some analogues such as the *Weddynge of Sir Gawene and Dame Ragnell* and 'A Marriage of Sir Gawain.'[3] Gower has exquisitely moulded an excellent romance out of folktales and courtly literature. R.A. Peck suggests that Gower's tale is 'apparently based on the same source as Chaucer's "Wife of Bath's Tale," a source which joins folk motifs of the 'loathly lady' transformed through love and the answering of a riddle to save one's life.'[4] Unlike Gower, Chaucer has the Wife of Bath tell the tale in an Arthurian setting. J. A. W. Bennett has pointed out some typical differences in the 'presentation and emphasis' between them.[5] Derek Pearsall emphasizes Gower's excellence in the narrative art and he goes on to say that 'By any conventional standards, Gower's realization of the story is much superior to Chaucer's.'[6]

The 'worthi' but 'wifles' knight Florent, nephew to an emperor, was 'chivalerous and amorous' as is familiar in Medieval romances (see 5.653-54). He slayed Branchus, son and heir to the captain through fortune, 'not because of his rape of a maiden'[7] as portrayed in Chaucer's tale. Immediately Branchus's parents resolved on vengeance against Florent, but they hit upon 'his worthinesse / Of knyhthod and of gentilesse, and of cousinage / To themperour.' We should bear in mind that it is Fortune that made Florent kill Branchus. First of all, close attention must be paid to the words and phrases Gower makes conscious use of. The word 'schapen' and its derivatives (1421, 1509, 1514, 1544, 1551, 1730, 1736)[8] are repeatedly used to mean 'to bring about,' 'looks' and so forth. So his parents were 'in gret desputeisoun ... Among hemself, what was the beste.' (1440-41). What we have to point out in advance is that the words 'worthinesse' and 'gentilesse' are value-words in the Middle Ages. So 'worthi' and its derivatives (1408, 1432, 1435, 1472) are repeated in this tale.

Derek Pearsall has observed that 'One quality of the *Confessio* remains to be mentioned, without which it would be nothing: its verbal artistry.[9] Consequently, Gower's use of words will be examined principally from the aspects of verbal artistry.

The phrase 'what is the beste' (1441, 1626, 1817, 1827) is repeated four times, except for 'what was best to do' (1525) and 'what is best to sein'(1570).The word 'beste' here is a play on word, meaning the superlative degree of 'good' and at the same time, 'beast' as in 'This beste wedde to his wif' (1741). Finally his 'gentilesse' (1336, 1726) or good and knightly breeding will be proved.

What attracts our attention in this tale is that the word 'old'(1444, 1713) or 'olde' (1407, 1548, 1582, 1634, 1672) is frequently repeated. There is a lady who is so old that she can hardly walk. She is grandmother to Branchus. She sends for Florent and asks a difficult question of him: 'what alle wommen most desire' (1481). While he is wandering about trying to obtain the correct answer from people in the street, he comes upon a 'foul' woman sitting under a tree. At first it must be mentioned that the verb 'syh,' repeated twice, plays a significant part in this tale, especially in drammatic scenes (1675, 1802):

In a forest under a tre
He *syh* wher sat a creature,
A lothly wommannysch figure,
That forto speke of fleisch and bon
So foul yit *syh* he nevere non. (1528-32)

Gower makes grammatical uses of the word 'foul' and its derivatives (1532, 1734,1718, 1759, 1785), repeated five times in all. Like the word 'beste,' he deftly uses them as the comparative degree and the superlative degree in her ugly portraiture as in 'foulere on to se' (1759) and 'the fouleste of alle' (1718) respectively. Maria Wickert has suggested: 'Bei der ersten Begegnung war ihm das Phänomen abstoßender Häßlichkeit als Gesamterscheinung entgegengetreten.'[10] The identity of this 'lothly wommannysch figure' will be miraculouly disclosed later in great details (1678ff.). It is a mystery that 'this olde wyht'(1548, 1582, 1634, 1672)–a similar phrase repeated four times–should know his name and dilemma before teaching him the answer of a riddle in exchange for her marriage to Florent:

And thus his trowthe he leith to wedde. (1588)

Because he is forced into a corner, he is reluctant to accept her offer. But this promise is a written contract under seal, i.e. a legal bond (1798) of marriage, which is used synonymously with 'covenant' (1450, 1590, 1636, 1696) and 'trowthe' (1512, 1559, 1588, 1594, 1667,1671, 1715), repeated four times and seven times respectively. Finally his truth will be proved.

> And thus this yonge lusti knyht
> Unto *this olde lothly wiht*
> Tho seide: (1581-83)

The 'olde lothly wiht' (1582) has taught the 'lusti' Florent a secret of a woman's right to sovereignty. 'A lusti Lady' (1773) is an echo of 'lusti knyht' (1581). As is more explicit later, here lies the theme of 'love' and 'sovereinete' (1847):

> upon this Molde
> That alle wommen lievest wolde
> Be soverein of mannes love. (1607-9)

'Soverein' and its derivative (1609, 1834, 1847) occur three times and they are structually related each other. Her ugliness is further emphasized with a sharper and more poignant phrase:

> such on which of alle kinde
> Of wommen is *thunsemlieste*. (1625-26)

He is completely bewildered about 'what is the best,' but he goes to the castle where Branchus's parents are waiting. The fluctuation of mind such as conflict, indeterminacy and perplexity is realistically described by phrases such as 'Now goth he forth, now comth ayein' (1569), 'rod to and fro' (1571), 'Or forto take hire to his wif Or elles forto lese his lif' (1573-74), 'Bot be him lief or be him loth' (1627), 'Or forto deie or forto live' (1630), and so forth. Then the lord sends for the lady, i.e. 'that olde Mone':

> He sende up for the lady sone,
> And forth sche cam, that olde *Mone*. (1633-34)

The *OED* suggests that Gower probably adopted 'mone' from ON. *mona* 'mammy,' the meaning of which is 'an old woman, a crone,' cited in the *OED* as a sole instance. It is from the figurative phrase 'lich unto the wollesak' that we take 'mone' to mean 'moon.' Suddenly, she presses Florent for kissing, contrary to the precepts of courtly love:

> Bot *lich unto the wollesak*

Sche proferth hire unto this knyht. (1692-93)

Here we wish to repeat J.A.W. Bennett's comment that 'the frouncing of the "olde mones" brow, her profer of a body "lich unto the wollesak," Florent lifting up his "wofull heved"–these are all characteristic touches.'[11]

Florent answers to the 'Matrone' as he was taught by 'that olde Mone.' When the secret is disclosed, she becomes furious, saying that she would burn him at the stake:

And whan that this *Matrone* herde
The manere how this knyht ansuerde,
Sche seide: 'Ha treson, wo thee be,
That hast thus told the privite,
Which alle wommen most desire!
I wolde that thou were afire.' (1657-62)

'Matrone' means 'a married woman, usually of mature years and socially respectable' (*MED*), cited as a sole instance in the *MED*.

Florent sees 'this olde wyht' (1672) sit waiting for him to come back. At last her ugly feature, likened to 'a moor,' is exaggeratedly and facetiously described in full. M. Wickert, as stated above, makes an interesting comment that 'Die Annäherung erfolgt widerum nach Gowers Technik des subjektiven Erlebens. Aber nun folgt eine Bestandsaufnahme aller abstoßenden Einzelheiten, die objektiven Charakter trägt':[12]

Florent his wofull heved uplefte
And syh this *vecke* wher sche sat,
Which was the *lothlieste what*
That evere man caste on his yhe:
Hire Nase bass, hire browes hyhe,
Hire yhen smale and depe set,
Hire chekes ben with teres wet,
And rivelen as an empty skyn
Hangende doun unto the chin,
Hire Lippes schrunken ben for age,
Ther was no grace in the visage,
Hir front was nargh, hir lockes hore,
Sche loketh forth as doth a More,
Hire Necke is schort, hir schuldres courbe,
That myhte a mannes lust destourbe,
Hire body gret and nothing smal,
And schortly to descrive hire al,
Sche hath no lith withoute a lak; (1674-91)

(He saw the old hag where she sat, / And a more loathsome thing was that
Than ever met the human eye: / Her nose was flat, her eyebrows high;

> Tiny her eyes, and deeply set; / With dripping tears her cheeks were wet,
> And wrinkled as an empty skin, / And they hung down upon her chin;
> Her lips had shrunk, she was so old. / She had no beauties to behold:
> Her forehead narrow, her locks hoar / (And she peers out as does a Moor),
> Such as no pleasure could support; / Her body thick, by no means small;
> And, shortly to describe her all, / Never a limb without a lack.)[13]

'Wofull' in 'his wofull heved' may be a transferred epithet. 'Vecke,' derived from It. *vecchia*, feminine of *vecchio* 'old,' means 'an old woman' as the *OED* explains:

> As direct adoption from Italian would be remarkable in the 14th c., it is possible that the *vecchio* existed in OF. colloquial use. The word *vecke* 'an old woman' is apparently adopted from the Italian word *vecchia*, a feminine of *vecchio* 'old.'

J.A.W. Bennett has noted as 'A restrained and effective variation on the traditional theme...of female ugliness,' i.e. 'the depiction of Jealousy as a 'rympled vekke' (*Romaunt of the Rose*, 4495-6) and of the 'auncian' (*Sir Gawain and the Green Knight*, 948ff.).[14]

Macaulay refers to 'what' as 'the use of 'quoy' in French, e.g. *Mir*.1781.'[15] 'What' in this case means 'thing,' implying, without doubt, a person. The last instance, according to the *MED*, is cited from Gower.

Florent has to keep words as he has promised. His youth is about to be wasted on an old and loathly woman 'as the weie.' L.J. Owen takes the phrase 'as the weie' to mean 'like the whey.'[16] Consequently 'weie,' meaning 'the serum or watery part of milk which remains after the separation of the curd by coagulation, esp. in the manufacture of cheese' (*OED*), has two senses of 'way' and 'whey,' so it means 'whey,' exploited as a simile like 'old and lothly as the weie.' In addition, 'this olde lothly whit' (1582), synthetically combined by attributive epithets, occurs later in the analytical form of descriptive epithets like 'old and lothly' below:

> His youthe schal be cast aweie
> Upon such on which *as the weie*
> Is *old* and *lothly* overal. (1711-13)

The peculiar word 'coise' below, of uncertain etymology and meaning as the *OED* notes, has the pejorative senses of 'ugly woman, monster, body, mistress.' As he has made a marital vow, he has to take her to the castle on horseback at night so as to be seen by nobody. Moral Gower humourously portrays her ugly figure by using a Homeric simile like 'as an oule':

In ragges, as sche was totore,
He set hire on his hors tofore
And forth he takth his weie softe;
No wonder thogh he siketh ofte.
Bot as an oule fleth be nyhte
Out of alle othre briddes syhte,
Riht so this knyht on daies brode
In clos him hield, and schop his rode
On nyhtes time, til the tyde
That he cam there he wolde abide;
And prively withoute noise
He bringth this foule grete *Coise*
To his Castell in such a wise
That noman myhte hire schappe avise. (1723-36)

Special mention is made of the problematic word 'coise' here. "In line with the *OED*," J.D. Shaw demonstrates, "I would like to propose a separate etymology and different meaning for Gower's term: *coise* n. [OF *coi* what] = thing." Further he goes on to say that "the editors of the *OED* define 'what' in line 1676 as 'thing,' a definition that could equally well apply to the succeeding epithet. In attempting to explain Gower's uncharacteristic use of 'what' in this passage. Macaulay refers us in his note to 'the use of 'quoy' in French, e.g. *Mir*. 1781.This further association of *thing* and *what* in the same passage argues for the proposed etymology and meaning of *coise*. Indeed, it would appear that both substantives used to describe the loathly hag are variants of the same French word, differing only in that one is a translation and the other a borrowing."[17]

It is a comic but interesting scene in which she takes up a strightforward and pragmatic attitude when she attempts to induce Florent to bed, by saying:'My lord, go we to bedde, / For I to that entente wedde, / That thou schalt be my worldes blisse' (1769-71). He cannot escape from lying naked with her in bed. He feels as if 'his heart were in purgatoire' (1776). Though he wishes to hide his eyes from looking at her, he dares to turn toward her:

He torneth on that other side,
For that he wolde hise yhen hyde
Fro lokynge on that *foule wyht*. (1783-85)

She is depicted as 'that foule wyht' (1785) who gladly holds her husband in her arms, while lying naked in bed:

This newe *bryd* which lay withinne,
Thogh it be noght with his acord,

In armes sche beclipte hire lord. (1789-90)

It is noteworthy of the phrase 'this newe bryd,' which undoubtedly has two meanings of 'bride' and 'bird.' 'That foule wyht,' compared above to 'an oule' (1727), i.e. hag, has been transformed into a bird, i.e. bride.

Then he sees a lovely lady of eighteen years old lying near by him:

And as it were a man in trance
He torneth him al sodeinly,
And *syh* a lady lay him by
Of eyhtetiene wynter age,
Which was the faireste of visage
That evere in al this world he *syh*: (1800-5)

This supplies a distinct and visual contrast between 'the lothlieste' old woman and 'the faireste' young lady.

The moment he holds a lovely young lady in his arms, she offers a difficult problem to him and demands him to choose one of the two things:

He mot on of tuo thinges chese,
Wher he wol have hire such on nyht,
Or elles upon daies lyht,
For he schal noght have bothe tuo. (1810-13)

It is the second time that he finds himself in the dilemma of choosing and finally swears to become her 'maistresse.' In this way he has obeyed her in love.

She begins to disclose her secrets. According to her story, she is the daughter of the king of Sicily who has been made into a 'foule wyht' (1785) by a wicked stepmother. She can not return to what she used to be until she marries a famous knight.

As has been stated, Gower's 'Tale of Florent is rich in the association of words and phrases, wordplay and so forth. The germinal words 'old' and 'foul' give rise to 'a lothly wommannysch figure, olde lothly wiht, thunsemlieste, olde Mone, vecke, lothlieste what, foule grete Coise, this foule wyht, and this beste.' Indeed, Gower is 'certainly a more daring innovator than Chaucer.'[18] This tale is interesting to read as well as to hear. Gower is clear and skilled in using words. His choice of words, though seemingly artless, is firmly based on accurate calculation.

Notes

1. Macaulay, G. C., ed., *The Complete Works of John Gower*. 4 vols. (Vol.I: French Works; Vol.II-III: English Works; Vol.IV: Latin Works), (Oxford, 1899-

French Works; Vol.II-III: English Works; Vol.IV: Latin Works), (Oxford, 1899-1902; rpt. Grosse Pointe, Mich., 1968). All quotations are quoted from this edition.

2. *Andreas Capellanus on Love*, ed. P. G. Walsh (London: Duckworth, 1982), pp.116-17. VII. Dominarum praeceptis in omnibus obediens semper studeas amoris aggregari militiae (7. Be obedient in mistresses' commands in all things, and always be eager to join the service of Love).

3. Sands, Donald B., ed., *The Wedding of Sir Gawain and Dame Regnell: Middle English Verse Romances* (New York: Holt, Rinehart and Winston, 1966), pp.323-347; *Sources and Analogues of Chaucer's Canterbury Tales*, ed. by W. F. Bryan and G. Dempster (Atlantic Highlands: Humanities Press, 1941; Copyright 1958), pp. 223-268.

4. Peck, R. A., ed. *Confessio Amantis* (New York: Holt, Rinehart and Winston, 1968), p.503.

5. Bennett, J.A.W., ed., *Selections from John Gower* (Oxford, 1968), pp.141-143.

6. Pearsall, Derek, *Gower and Lydgate: Writers and Their Work* (Longmans, 1969), p.21.

7. Bennett, J. A. W., *op. cit.*, p.142.

8. Pickles, J. D. and J. L. Dawson, eds., *A Concordance to John Gower's Confessio Amantis* (D.S. Brewer, 1987).

9. Pearsall, *op. cit.*, p. 21.

10. Wickert, Maria, *Studien zu John Gower* (Kölner Universitäts Verlag, 1953), p.194.

11. Bennett, *op. cit.*, p.143.

12. Wickert, *op. cit.*, p.194.

13. Tiller, T., trans. *Confessio Amantis* (Baltimore: Penguin Books, 1963), pp. 70-71.

14. Bennett, *op. cit.*, p.144.

15. Macaulay, *op. cit.*, p.473.

16. Owen, L. J. and N. H. Owen, eds., *Middle English Poetry: An Anthology* (New York: The Bobbs-Merrill, 1971), p.189.

17. Shaw, J. D., "An Etymology of the Middle English *coise*," *ELN*, (1985), 11-13.

18. Casson, Leslie F., "Studies in the Diction of the *Confessio Amantis*," *ES*, (1934), 184.

Chaucer's *Semely* and Its Related Words from an Optical Point of View

Yoshiyuki Nakao

1. Introduction: The aim of this paper

Ways of seeing are antecedent to ways of epistemology (cognition). Limited seeing leads to limited epistemology, whereas unlimited seeing leads to unlimited epistemology–the divine view. These two ways of seeing are manifested in Chaucer's descriptions of love, wishes, etc. with varying degrees of emphasis. Limited seeing or epistemology is typically shown in secular romance contexts such as Troilus framed in sieged Troy; Criseyde looking at Troilus through the window of her house; Aryadne accessing Theseus through a *foreyne* ('privy'); Arcite bound in the prison looking at Emelie; the old blind husband Januarie looking at *freshe* May in the enclosed garden. These characters are all involved in romantic love or expectation and all betrayed owing to their limited view. On the other hand, as regards philosophical and religious works such as *Boece* and the Parson's Tale, we have a different story. There the divine view is brought into focus as a final goal. In *Boece*, Chaucer's translation of Boethius' *Consolatione Philosophiae*, we find four distinguished stages of cognition: *wit* or *sensus* as the most limited view (attributed to an immovable oyster); *ymaginacioun* or *imaginatio* as the second limited view (attributed to a movable animal); *resoun* or *ratio* as the human view; and finally *intelligence* or *intellegentiae* as the least limited or the divine view. The same is true of the Parson's Tale, the last tale of the *Canterbury Tales*. The divine light of the New Jerusalem or heavenly bliss is demonstrated as attainable after people have confessed their sins and performed their penance.

This paper is an attempt to explore implications of Chaucer's *semely* in relation to the mechanism of optics. This word is a case in point in that it can mediate the physical/visual and cognitive/spiritual worlds. Chaucer's use of it captures our attention because it is nearly limited to secular romantic contexts, or to be more precise, to romantic expectations, as typically shown in Aryadne's observation of Theseus, 'A *semely* knyght was Theseus to se' LGW 2074).[1] Burnley's (1983:

246) notes on *semely* merit attention: 'Indeed *semely* is as nearly restricted to satirical use in Chaucer's works as is the word *hende*.' However, he is reticent as regards how this word is likely to be 'satirical.' My assumption is that optics plays an important role there. There have been no studies on the relationship between Chaucer's *semely* and optics. I will re-examine this word from an optical point of view.

2. Our viewpoint: The concept of 'optical'

The word 'optical' here is used to mean 'seeing through from a framed space,' both literally and metaphorically. In the literal sense it concerns 'Pertaining or relating to light, as the medium of sight, or generally in relation to its physical properties' (OED s.v. optical 2. 1570-) and then 'the actual objects when viewed from a particular point' (OED s.v. perspective 3.a). In the metaphorical sense, it concerns 'the aspect of a matter or object of thought, as perceived from a particular mental 'point of view.'' (Cf. OED s.v. perspective 3.d.)

Optics as the science of sight (OED s.v. optics) in Chaucer's day operated in four areas of experiment or speculation according to Holley (1990: 17).

(1) a. physiological (the physiognomy of the eye)
  b. physical (measuring of the force of light rays)
  c. epistemological (cognitive theory, that is, how do we truly know something?)
  d. metaphysical (linking physical vision with perception of the Divine)

Chaucer did not handle these four areas systematically. However, they seem to have been behind and affected his use of optical words. *Semely* is just one of those vision-related words. My primary concern here is with the intralexical (semantic) as well as interlexical (lexical network) structure of these words. The discussion of the science of seeing as a whole goes beyond the scope of the paper. I will first take up the semantic aspect of *semely*, and then its pragmatic aspect with a special focus on optics.

3. The semanctics and pragmatics of Chaucer's *semely*

3.1. The semantics of *semely*

The semantic development of *semely* is, according to the OED, as follows:

(2) OED s.v. seemly [ON *saemiligr,* fr *saem-r* becoming]
1. Of a person, his figure, etc. Of a pleasing or goodly appearance, fair, well-formed, handsome, 'proper'. *Obs.* ex. *dial.* In early use chiefly applied to a person of high rank or lineage. Frequently used alliteratively, as *seemly to see*, *seemly in* or *to sight*. a1225-1513. *The Life of Saint Katherine* 1456-7 [St Katherine]
2. Of things: Pleasant (*esp.* to the sight); handsome in appearance; of fine or stately proportion. a1310-
3. Of conduct, speech, appearance: comfortable to propriety or good taste; becoming, decorous. a1225-
†4. Suitable to the person or the occasion; appropriate. c1350-1634
†5. [Influenced by SEEM *v*.2]
a. Likely. c1400-1496
b. Apparent, seeming. *Obs.* c1400-1800

Semely was introduced to English from ON *saemiligr*, whose etymological meaning is 'becoming' or 'fitting.' This was found in English texts around the early 13th century. It should be noticed that this word is related to the speaker's judgment from the beginning. In English, besides this etymological meaning, several derived senses can be seen. Here optics seems to have played an important role in such semantic development. A person/thing 'becoming' is perhaps visibly beautiful. The relation between the two words *sight* and *semely* is very strong. So much so that it is grammaticised as an alliterative phrase such as *semely to see*, *semely in* or *to sight*. This point is reinforced by the OED. In the final stage, *semely* developed an epistemic sense 'apparent' or 'be likely to' influenced by its etymologically cognate word *seem*. We have to note that this word has increasingly strengthened as regards its subjective force, and has come to have a modalizing[2] function.

The MED's treatment of this word is more or less the same as the OED's except that the former distinguishes between physical beauty and spiritual beauty (MED s.v. semely 4. (a) honorable, (b) virtuous, pure, (c) as noun: a righteous, worthy, or honorable person; also used of God, Christ, the Virgin Mary) while the latter leaves them as implicit.

3.2. The semantic relation between *semely* and its synonymous words

There are no exact words to which *semely* can semantically correspond. Some synonymous candidates are shown in Table 1. I made a componential analysis of these words based on the definitions of the OED and Davis (1979).

Table 1

(words)	semely	shene	bright	fayr	sittyng	worthy	gentil	courteous	pure
(senses)									
beautiful	+	+	+	+					
favorable				+				+	
clement				+			+		
peaceable				+					
desirable				+					
shining		+	+						
honourable	+					+	+	+	+
refined							+	+	
distinguished						+			
strong						+			
fitting	+				+	+			
apparent	+								
likely	+								

In the English of Chaucer's times, *semely* retains an etymological 'fitting,' and has derived such senses as 'beautiful' and 'honourable'/ 'pure,' and is developing a new modal (epistemic) sense 'apparent' or 'likely.' This combination of senses is unique to *semely* and seems to contribute to the semantic complexity in Chaucer's use.

3.3. The pragmatics of *semely*

To make the full potential of Chaucer's use of *semely*, the semantic or lexicographical information is only part of the whole picture. This word is likely to be used in relation to romantic love or expectation, as is detailed later, and as a result to ways of perception and cognition of those participants involved in it. *Semely* is one of those linked words. Optics seems to be functional here as a system of perceived associations. Love, needless to say, begins with the hero 'seeing' the heroine or vice versa. Ways of seeing lead to ways of cognition. *Semely* is an outcome of the observer's cognition. Chaucer's *semely* needs to be investigated with this pragmatic/discourse structure in mind. I think that this structure is an important element constituting Chaucer's architecture of *semely*. (Cf. For the 'architecture,' see Burnely (1983: 214-5–a system of perceived associations between semantic structure, collocations, language varieties, and other patterns of usage….)

4. The optical structure of Chaucer's *semely*: A descriptive framework

Chaucer's *semely* tends to be found in relation to romantic love. According to the development of love or how the participants' sight/ vision is involved in it, I have set up six elements on which to describe the optical structure. It should be noticed that the elements from A to F in (3) are gradable.[3] With these two points in mind, we have the following framework:

(3) The optical structure of Chaucer's *semely*
 A. who sees: **a limited-view character/narrator** ↔ the omniscient narrator
 B. where he/she sees: a small place (***foreyne*** 'privy', etc.) ↔ a large place (*the eighth sphere*, etc.)[4]
 C. what he/she sees: physical features (***chere, contenaunce***, etc.) ↔ spiritual ones (*trouthe, honeste,* etc.)
 D. how he/she sees (words of perception; some have developed cognitive senses): positive vision (***see***, etc.) ↔ negative vision (*blynd*, etc.); narrow vision (*piken*, etc.) ↔ wide vision (*purveien*, etc.)[5]
 E. how far (certainly) he/she sees: with regard to words of cognition
 objective cognition ↔ subjective cognition
 verbs: *know*, etc. ↔ *gesse*, *leve*, ***think***, *seme*, etc.
 modal auxiliaries: *moot*, etc. ↔ *may*, ***oughte***, etc.
 adjectives: *certain*, etc. ↔ ***likely to***, *possible*, etc.
 adverbs: *certain*, *trewely*, etc. ↔ *paraventure*, etc.
 F. how far (validly) he/she sees: with regard to words of evaluation
 weakly subjective ↔ strongly subjective
 gentil: weakly subj. ↔ strongly subj., ***semely,*** *weldy*, etc.

Semely is situated in the F of the discourse structure above. It should be noticed, however, that F is only part of the coherent as well as cohesive structure of optics.

Let us take an example by looking at the bold types in the framework above. A heroine is characterised with a limited view although she belongs to the group of 'good women.' She has a chance to see a hero through a *foreyne* ('privy') which mediates between the prison in which he is and the chamber in which she sleeps. She sees and is attracted by his *contenaunce* and *chere* 'appearance.' She falls in love with him, and as far as she sees, he is a *semely* knight. Finally she is deceived by him. Who is she? Different combinations of the elements of A to F with varying gradience make different types of stories.

5. Chaucer's *semely* from an optical point of view

5.1. *Semely* in Chaucer's earliest works: *Rom* and *BD*

In Chaucer's earliest works, the *Romaunt of the Rose* and the *Book of the Duchess*, Chaucer used *semely* as typically shown in traditional romances such as *Emare*, *Amis and Amiloun*, and the *Romance of Guy of Warwick*.[6] In *Rom*, the narrator is in a dream vision. Entering a garden of love, he observes and is charmed by allegorical characters such as Ideleness and Gladness and their belongings. *Semely* is used four times in Fragment A, all by the narrator to describe their beauty (adj.: *Rom* 563, 586, 1271; adv. 748). There his use is straightforward with little modalization if any. The same is true of *BD*. The narrator in a dream vision sees a man in black in great sorrow. The man begins to open his mind to the poet narrator. In his romantic recollection of his lady, he describes her excellent character. Her lady's name is *Whyte*. She is symbolic of madame Blanche, the first wife of John of Gaunt, who died of the pest. She gives light to the beholder, the black knight. She is *so semely on to see* (*BD* 1177), and *fair and bright* (*BD* 1180). The knight's praise of her runs throughout the narrative with little hint of scepticism.

5.2. *Semely* in Chaucer's later works

There are no examples of *semely* in *HF, PF, Bo, Tr*, and it emerges again some 20 years after in the *Legend of Good Women*, one of Chaucer's later works. Two examples are found there. And in the *Canterbury Tales,* we find seven examples. In these works the function of *semely* seems to become complicated involving degrees of modalization.

5.2.1. *Semely* in *LGW*

The *Legend of Good Women* is back to the dream vision, and women's response is in a sense affected by this vision, or to be more precise, *illusioun*. The dichotomy of good women and false men is too arbitrary to Chaucer. Women are good only to the extent that they are beguiled and betrayed, and those betrayers are men. Chaucer is sensitive to some human weaknesses in women. The typical pattern there is that the heroine sees the hero in a predicament, is captivated by his appearance, sympathizes with and loves him, and finally is betrayed by him. This pattern accords with the optical structure both physically and spiritually. We find two instances of *semely*: one with reference to Jason,[7] the betrayer of Medea, the other one to Theseus, betrayer of Aryadne.

I will limit myself to the legend of Aryadne. Aryadne is a daughter of the King of Crete. His castle has a prison, and there the knight Theseus is imprisoned. At the beginning of the story, the narrator sees through Theseus: Of Theseus the grete *untrouthe* of love; (*LGW* 1890). The audience is given information about his true character. Then the narrator touches upon, significantly enough, in what way Adryane comes to know him, or where she sees him (B) according to my framework. This is shown in (4):

(4) The tour there as this Theseus is throwe
Doun in the bottom derk and wonder lowe,
Was joynynge in the wal to a *foreyne*;[8]
And it was longynge to the doughtren tweyne
Of Mynos, that in hire chaumbres grete
Dwellten above, toward the mayster-strete
Of Athenes, in joye and in solas. (*LGW* 1960-6)

She gains access to Theseus through the unromantic 'foreyne' or 'privy' which mediates between the prison which Theseus is in and the bedchamber Adryane sleeps in. This *foreyne* seems to function both literally and metaphorically. Metaphorically her sight is framed in this narrow and dark *foreyne*. Her love begins when she sees Theseus. However, what she sees is limited to his appearance, or his youth (*yong*) and countenance (*contenaunce*), although she is expected to see him holistically as a princess. The narrator brings into focus Theseus's *seemly*, as shown in (5):

(5) A *semely* knyght was Theseus to *se*,
And yong, but of a twenty yer and thre.
But whoso hadde seyn his contenaunce
He wolde have wept for routhe of his penaunce;
For which this Adryane in this manere
Answerde hym to his profre and to his chere: (*LGW* 2074-9)

Semely in a typical romance is functional in such a way that the hero/heroine is beautiful both externally and internally. This is shown for instance in Emare. *Semely* there is used by the omniscient narrator.[9] However, with regard to Aryadne, the narrator is not omniscient, but slides into her way of seeing and cognition. Theseus is observed through her romantic expectations, which are framed as narrowly as the unromantic *foreyne*.

How far Adryane knows about her future life (E) is repetitively modalized as shown in (6).

(6) Yit *were* it betere that I *were* youre wyf,
Syn that ye ben as gentil born as I, (*LGW* 2089-90)
"Now be we duchesses, bothe I and ye,
And sekered to the regals of Athenes,

> And bothe hereafter *likly to ben* quenes; (*LGW* 2127-9)
> *Me thynketh* no wight *oughte* us herof blame,
> Ne beren us therefore an evil name." (*LGW* 2134-5)

All her visions of the future will go unrealized. She is betrayed by Theseus, who forsakes her and takes up her sister, ironically enough because she is more beautiful. To those readers who know Boethius, her vision is framed in her *wit* or *sensus*, only seeing Theseus' physical/ handsome features, or possibly extended also to *ymaginacioun* or *imaginatio* expecting his honourable or virtuous features, but with an anticlimactic illusion. The usual alliterative phrase 'semely knyght ... to se' seems to be operative not in a unitary sense but compositionally to the effect that Theseus is 'seemly' as far as she sees, or as far as seeing is concerned.

5.2.2. *Semely* in the *Canterbury Tales* (GP): The Prioress's *semely*

Among the seven examples in the *Catnerbury Tales,* five appears in Fragment I, one in Fragment VII, and one in Fragment IX, according to the Ellesmere order. First, let us look at Fragment I. There are three instances of *semely* in the portrait of the Prioress in the General Prologue. The portarait is forty-five lines long (one per 15 lines). This repetition and frequency is conspicuous compared with Chaucer's other works and also works of other romance writers. Compare twice in *LGW* of 2723 lines; once in the Manciple's Tale of 362 lines; once in *Orfeo* of 602 lines; 13 times in *Amis and Amiloun* of 2508 lines (one per 192.9); and once in the *Romance of Guy of Warwick* of 10894 lines. The intensification of *semely* by 'ful' is also worth noticing in that the use is consistent with the Prioress, and by comparison there are no instances of intensification in *Emare*'s *semely. Semelys* here are all used as a manner adverb to focalize her action to imitate courtly behaviour. It is used adverbially four times in total in Chaucer. Three of these cluster here. First her way of intoning in her nose is focused on (Entuned in hir nose ful *semely; CT* I (A) 123); second her way of reaching after the meal (Ful *semely* after hir mete she raughte. *CT* I (A) 136); and third her way of pleating the headdress (Ful *semyly* hir wympul pynched was, *CT* I (A) 151). She sees only what she wants to see: courtly manners. Her sight is not extended to the internal aspect, say, devotion to divine love. Her sight might go to the mouse caught in a trap (*CT* I (A) 144-5), but perhaps not to human misery. The narrator pays attention to her 'eyen' and describes it as 'greye as glas' (*CT* I (A) 152). Typical of a romance heroine, we do not know how far this feature contributes to her internal view. *Semely* used for Emare and St

Katherine refers to their internal as well as external features with no restriction, and no reference to table manners. However, here *semely* is only functional or 'fitting' or 'visibly beautiful' in such a way that it applies to courtly behaviour 'cheere of court,' a big deviation from her religious order. The narrator, Chaucer the pilgrim, seems to sympathize with and align himself with the Prioress's romantic expectations, and show his cognition through her eyes.

5.2.3. *Semely* in the *Canterbury Tales* (GP): The Host's *semely*

Semely is used again in the final part of the General Prologue. Here it is used straightforwardly to describe the unromantic character Host. He was not born as noble, and perhaps is not so noble in character. He is a manager of the Tabard Inn. But he is 'fitting' (MED 3. (b)) to the extent that he is a master of ceremonies (A *semely* man OURE HOOSTE was withalle / For to been a marchal in an halle. *CT* I (A) 751-2).

5.2.4. *Semely* in the *Canterbury Tales* (KnT) : Venus's *semely*

Semely is used in the Knight's Tale to describe Venus's head with a rose garland. This functions in the sense of 'visibly beautiful' or 'becoming' (And on hir heed, ful *semely* for to *see* / A rose gerland, *CT* I (A) 1960-1). This feature is cohesive to her son Cupid and his blindness. This is suggestive enough of the blind love in which Palamon and Aricite are involved.

5.2.5. *Semely* in the *Canterbury Tales* (Thop): Thopas's *semely*

Semely does not appear until Fragment VII according to the Ellesmere order (the Hengwrt order: B2). In this Fragment varieties of genre are brought into focus with plenty of meta-narrative as well as metalinguistic comments. Sir Thopas is one of those tales, and there *semely* is used to highlight the hero's beautiful nose. The narrator is Chaucer the pilgrim, reproducing a typical romance and yet reinterpreting from a fresh perspective. Sir Thopas is praised with traditional romance words and phrases, but as already noted, these are not appropriate for a knight, but for a woman who is in a kitchen or chamber, or a child who is restricted a great deal in activity or power. Some of these features are shown in (7):

(7) Sire Thopas wax a doghty swayn;
Whit was his face as payndemayn,
His lippes rede as rose;
His rode is lyk scarlet in grayn,
And I yow telle in good certayn
He hadde a *semely* nose. (*CT* VII Thop 724-9)

I will examine the above *semely* in terms of its collocability. Let us first see words collocating with *semely*, and then words collocating with nose. I have collected eighty nine examples of *semely*, but except for Sir Thopas I have found none collocating with a nose. *Semely* can collocate with both persons and things such as a man, knight, jewels, hall, garland, etc. But perhaps not so often with a nose. Sir Thopas's example seems to capture our attention. On the other hand, words collocating with nose have two tendencies. One tendency is that evaluative adjectives or phrases collocate with a nose such as *heigh* referring to Aricite's nose in the Knight's Tale; the other is that derogatory adjectives collocate with it such as *kamus* (stubbed) referring to the wench's, or the miller's daughter's nose in the Reeve's Tale.[10] Which tendency is applied to Sir Thopas? It seems that Chaucer praises his beautiful nose in the same way as he did the Prioress's nose by using a déclassé word like 'hire nose tretys' (*CT* I (A) 152). His *semely* nose is more appropriate for a woman or child than a knight in the same way as the Prioress's *tretys* nose is more appropriate for a romance heroine than her religious order. The sight of Sir Thopas is narrowed down and framed within a kitchen or a child way of moving (B). The function of *semely* is limited and minituarized, fitting/beautiful as far as his nose is concerned, not in terms of a knight as a whole, as typically shown in (8):

(8) & seyd, "So god ȝou spede,
Who was hold þe douȝtiest kniȝt
& *semlyest* in ich a siȝt
& worþliest in wede,
& who was þe fairest man
þat was yholden in lond þan,
& douȝtiest of dede?" (*Amis and Amiloun* 450-6)
It is sir Amis, þe kinges boteler; (*Amis and Amiloun* 463)

5.2.6. *Semely* in the *Canterbury Tales* (ManceT): Phebus's *semely*

The last example is found in the Manciple's Tale belonging to Fragment IX, the penultimate tale in the *Canterbury Tales*. Immediately before this tale starts, the pilgrims arrive at *Bobbe-up-and-doun* (Woot ye nat where ther stant a litel toun / Which that ycleped is *Bobbe-up-and-doun*, / Under the Blee, in Caunterbury Weye? *CT* IX (H) MancP 1-3. bob 'to move up and down'). This place indicates the situation 'moving up and down' not only physically but metaphorically with an implication of the development of the story. And Phebus the hero of this tale lives down on the earth, not in heaven (Whan Phebus dwelled heere in *this erthe adoun*, CT IX (H) 105). From an optical point of view, these two elements are significant enough to show the place where Phebus sees (B). Phebus, a god of light, is expected to have sufficient vision to see through the humans and human events. But as the tale unfolds, it turns out that he is short-sighted and betrayed.

He is praised as an ideal knight. Various knightly virtues are accumulated as shown in (9):

(9) Therto he was the *semelieste* man
That is or was sith that the world began.
What nedeth it his fetures to discryve?
For in this world was noon so faire on-lyve.
He was therwith fulfild of gentilesse,
Of honour, and of parfit worthynesse.
This phebus, that was flour of bachilrie,
As wel in freedom as in chivalrie, (*CT* IX (H) MancT 119-26)

Semely is one of his knightly virtues. However, these virtues of Phebus's turn out to be useless when he is cuckholded by his unnamed wife's liaison with an unnamed worthless man. The narrator's view of Phebus is upside down. Phebus sees only what he wants to see about his wife. He is not aware of how much she wants to do *natureelly* (*CT* IX (H) MancT 162). The cuckholding is observed by a crow Phebus has at his house. The crow discloses his wife's betrayal to him and criticizes his ignorance. We have words of perception with respect to a negative type (D), as shown in (10):

(10) Phebus, "quod he, "for al thy worthynesse,
For al thy beautee and thy gentilesse,
For al thy song and al thy mynstralcye,
For al thy waityng, *blered is thyn ye*
With oon of litel reputacioun, (*CT* IX (H) MancT 249-53)

The crow's words are truthful, but to the effect that Phebus makes a fatal mistake. He is short-tempered with no vision of the future. His chivalric artifice (bowing) ought to be used to kill soldiers on a battlefield, but here is used to kill his important wife at home. He is an expert at bowing, but he does not know when to use it, to whom, nor for what purpose. His blindness is also manifested in his recognition of his ignorance itself. Despite his evaluation of his wife being *gilteles*, she is in fact guilty (F). This can be seen as follows:

(11) "Traitour," quod he, "with tonge of scorpioun,
Thou hast me broght to my *confusioun*; ...
O rakel hand, to doon so foule amys!

O trouble wit, O ire recchelees,
That *unavysed* smyteth gilteles! (*CT* IX (H) MancT 271-80)

He is completely blind to the truth despite the affluence of his light (being attributed to a god of light). Apart from his handsome appearance, he is not at all fitting nor honourable as a knight nor as a husband. The link between the signifying *semely* and its signified is upside down, although the narrator asserts 'The word moot nede accorde with the dede' (*CT* IX (H) MancT 208). This is a typical tale as ascribed to Fragment IX or what Rogers (1986) classifies as 'The Problem of Language.' This is an extreme case in opposition to the prototypical *Emare* and *Amis and Amiloun*. To those readers who know Boethius, Phebus loses human *resoun*, and is degraded to an animal with *ymaginacioun* (*illusioun*), and even worse to an immovable oyster with only *wit*.

6. Summary and conclusion

From the above discussion, the following can be summarized. We examined Chaucer's *semely* and its related words from an optical point of view. In Chaucer's earliest works, *semely* is used in romantic contexts with little or no defectiveness of vision. On the other hand, in Chaucer's later works, *semely* is used through romantic expectations in unromantic contexts. There we have found that it is used with varying degrees of limitedness of vision. This will induce us to say that *semely* in Chaucer tends to be used in the direction of déclassé. The optical structure of *semely* with regard to Chaucer's later works can be summarized as follows:

A. The limited viewer: Aryadne, Prioress, Phebus, etc.
B. Narrowed frame within which he/she sees: *foreyne*, *Bobbe-up-and-doun*, etc.
C. Emphasis on physical features (not corresponding to spiritual features): *chere, contenaunce,* table-manners, etc.
D. Words of perception: [positive] see, lok, etc. [negative] *blered, blynd, confusioun, unavysed*, etc.
E. Words of cognition (degrees of subjectivity): *me thynketh, be likly to ..., lyk*, etc.
F. Evaluation (restricted sense, upside-down sense): *semely, gentil, parfit worthynesse*, etc.

From the above findings, we can arrive at the following conclusion. Chaucer's use of *semely* differs from contemporary northern poets' as well as provincial romance writers' in that it is applied to the characters' limited views, not to the omniscient narrator's. The characters' visions (A) are made relative so much so that they are narrowed down to a small area of sight (B), misplaced, miniaturized, and even upside down. What they see is superficiously limited (C). To this extent the function of *semely* is limited. Those words representing visions (*blered, confusioun, unavysed*, etc.) are significantly related (D). In the case of 'fitting' or 'beautiful,' it is only to the extent that it works within a limited frame, therefore the two are not necessarily compatible: beautiful but not fitting. There the etymological sense 'fitting' contributes to strengthening ironies because it evokes social appropriateness. In the case of 'beautiful' or 'virtuous' it is reduced to the extent that there is very little correspondence between them (C). Further, the newest modalized (epistemic) sense of *semely* 'apparent'/'likely' is very close at hand. From the above examination it can be concluded that *semely* (F) is susceptive to who sees (A), where he/she sees (B), what he/she sees (C), how he/she sees (D), and how far he/she sees (E), in one word, modalization. This provides a possible answer to why *semely* is likely to be what Burnely describes as 'satirical.'

Notes

* I read an earlier version of this paper at Symposium II "Twenty Years from Burnley's *Guide*: Studies on Chaucer's Language (The Nineteenth Congress of the Japan Society for Medieval English Studies, Tokyo University of Foreign Languages, 14 December, 2003). I would like to express my heartfelt thanks to Dr. Michiko Ogura, the organizer of this Symposium, for helpful comments on my paper.

1 Quotations from Chaucer are taken from Benson (1987). The abbreviations of Chaucer's works are also taken from Benson (1987). Italics and underlinings are mine.

2 'Modalizing' is used to show 'many kinds of 'in-between' or qualified sentences, which, revealingly, are less than absolute about something being or not being the case' (Toolan 1998: 46-7).

3 Regarding 'gradability in cognition in Boethian terms,' see for instance *Bo*, 5.p.4.151-4 and 5.p.5.26-6. And for 'gradability in cognition demonstrated in the *Cloud of Unknowing,'* see Chapters 3 and 4.

4 door-hole, window, bedchamber, house, garden, sieged Troy, the dream vision, etc.

5 Words of positive vision: aspie (search out), avisen (look at, consider, instruct), beholden (look at, gaze on, notice), brighte, cape (gaze), devisen (inspect upon, look on, think about, design), eye, gapen (stare), gauren (stare at), kiken (stare), lighte (brighten, shine), loken (look, appear, look to, find out), observen (attend to), percerven (understand with the senses), percen

(pierce with the eye, look straight into), perspectives (CT V (F) SqT 234), piken (peek), pouren (pore, gaze intently, peep), prien (peer, gaze), purveien (foresee, foreknow), sen, sighte, spie (espy, discover), staren (stare), vigil, take hede (heed, attention), visage (put a bold face on), visible, visioun, waiten (watch, await, observe), waken (be, remain awake), ware (aware, discreet), etc.

Words of negative vision: blenden (blind), blere (blear, deceive), blind, deceyve, derk, overloken, unaspied, unavised, unwar, winken (close one's eyes, sleep), wrien (cover, conceal), etc.

6 *Semely* in terms of dialect, period, register and frequency.

works	dialect	period	register	Frequency
St Katherine	South West	c1220	Lives of saints	2
Genesis and Exodus	Midland	early 13c	Biblical	2
Religious Lyrics	various	14c	religious lyrics	5
Langland: Plowman	West Midland	late 14c	homily	0 (B-text)
Gawain-poet	North West	late 14c		
Pearl			religious	3
Cleanness			religious	9
Patience			Biblical	0
Sir Gawain			romance	13
Metrical romances				
Athelston	North Midland	1350-1400	romance	1
Emare	Northeast Midland	late 14c	romance	12
Launfal	Sourthern	c1350	romance	3
Toulous	Northeast Midland	after 1350	romance	2
Auchinleck MS	London	c1330		
Amis and Amiloun			romance	13
The Romance of Guy of Warwick			romance	1
Of Arthour and Of Merlin			romance	0
Orfeo			romance	1
London English		late 14c		

Thomas Usk			testament	4
A Book of London English		late 14c and 15c	Parlimament laws	0
Chaucer Rom (Frag A)	London	late 14c	romance, etc. romance	14 4
BD			elegy (Madam Blanche)	1
LGW			secular hagiography (Betrayers: Jason, Theseus)	2
CT:GP			Introduction (Prioress 3, Host 1)	4
CT: KnT			romance (Venus)	1
CT: Thop			parodied romance (Thopas)	1
CT: MancT			problem tale (Phebus)	1
Gower: Confessio Amantis	London, Kent	late 14c	homily	2

7 Now was Jason a *semely* man withalle,
And *lyk* a lord, and hadde a gret renoun,
And of *his lok* as real as a leoun,
And *goodly of his speche*, and familer, ...
She wex enamoured upon this man. (*LGW* 1603-10)

8 MED s.v. forein 3. An outer room used as a privy, a privy attached to the outer wall of a building. c1390-LGW 1962 (final cit.)

9 *Emare* is a tail rime romance of 1035 lines, written in North East Midland dialect around 1400. *Semely* is used 12 times with a particular stress on the attributes of the heroine's character and people and things related to her. This word refers to the persons and things such as: Virgin Mary (7), Emare (48, 423, 501), jewels (93, 141), cloth (135, 171), hall (459), great lords (471), the king of Galacia and his great lords (486), Sir Kadore and other lords (943). The narrator's evaluation of her and her related persons and things by *semely* is destroyed with little or no hint of a critical view (modalization)(E). The romance *Emare* comes close to being homiletic.

10 Words collocating with nose in Chaucer [male 5 : female 7] (Cf. Burnley 1983: 215). Bold typed words show a positive evaluation of nose, and underlined words a negative evaluation.

Entuned in hir *nose* ful semely (*CT* I (A) GP 123: Prioress [female])

Hir *nose* **tretys** (*CT* I(A) GP 152: Prioress [female])
Upon the cop right of his *nose* he hade / A werte,
(*CT* I (A) GP: 554-5 Miller [male])
His *nose* was **heigh** (*CT* I (A) KnT 2167: Arcite [male])
camus was his *nose* (*CT* I (A) RevT 3934: miller [male], camus=snubbed)
This wench thikke and wel ygrowen was, / With kamus *nose* and eyen as glas, (*CT* I (A) RevT 3973-4: the miller's daughter [female])
'A fair womman, but she be chaast also, / Is lyk a gold ryng in a sowes *nose*.' (*CT* III (D) WBP 784-5 [female])
For, were it wyn or oold or moysty ale / That he hath dronke, he speketh in his *nose*, (*CT* IX (H) 60-1: the Cook [male])
Hir *nose* snorted up for tene, (*Rom* 155: Hate [female])
Hir *nose* **of good proporcioun**, (*Rom* 545: Ydelnesse [female])
His *nose* **by mesure wrought ful right**; (*Rom* 823: Myrthe [male])
Hir *nose* was **wrought at poynt devys**, / For it was gentyl and tretys,
(*Rom* 1215-6: Fraunchise [female])

References

Andrew, M.and R. Waldron. (1978) *The Poems of the Pearl Manuscript: Pearl, Cleanness, Patience, Sir Gawain and the Green Knight.* London: Edward Arnold.

Benson, L. D. ed. (1987) *The Riverside Chaucer: Third Edition Based on The Works of Geoffrey Chaucer Edited by F. N. Robinson.* Boston: Houghton Mifflin Company.

Brown, C. ed. (1924, rpt. 1952) *Religious Lyrics of the Fourteenth Century.* (2nd ed. rev. G. V. Smithers). Oxford: Clarendon Press.

Burnley, J. D. (1983) *A Guide to Chaucer's Language.* London: Macmillan.

Chambers, R. W. and M. Daunt eds. (1967) *A Book of London English 1384-1425.* Oxford: At the Clarendon Press.

Davis, N. et al. eds. (1979) *A Chaucer Glossary.* Oxford: Clarendon Press.

French, W. H. and C. B. Hale. eds. (1930) *Middle English Metrical Romances.* New York: Russell & Russell.

Hodgson, P. ed. (1944) *The Cloud of Unknowing.* EETS OS. 218. Oxford.

Holley, L. T. (1990) *Chaucer's Measuring Eye.* Houseton, Texas: Rice University Press.

Eikenkel, E. ed. (1978, orig. publ. 1884) *The Life of Saint Katherine.* From the Royal MS. 17 A. XXVII. With Its Latin Original. EETS OS 80. Millwood, N.Y.: Kraus Reprint CO.

Kurath, H., S. M. Kuhn, and R. E. Lewis. eds. (1952-2001) *Middle English Dictionary.* Ann Arbor: The University of Michigan Press.

Leach, M. ed. (1960) *Amis and Amiloun.* EETS OS. 203. London / New York / Toronto: Oxford University Press.

Macaulay, G. C. ed. (1900, 1901) *The English Works of John Gower*, 2 Vols, EETS ES. 81, 82. London/New York/Toronto: Oxford University Press.

Macrae-Gibson, O. D. ed. (1973, 1979) *Of Arthour and of Merlin*, 2 Vols. Chicago & London: The University of Chicago Press.

Rogers, W. E. (1986) *Upon the Ways: The Structure of The Canterbury Tales. English Literary Studies.* B. C., Canada: The University of Victoria.

Schmidt, A. V. C. ed. (1995) *William Langland The Vision of Piers Plowman: A Critical Edition of the B-Text Based on Trinity College Cambridge MS B.15.17.* J. M. Dent: London.

Simpson, J. A. and E. S. C. Weiner. eds. (1989) *The Oxford English Dictionary.* 2nd ed. Oxford: Clarendon Press.

Skeat, W. W., ed. (1897, rpt. 1972) *Chaucerian and Other Pieces.* Oxford: Oxford University Press.

Stewart, H. F., E. K. Rand and S. J. Tester. eds. and trs. (1973) *Boethius: The Consolation of Philosophy.* The Loeb Classical Library. Cambridge, MA: Harvard University Press.

Sutherland, R. ed. (1968) *The Romaunt of the Rose and Le Roman de la Rose– A Parallel-Text Edition.* Oxford: Basil Blackwell.

Toolan, Michael. (1998) *Language in Literature: An Introduction to Stylistics.* London / New York / Sydney / Auckland: Arnold.

Zupitza, J. ed. (1966) *The Romance of Guy of Warwick.* EETS. ES 42, 49, and 59. London / New York / Toronto: Oxford University Press.

Lexicological Multiplicity in Chaucer: With Special Reference to Words Related to "Heart"*

Hideshi Ohno

1. Introduction

The aim of this paper is to present one aspect of multiculturalism in the fourteenth-century England from the lexicological viewpoint. Especially, by analysing Chaucer's words, this paper focuses attention on the lexicological multiplicity, in which synonyms of Old English and Old French origins existed with different connotations and different semantic backgrounds.

First of all, let us take a general view of the linguistic picture in the fourteenth-century England. Since the Norman Conquest, Anglo-Norman had been "the dominant language of record for guilds, government administration, law and noble households" (Crane 55-56). However, partly because it "had the characteristics of a dialect from the mid-twelfth century" (Crane 56), its status started to decline by the beginning of the thirteenth century. English, on the other hand, restored its status as an official language, so that in 1362 the opening of Parliament was announced in English. This period, mainly from 1200 to 1350, saw a hoard of lexical borrowings from French (Dekeyser 264), which, along with those from Latin, gave English "the layered lexicon" (Crane 57).

Under the foresaid circumstance Chaucer used English in writing his works, though "French was a second native tongue" (Wimsatt 110) to him. Although about 52% of his total vocabulary is of Romance origin (Mersand 43), his single work has about 12% of borrowings from French on average (Serjeantson 149-50), fewer than those in Langland and other contemporary poets (Hughes 126).

The question now arises: what lexical status or semantic function did the borrowings from French have in Chaucer's works? It is generally said that juxtaposed synonyms had rhetorical and stylistic effects in those days (Mossé 94). In order to solve the question we need to research each loanword, and this paper will examine the words related to "heart," specifically *corage* of Old French origin, comparing it with *herte* of Old English origin.[1] The comparison will treat the statistic aspects such as their frequency in Chaucer's work (in Section 2) and the semantic aspects, such as their collocations and connotations (in Section 3).

Prior to the examination, we need to trace a brief history of *corage*. In Old French, the word meant "heart, innermost feelings, intentions, thoughts; disposition, temper" (Hindley, et al. 152). It seemed to maintain these meanings after its first appearance in English around 1300[2] and by around 1600 the meanings were narrowed to the current definition "valour." According to Knapp, in Chaucer's time "*corage* has three quite distinct senses: 'heart,' 'valor,' and 'lust'" (2000, 13-14). Concerning the last meaning "lust", the MED sides with him, but the OED does not, citing the examples from the works dated around 1600 only (s.v. *courage*, n. 3. e.).

The works the OED or the MED cites whose composition dates are thought to be earlier than Chaucer's works are: *King Alisaunder*, *Handlyng Synne*, *The Seven Sages of Rome*, *Chronicle of England Pt.1*, and *Ayenbite of Inwit*. Most of them are romances and religious works. Among them, according to the MED, the example from *Handlyng Synne* means "lust":

(1) Yn drunkenes men wyl rage, And, ragyng wyl reyse *korage*.[3]
(MED, s.v. *corage* n. 2. (b))

2. Statistical Aspects

2.1. Frequency

This section deals with some statistical aspects of *corage* and *herte*. First, the section treats the frequency of each word. The frequencies appearing in Chaucer are shown in Table 1:

Table 1

	CT	BD	HF	Anel	PF	Bo	Tr	LGW	SP	RomA	Ast
corage	35	1	0	0	0	45	5	2	0	6	0
herte	368	35	12	19	10	18	344	63	39	20	0

This table indicates that *herte* appears more frequently in all works except *Boece*, where *corage* is more than double in number. This is because Chaucer uses *corage* preferably when translating the Latin word *animus* in Boethius. *Corage* is "clearly one of the *termes of philosophie*" (Burnley 1983, 216).

Furthermore, when each tale of the *Canterbury Tales* is taken into consideration, it is clear that *corage* is used relatively frequently for "ethical" (Burnley 1982, 27) tales, such as the *Clerk's Tale* and the *Parson's Tale*, while there are some tales with no example of it, as Table 2 shows.

Table 2

	corage	*herte*
GP	2	4
KnT	2	43
MilT	0	2
RvT	0	4
MLT	1	11
WBT	0	18
FrT	0	2
SumT	0	4
ClT	8	30
MerT	5	20
SqT	1	16
FranT	0	28
PhyT	0	5
PardT	0	8
ShipT	0	1
PrT	0	3
Thop	1	1
Mel	2	34
MkT	2	4
NPT	1	16
SNT	1	5
CYT	0	6
MancT	1	2
ParsT	8	95

This tendency is similar to that of the earlier works mentioned above.

2.2. Rhyme

Next, the focus is placed on rhyme in which *corage* and *herte* appear as rhyme words. In Chaucer's verse, *corage* occurs more frequently in the rhyme position and rhymes with more words than *herte*, as in Table 3.

Table 3

	Examples in Verse	In Rhyme Position	Ratio (%)	Rhyme Fellows
corage	39	29	74.4	17 words, such as *age, marigae*
herte	763	114	14.9	7 words, such as *smerte, sterte*

This tendency is true with Chaucer's contemporary poets: Gower's *Confessio Amantis* has about 90% of *corage* in the rhyme position, while Langland's *The Vision of Piers Plowman*, which does not rhyme, has no example of *corage*. Concerning this, Masui says that words with *-age* ending are frequently used in the rhyme position (1964, 26). Therefore, there may be no denying that *corage* is preferred for the sake of rhyme.

This section has discussed *corage* and *herte* on the basis of their objective evidence, but in other words, the focus has been placed on the superficial tendencies. In order to have true understanding of *corage* and *herte*, it is vital that each individual example is examined fully with its context taken into consideration.

3. Semantic Aspects

3.1. Collocation

This section will treat the semantic aspects of *corage* and *herte*. The aspects may be well described in the collocations of these words,[4] which will be examined first. The following words are looked into: (i) adjectives or adjectival phrases modifying *corage* / *herte*, (ii) verbs which take *corage* / *herte* as their subject or object, (iii) nouns juxtaposed with *corage* / *herte*, (iv) words followed by prepositional phrases of *corage* / *herte* (e.g. *slydynge* in the phrase *slydynge of corage*), and (v) nouns preceded by the genitive cases of *corage* / *herte*.

The result, briefed in Table 4, is that *corage* collocates with those words denoting strong emotions, such as *emprise*, *fers* and *sharp*; whereas *herte* collocates with: (i) words associated with the physical organ such as *breken* and *bresten*, (ii) those denoting destruction and grief such as *dien* and *sorrowful*, (iii) those denoting thinking such as *desiren* and *thinken*, and (iv) those denoting sensitivity such as *pite* and *gentil*.

Table 4

Collocating with	Words
corage only	*emprise, magnanimite, gret, heigh, fel, fers, kene, sharp, demen,* rehersen,* sechen,** etc.
herte only	*dien, breken, bresten, destroien, esen, desiren, thinken, mercy, pite, gentil, dredful, sorrowful,* etc.
both *corage* and *herte*	*awaken, ben, chaungen, given, haven, slen, stiren, turnen, cruel, glad, hardi, noble, sad, mannes / of man, entente, might, wil, repairen,* sechen,* percen,* of folk,* fre,* bodi**

* Words collocating with *corage* in *Boece* only

Additionally, *herte* frequently collocates with the prepositions of space: *in*, *from*, *thurgh*, *to*, *withinne*, and so forth, which means that *herte* is closely connected to an image of a receptacle. These facts may be reflected in quotations (2)-(5):

(2) Debonairetee withdraweth and refreyneth the stirynges and the moevynges of mannes *corage* in his *herte*, in swich manere that they ne skippe nat out by angre ne by ire. (ParsT 655)

(3) Quod Pandarus, "Thow *wrecched mouses herte*,
Artow agast so that she wol the bite? (Tr 3.736-37)

(4) Save wyn and wommen, no thing myghte aswage
His hye entente in armes and labour,
So was he ful of *leonyn corage*. (MkT 2644-46)

(5) But pite renneth soone in *gentil herte*; (LGW F 503)

In (2) *corage* is seen as an emotion which dwells within *herte*. In (3) *herte*, which appears in an address, co-occurs with the words denoting frailty: *wrecched mouses*, while in (4) *corage* with that denoting gallantry: *leonyn*. In (5), which is "Chaucer's favorite line" (Benson 1988, 834), *herte* collocates with the word denoting sensitivity: *gentil*.[5]

A salient characteristic of *herte* is also found, as (6) and (7) represent:

(6) … But certeyn, at the laste,
For this or that, he into bed hym caste,
And seyde, "O thef, is this a *mannes herte*?" (Tr 3.1096-98)

(7) How dorste ye seyn, for shame, unto youre love
That any thyng myghte make yow aferd?
Have ye no *mannes herte*, and han a berd?
Allas! And konne ye been agast of swevenys? (NPT 2918-21)

In (6) Pandarus denounces Troilus, who has fainted in the presence of Criseyde in the bedroom, and in (7) Pertelote denounces Chaunticleer, who is cowed by his dream in which a hound-like beast killed him. In both these quotations *herte*, collocating with *mannes*, expresses masculinity which a male is thought to possess by nature. No example of *corage* in this usage can be found in Chaucer. This phenomenon can be explained by Wrenn's comment that native words "have a far deeper content of feeling" (35) than loanwords.

In *Boece*, however, as in Table 4, *corage* appears with *percen*, *bodi*, *demen*, *rehersen*, and so forth, which have a close connection with *herte* in the other works. That may mean that *corage* and *herte* are used more similarly or synonymously in this work.

3.2. Connotation and Context

Now let us attempt to extend the observation into the contexts in which *corage* and *herte* appear and into their connotations, as seen in (6) and (7). As Knapp (2000) suggests, the remarkable use of *corage* can be found in the *Clerk's Tale* and the *Merchant's Tale*.

The *Clerk's Tale* concerns Grisilde's "vertuous suffraunce" (1162), who is hallowed, being described as "from hevene sent" (440). In this tale *corage* appears eight times, as in Table 2. Six out of the eight refer to Grisilde's heart and the other two to Walter's. The fact that *herte* numerically equals *corage* in this tale (14 examples to Grisilde's and 12 to Walter's) proves the inclination of *corage* towards Grisilde's. A couple of examples of *corage* referring to Grisilde's heart are as follows:

(8) But thogh this mayde tendre were of age,
Yet in the brest of hire virginitee
Ther was enclosed rype and sad *corage*;
And in greet reverence and charitee
Hir olde povre fader fostred shee. (ClT 218-22)

(9) "Ther may no thyng, God so my soule save,
Liken to yow that may displese me;
Ne I desire no thyng for to have,
Ne drede for to leese, save oonly yee.
This wyl is in myn herte, and ay shal be;
No lengthe of tyme or deeth may this deface,
Ne chaunge my *corage* to another place." (ClT 505-11)

In these quotations, *corage* does not take the rhyme position, and therefore it is likely to be used because of its connotation, although one cannot deny that it may be preferred for metrical reasons. In writing this tale, Chaucer follows Petrarch, who turned the original story of

Boccaccio "into an exemplum" (Cooper 189) and "overtly Christianizes and moralizes the tale, ... casting it into the language and rhetorical style that would suit the new dignity of the subject matter" (Mascatine 191). The Christianization and moralization can be seen in the use of *corage*, although a minute comparison among Boccaccio, Petrarch, and Chaucer has not been done. This idea is also supported by Héraucourt, who explains Chaucer's *corage* on the basis of the cardinal virtues.[6]

For the discussion about the use of *corage* above mentioned, it will be necessary to refer to *corage* in *Troilus and Criseyde*. In the story *corage*, collocating with *noble*, *heigh*, and *ordeyne* from the beginning, expresses exemplary or ideal spirit of human beings. Quotation (10), which is the last one in the story, is the narrator's description of Criseyde, who has betrayed her promise to come back to Troilus and given her heart[7] to Diomede.

(10) She sobre was, ek symple, and wys withal,
The best ynorisshed ek that myghte be,
And goodly of hire speche in general,
Charitable, estatlich, lusty, fre;
Ne nevere mo ne lakked hire pite;
Tendre-herted, slydynge of *corage*;
But trewely, I kan nat telle hire age. (Tr 5.820-26)

It is safe to say that this *corage* also connotes morality, as Burnley (1982) explains *slydyng of corage* shows "a failure in rationality" (32) and "moral weakness" (37).

Now let us return to the *Clerk's Tale*. It is noticeable that *corage* is used twice to mention Walter's heart. One example is (11), in which *corage* is juxtaposed with *herte*:

(11) "Wyf," quod this markys, "ye han herd er this
My peple sikly berth oure mariage;
And namely sith my sone yboren is,
Now is it worse than evere in al oure age.
The murmur sleeth myn *herte* and my *corage*,
For to myne eres comth the voys so smerte
That it wel ny destroyed hath myn herte. (ClT 624-30)

There are differences in the interpretation of *corage* among scholars: Benson (2002) says it means "feelings," Sasamoto says it means "valour" (186), and Masui says *herte and corage* means "mind and body" (1995, 139). However, the results of its collocation considered, there seems to be general agreement among them that *corage* represents an emotion dwelling within the *herte*. Furthermore, in addition to the three opinions, *corage* may mean the moral sense of Walter as marquis and lord, as seen in Grisilde's case.

The other example is (12), in which Janicula criticizes Walter.

(12) For out of doute this olde poure man
Was evere in suspect of hir mariage;
For evere he demed, sith that it bigan,
That whan the lord fulfild hadde his *corage*,
Hym wolde thynke it were a disparage
To his estaat so lowe for t'alighte,
And voyden hire as soone as ever he myghte. (ClT 904-10)

It may be adequate to interpret this *corage* as "desire," or as "lust" as both Benson (1987, 1232) and the MED say. At least this *corage* has secular or profane connotations in contrast to the *corage* discussed so far.

The use of *corage* with secular connotations can be found in the *Merchant's Tale*, which, like the *Clerk's Tale*, deals with the married life of Januarie and May, but, unlike it, is a fabliau in that May has a love affair with Damian. Although there are some examples of *corage* meaning "courage" in the tale, close attention should centre on Januarie's *corage*, as seen in (13)-(15).

(13) Bacus the wyn hem shynketh al aboute,
And Venus laugheth upon every wight,
For Januarie was bicome hir knyght
And wolde bothe assayen his *corage*
In libertee, and eek in mariage;
And with hire fyrbrond in hire hand aboute
Daunceth biforn the bryde and al the route. (MerT 1722-28)

(14) But nathelees yet hadde he greet pitee
That thilke nyght offenden hire moste he,
And thoughte, "Allas! O tendre creature,
Now wolde God ye myghte wel endure
Al my *corage*, *it* is so sharp and keene!
I am agast ye shul *it* nat susteene.
But God forbede that I dide al my myght! (MerT 1755-61)

(15) He drynketh ypocras, clarree, and vernage
Of spices hoote t'encreessen his *corage*;
And many a letuarie hath he ful fyn,
Swiche as the cursed monk, daun Constantyn,
Hath writen in his book *De Coitu*;
To eten hem alle he nas no thyng eschu. (MerT 1807-12)

In (13), which describes the marriage feast, the appearance of Bacchus and Venus gives sexual imagery to the scene. Concerning (15), according to Galenic medicine on which *De Coitu* is based, *corage* is spirit or humour which is necessary for sexual intercourse (Delany 561). When a word takes on sexual connotations in the "courtly" (Cooper 203) style used in a fabliau, one can say that *corage* functions as a euphemism. This idea is supported by Marchand (43-44), who says that loanwords and even biblical terms are used euphemistically.

Both the *Clerk's Tale* and the *Merchant's Tale* handle the same theme, but there is a big difference in the use of *corage* between them. McMahon states that "Borrowed and native words consequently come to occupy different registers. ...the existence of such register differences provides a useful source of euphemisms. Translating between registers can also produce humorous or peculiar effects" (202), but additionally, it can be said that there are different registers in the one word *corage* and they make the contrast between the two tales and between Grisilde's and Walter's hearts presented effectively.

4. Conclusion

In Chaucer's works, *corage*, as a loanword, can coexist with *herte* by expressing images and values native *herte* cannot express because of its inextricable link to the physical organ. Moreover, different images and values coexist in *corage* itself. By using these words and the different registers, Chaucer tells his stories and describes his characters' hearts vividly. At the same time, there existed the linguistic environment which was able to allow the lexicological multi-culture in the fourteenth-century England.

Notes

* This is a revised version of the paper read at the symposium, "Multiplicity in Medieval European Culture: With Special reference to England," in the 18th Congress of Japan Society for Medieval English Studies, which was held at Hiroshima University on 8 December 2002. I would like to thank Prof. Akiyuki Jimura, Prof. Noboru Harano, Prof. Hiromichi Yamashiro, Prof. Hidemi Mizuta, Prof. So Shitanda, and Prof. Yoshiyuki Nakao for their detailed comments and suggestions.

1 Burnley observes just that "Although it would be incorrect to assert that the words *corage*, *herte*, *thought*, *soule* and *spirit* are clearly distinct in Chaucer's usage as a whole, it is apparent that in some contexts, and consequently in their connotations, they can be distinguished" (1983, 217).

2 The first example cited in the OED is from *King Alisaunder*.

3 The italics are mine in each quotation.

4 Henceforth, the pronouns denoting *herte* and *corage* are also included in the research data.

5 Burnley states that "*gentil herte* is 'fulfild of pitee' (CT. II, 660)" ... *Pitee*, too, is a quality of the *gentil* man; ... Sympathetic identification between members of the courtly community is as important a concept as it is between Christians. The capacity for feeling this compassion defines a particular kind of heart which Chaucer often refers to as a 'pitous herte', but alternatively, it may be called a 'gentil herte'" (1979, 153).

6 Courage or fortitude is one of them, the others being wisdom, temperance and justice.

7 In love, *herte* is used but *corage* is not. See Oka and Jimura (1991).

References

Benson, L. D., ed. (1987) *The Riverside Chaucer*. 3rd ed. Boston: Houghton Mifflin.

Benson, L. D., ed. (1993) *A Glossarial Concordance to the Riverside Chaucer*. Vol. I. New York: Garland.

Benson, L. D. (2002) "The Clerk's Prologue and Tale: An Interlinear Translation." *The Geoffrey Chaucer Page*. (Online. 5 Nov. 2002).

Burnley, J. D. (1979) *Chaucer's Language and the Philosopher's Tradition*. Cambridge: D. S. Brewer.

Burnley, J. D. (1982) "Criseyde's Heart and the Weakness of Women: An Essay in Lexical Interpretation." *Studia Neophilologica* 54: 25-38.

Burnley, J. D. (1983) *A Guide to Chaucer's Language*. London: Macmillan.

Cannon, C. (1998) *The Making of Chaucer's English*. Cambridge: Cambridge UP.

Cooper, H. (1996) *Oxford Guides to Chaucer:* The Canterbury Tales. 2nd ed. Oxford: Oxford UP.

Crane, S. (1999) "Anglo-Norman cultures in England, 1066-1460." *The Cambridge History of Medieval English Literature*. Ed. David Wallace. Cambridge: Cambridge UP, 35-60.

Davis, N. (1974) "Chaucer and Fourteenth-century English." *Geoffrey Chaucer: the Writer and His Background*. Ed. Derek Brewer. Cambridge: D. S. Brewer, 58-84.

Davis, N., et al., eds. (1979) *A Chaucer Glossary*. Oxford: Clarendon.

Dekeyser, X. (1986) "Romance loans in Middle English: a re-assessment." *Linguistic Theory and Historical Linguistics*. Ed. Dieter Kastovsky and Aleksander Szwedek. Berlin: Mouton, 253-65.

Delany, P. (1967) "Constantinus Africanus and Chaucer's *Merchant's Tale*." *Philological Quarterly* 46: 560-66.

García, B. C. (2000) "Historical background of multilingualism and its impact on English." *Multilingualism in Later Medieval Britain*. Ed. D. A. Trotter. Cambridge: D. S. Brewer, 25-36.

Héraucourt, W. (1941) "Chaucers Vorstellung von den Geistig-Seelischen Kräften des Menschen." *Anglia* 65: 255-302.

Herbermann, C. G., et al, eds. (1908) *The Catholic Encyclopedia*. Vol. 3. New York: Robert Appleton. (*New Advent*. Online. 22 Nov. 2002).

Hindley, A., et al., eds. (2000) *Old French-English Dictionary*. Cambridge: Cambridge UP.

Hughes, G. (2000) *A History of English Words*. Oxford: Blackwell.

Jimura, A. (1991) "Chaucer's Use of 'herte' in *The Book of the Duchess*." *Language and Style in English Literature: Essays in Honour of Michio Masui*. Ed. Michio Kawai. Tokyo: Eihosha.

Jimura, A. (2002) "Multiplicity in Chaucer's English." *Multiplicity in Medieval European Culture*. (in Japanese) Hiroshima: Keisuisha, 79-118.

Kastovsky, D. and A. Mettinger, eds. (2001) *Language Contact in the History of English*. Frankfurt am Main: Peter Lang.

Knapp, P. A. (2000) *Time-Bound Words: Semantic and Social Economies from Chaucer's England to Shakespeare's*. Basingstoke: Macmillan Press.

Kurath, H., et al., eds. (1952-2001) *Middle English Dictionary*. Ann Arbor: The University of Michigan Press.

Marchand, J. W. (1999) "'Quoniam', 'Wife of Bath's Prologue' D.608." *Neuphilologische Mitteilungen* 100: 43-49.

Masui, M. (1964) *The Structure of Chaucer's Rime Words: An Exploration into the Poetic Language of Chaucer*. Tokyo: Kenkyusha.

Masui, M., trans. (1995) *The Canterbury Tales*. (in Japanese) 3 vols. Tokyo: Iwanami.

Matsushita, T., ed. (1998) *A Glossarial Concordance to* William Langland's The Vision of Piers Plowman: The B-Text. Tokyo: Yushodo.

McInerney, M. B. (1998) "'Is this a mannes herte?': Unmanning Troilus through Ovidian Allusion." *Masculinities in Chaucer: Approaches to Maleness in the* Canterbury Tales *and* Troilus and Criseyde. Ed. P. G. Beidler. Cambridge: D. S. Brewer, 221-235.

McMahon, A. M. S. (1994) *Understanding Language Change*. Cambridge: Cambridge UP.

Mersand, J. (1939) *Chaucer's Romance Vocabulary*. New York: Comet Press. Reissued. Washington: Kennikat Press, 1968.

Mossé, F. (1947) *Esquisse D'une Histoire de la Langue Anglaise*. Lyon: Rue Victor-Lagrange.

Muscatine, C. (1960) *Chaucer and the French Tradition*. Berkeley: University of California Press.

Oka, F. (1997) *Investigations on Courtly Words and Others*. Tokyo: Kokubunsha.

Pickles, J. D. and J. L. Dawson, eds. (1987) *A Concordance to John Gower's* Confessio Amantis. Cambridge: D. S. Brewer.

Sasamoto, H., trans. (2002) *The Canterbury Tales*. (in Japanese) Tokyo: Eihosha.

Serjeantson, M. S. (1935) *A History of Foreign Words in English*. London: Kegan Paul.

Simpson, J. A. and E. S. C. Weiner, eds. (2002) *The Oxford English Dictionary*. 2nd ed. CD-ROM. Ver. 3. Oxford: Clarendon.

Thomas, P. R. (1998) "'Have ye no mannes herte?': Chauntecleer as Cock-Man in the *Nun's Priest's Tale*." *Masculinities in Chaucer: Approaches to Maleness in the* Canterbury Tales *and* Troilus and Criseyde. Ed. Peter G. Beidler. Cambridge: D. S. Brewer, 187-202.

Wimsatt, J. I. (1974) "Chaucer and French Poetry." *Geoffrey Chaucer: the Writer and His Background.* Ed. Derek Brewer. Cambridge: D. S. Brewer.

Wrenn, C. L. (1949) *The English Language.* London: Methuen. Reprinted 1954.

"Pendragon" and "Tyntagill" in *The Destruction of Troy*: A Conjecture

Hiroyuki Matsumoto

It is strange that there are two proper names related to the Arthurian legend in *The Destruction of Troy* (hereafter *D.Troy*): "Pendragon" in line 5436 and "Tyntagill" in line 1670. Why did the poet use those names in the Troy legend? There might be some reasons hidden behind his use of those names. This paper, therefore, aims to consider the reasons.

1. Pendragon and Pandarus

1.1. *D.Troy*

> *Pendragon* þe pert prestly was on,
> And Thabor þat tother, a tor man of strenght,
> Adasthon the doghti þat derfe was the þrid. (5436-38)

This is a descriptive part of kings and lords who came to help Troy and in which "Pendragon" is listed first among them. Since the source of *D.Troy* is Guido's *Historia Destructionis Troiae*, it may be worthwhile to look at the corresponding lines in the source:

1.2. Guido's *Historia*

> ...rex videlicit *Pandarus*, rex Thabor, et rex Andastrus. (p. 115)

Although Guido also mentions three kings, the first is not "Pendragon" but "Pandarus". In order to see the validity of the latter name, it is not useless to refer briefly to other sources. The source of Guido's *Historia* is *Le Roman de Troie* by Benoit de Sainte-Maure, whose sources are *De Excidio Troiae Historia* by Dares Phrygius and *Ephemeridos Belli Troiai* by Dictys Cretensis. The following citations are the corresponding lines in each source.

1.3. Benoit's *Roman*

> De Sezile i vint *Pandarus*,
> Ampon li vieuz e Adrastus. (6667-8)

1.4. Dares's *Excidio*

> ... de Zelia *Pandarus* Amphius Adrastus... (§ XVIII)

1.5. Dictys's *Ephemeridos*

> primus igitur portis erumpit *Pandarus* Lycaone genitus ex Lycia ...
> (§ 35)

In addition, it is worth looking at Homer's *Illiad*, though it is not the primary source of those two Latin prose works.

1.6. Homer's *Illiad*

> The men that lived in Zeleia...were led by the famous son of Lycaon, *Pandarus*... (Bk.II, l.827)

It should be noted that all these citations keep the name "Pandarus" in the corresponding lines except that of *D.Troy*. Therefore, it is apparent that the Troy-poet, John Clerk changed "Pandarus" to "Pendragon". What made him change the name? In order to find a clue to answer this question, it may be appropriate to see another Troy legend in Middle English, *Lydgate's Troy Book*. John Lydgate also translated Guido's *Historia* into Middle English. The following are the corresponding lines of his to those of *D.Troy*.

1.7.1. *Lydgate's Troy Book,* Book II

> þe first of hem was callid *Pandarus*,
> And as I rede, Thabor þe secounde,
> þe þridde Andastrus, licke as it is founde; (Bk.2, 7626-28)

As he is an ardent devotee of Chaucer, he goes so far as to insert an episode of his master's *Troilus and Criseyde* into his translation of Guido's, as in what follows:

1.7.2. *Lydgate's Troy Book,* Book III

> And in þis wise Troylus first be-gan
> To be a seruaunt, my maister telleth þus,
> Til he was holpe aftir of *Pandarus*, (Bk.3, 4214-16)

The first "Pandarus" in line 7626, Bk.II is referred to as one of the lords of the Trojan allies, as in the sources cited above, while the second in line 4216, Bk.III, as the famous character in Chaucer's work. Therefore the two Pandarus's surely come to confuse the reader.

Now, although John Clerk does not mention Chaucer's "Pandarus" as Lydgate does, the following lines seem to show that he knew Chaucer's *Troilus*:

Who-so wilnes to wit of þaire wo fir,
Turne hym to *Troilus* and talke þere ynoghe. (*D.Troy* 8053-54)

Since the lines corresponding to the above are not found in Guido's *Historia*, they are certainly the poet's original and so "Troilus" in line 8054 seems, as some critics point out[1], to refer to Chaucer's work, which suggests that he had known the tragic story. Although it is difficult to ascertain whether he had read *Lydgate's Troy Book*[2], it is most likely that his change of the personal name hints his intention to avoid the confusion caused by using such a well-known name. If this presumption is true, then the next questions are why he has adopted "Pendragon" , though he could have chosen any other names beginning with 'P' which is required by alliteration, and what he learned it from. Let us look at a brief survey of works which contain the name in order to solve the problems.

1.8. Geoffrey of Monmouth's *Historia Regum Britanniae*

> From that moment onwards he was called *Utherpendragon*, which in the British language means 'a dragon's head'. He had been given this title because it was by means of a dragon that Merlin had prophesied that he would become King. (Bk.VIII, §17, p.202)

1.9. Wace's *Roman de Brut*

> *Uther Pendragon.* Pendragon was his name in the Briton's tongue, but Dragon's head in that of Rome. (p.33)

1.10. *Laȝamon's Brut*

þene nome heo him laiden on: þet wes *Vđer Pendragon*,
Pendragun an Brutisc, Draken-hefd an Englisc. (9096-97)

1.11. *Of Arthour and of Merlin*

And þi lond þou fond to were
Vter Pendragoun and mani anoþer
And Aurilis Broslas his broþer (1720-22, Auchinleck MS)

1.12. The Prose *Merlin*

> "*Pendragon* taried not till he come to his brother Vter."
> (Chapter III; pp.46-47)

1.13. Henry Lovelich's *Merlin*

They ben the vesselis of *Pendragown*,
that to this Rewm hath good Resown;
and also vter, his brother so dere,

> jnto his Rewm with him cometh here
> of Fortager taken veniaunce, (3075-79)

The above citations show that "Pendragon" which originated from Geoffrey's *Historia* descended to Wace's *Brut* and *Laȝamon's Brut* or through the French Vulgate *Merlin* down to the later works of Merlin, *Of Arthour and of Merlin*, The Prose *Merlin* and Henry Lovelich's *Merlin*. Which of those works did the poet borrow the name from? The exact date of *D.Troy* is uncertain, so it is difficult to identify the source. However, some critics agree that the date would be about 1400.[3] If this is true, there is no possibility that the poet had read either The Prose *Merlin* or Henry Lovelich's *Merlin*, both of which are said to be written in about 1450, nor *Of Arthour and of Merlin*, the original of which was said to be composed between 1250 and 1300 and the Auchinleck MS in c.1330 and MS Lincoln's Inn 150 in a.1425. Since the source of *D.Troy* is the Latin prose of Guido's *Historia*, it may be natural to assume that the poet could read Geoffrey's *Historia*. Furthermore, one of the manuscripts of Guido's *Historia*, MS Harley 4123, in which many variant forms of proper names are similar to those of *D.Troy*, contains Geoffrey's *Historia*. From those circumstantial facts, it may be most likely that he adopted "Pendragon" from Geoffrey's *Historia*.

Why did he choose the name then? "Uther Pendragon" is, according to Geoffrey's *Historia*, the father of King Arthur. The original "Pandarus" in Guido's *Historia* is mentioned as the first lord who came to support Troy. Therefore the poet may have regarded "Pendragon" as suitable, though anachronistic, for the honorable first comer and thereby wanted to avoid any confusion caused by using the same name as Chaucer's "Pandarus".

2. Tyntagill

2.1. *D.Troy*

> For the souerayn hym-selfe was a sete riall,
> Pight full of peritoris and of proude gemys,
> Atyret with a tabernacle of *Tyntagill*[4] fyn. (1668-70)

This is part of the descriptive passage of the royal seat in the palace of new Troy. The name "Tyntagill" also comes from Geoffrey's *Historia* on to Wace's *Historia* and *Laȝmon's Brut* and down to the works of Merlin cited above:

2.2. Geoffrey's *Historia*

> As he [Gorlois, Duke of Cornwall] was more worried about his wife [Ygerne] than he was about himself, he left her in the castle of *Tintagel*... (p. 205)

2.3. Wace's *Brut*

> He [Gorlois] went into Cornwall...His wife [Igerne] he put in his castle of *Tintagel*, for this was the home of his father and of his race. (pp. 37-39)

2.4. *Laȝamon's Brut*

> And sugged Vđer Kinge at *Tintaieol* he mai me finden: (9277)

2.5. *Of Arthour and of Merlin*

> Ac al þai loked swiþe ȝerne
> After *Tintagel* and Ygerne. (2377-78)

2.6. The Prose *Merlin*

> "And Vterpendragon dide as Merlin hadde devised...and so thei wenten forth alle thre till thei com ner at *Tintagell*..." (Chapter IV; p.76)

2.7. Henry Lovelich's *Merlin*

> so longe alle thre to-gederis paste,
> that to *tyntagel* they comen atte laste. (5491-92)

All citations except that of *Of Arthour and of Merlin* disclose that "Tintagel" is the place name of Duke Gorlois of Cornwall and that it is the birthplace of Arthur, but there is no necessity to use the place name in the Trojan legend. The corresponding lines of Guido's *Historia* have no such mention:

2.7. Guido's *Historia*

> Sic et utroque latere mensarumordo distensus comodas dabat discumbentibus sessiones. (p. 50)
> (Meek's translation: "On each side of the tables, the long row of benches offered comfortable seats to the dinner guests.")

In the case of "Tyntagill", therefore, the proper name may be a scribal error for a common noun because the name is irrelevant to the context. A common noun which modifies the previous word "tabernacle" in the line would be best fitted.

Notes

* This is a revised version of my paper read at the Reunion of the Centre for Medieval English Studies in Tokyo held on 5th April, 2003.

1 E.B. Atwood, *English Versions of the Historia Trojana.* Diss. University of Virginia, 1932. 135-37. William Ringler, 'An Early Chaucer Allusion Restored', *Notes & Queries*, 174 (1938), 120. C.D. Benson, 'A Chaucerian Allusion and the Date of the Alliterative "Destruction of Troy"', *Notes & Queries*, 219 (1974), 206-7. Thorlac Turville-Petre, *Alliterative Poetry of the Late Middle Ages: An Anthology.* (Routledge; London, 1989), 170.

2 McKay Sundwall argues that *D.Troy* was written after 1420, on the grounds that the Troy-poet "drew upon Lydgate as a source for both the allusion" of Chaucer's work, 'Troilus' in line 8054 and Diomede's gesture in grasping Briseida's rein in line 8077. (*Review of English Studies*, 26, (1975), pp.313-17.) But even if the Troy-poet had not read *Lydgate's Troy Book*, he would have known the phrase 'toke the reyne' in line 8077 because the 'reyne' is so highly an alliterating word that the poet could use it without Lydgate's example.

3 Mabel Day. *The Siege of Jerusalem*, ed. E. Kölbing & Mabel Day. EETS. OS.188; Kraus Reprint 1971. xxix. E.B. Atwood, op.cit. C.D. Benson, op.cit.

4 The editors of the EETS edition transcribed the word as 'Eyntayill', but the manuscript shows that the correct form is 'Tyntagill'.

References

Barron, W. R. J. & S. C. Weinberg, eds. & trans., (1995) *Laȝmon's Brut.* Longman: London.

Bergen, H., ed. (1906-35) *Lydgate's Troy Book*, 4 parts. EETS. ES.97, 103, 106, 126. London; Kraus Reprint, 1973.

Constans, L., ed. (1904-12) *Le Roman de Troie par Benoit de Sainte-Maure.* Paris.

Eisenhut, W., ed. (1958) *Dictys Cretensis Ephemeridos Belli Troiani.* Leipzig.

Griffin, N. E., ed. (1936) *Guido de Columnis Historia Destructionis Troiae.* Cambridge, Mass.: The Medieval Academy of America.

Kock, E. A., ed. (1904-32) *Merlin, A Middle-English Metrical Version of A French Romance by Herry Lovelich.* EETS. ES.93, 112, 185. London.

Macrae-Gibson, O. D., ed. (1973, 1979) *Of Arthour and of Merlin.* 2 Vols. EETS. OS.268, 279. London.

Mason, E., trans. (1962) *Wace and Layamon: Arthurian Chronicles.* Dent: London.

Matsumoto, H., ed. (2002) *The Destruction of Troy: A Diplomatic and Color Facsimile Edition*, University of Michigan Press. (Citations have been punctuated by the editor.)

Meek, M. E., trans. (1974) *Historia Destructionis Troiae: Guido delle Colonne*, Bloomington & London: Indiana University Press.

Meister, F., ed. (1873) *Daretis Phrygii de Excidio Troiae Historia.* Leipzig.

Rieu, E. V., trans. (1950) *Homer: The Illiad.* London: Penguin Books.

Epistemic Adverbs in the *Paston Letters*

NAOKI HIRAYAMA

1. Introduction

The *Paston Letters* is a representative collection of correspondence of the fifteenth century. In the letters, using modal expressions (i.e. modal auxiliaries, epistemic verbs, subjunctive mood, etc.), the addressers indicate their attitude about what they say. They can also soften their tone by those expressions in order to keep good relationships with the addressees unless they are adopting businesslike manners. I have been examining those modal expressions in the text from the viewpoint of the speaker's involvement.

This paper is an attempt to make clear some features of epistemic adverbs (i.e. the adverbs indicating the speaker's attitude toward the propositional content of the sentence) from the above viewpoint, with special regard to their occurrence in the *Paston Letters*. I will use the text edited by Norman Davis as shown in (1). This paper will refer to part of the usage of epistemic adverbs in the fifteenth century.

(1) TEXT: Norman Davis ed. *Paston Letters and Papers of the Fifteenth Century*, Vols. 1, 2. London: Oxford, 1971, 1976.

2. Previous scholarship and problems

Swan (1998) has already conducted diachronic research into various adverbs. 'Epistemic adverbs' in this paper are equivalent to Swan's 'SA (sentence adverb(ial)(s)).' Although she has dealt with the *Paston Letters* as one of a large variety of works, she has investigated only 150 pages at the beginning of the first volume of Davis's text. Nor has she adopted the viewpoint of grammaticalization and subjectification very much. Her strong interest is in the relationship between the positions of adverbs and their development of SA usage. In this paper I will describe the epistemic adverbs in the whole text with regard to various points concerning grammaticalization and subjectification, which are not limited to the positions of the adverbs.

3. Methodology of grammaticalization and subjectification

3.1. Definition

Hopper and Traugott (1993) and Traugott (1972) define grammaticalization and subjectification as seen in (2).

(2) a. [G]rammaticalization is usually thought of as that subset of linguistic changes through which a lexical item becomes a grammatical item, or through which a grammatical item becomes more grammatical. (Hopper and Traugott 2)

b. '[S]ubjectification' refers to a pragmatic-semantic process whereby 'meanings become increasingly based in the speaker's subjective belief state/attitude toward the proposition', in other words, toward what the speaker is talking about. (Traugott 35)

3.2. Scale based on grammaticalization and subjectification

3.2.1. An illustrative example

In (3) I have picked up three types of *certainly* from the text to illustrate the gradience of the speaker's involvement. (3a) is an example of 'manner adverb.' It is clear that *certainly* modifies the verb "write" because it collocates with the emphatic adverb "right." Although (3b) is also an example of a manner adverb modifying the verb "knowe," we can also regard it as a somewhat epistemic one (i.e. 'intermediate adverb' in this paper), which makes a unity with the 'harmonic' (Coates 45) parenthetical "I knowe" (underlined). Placed within the propositional clause "tei wylle laboren," we can understand that the unity is expressing the speaker's subjective attitude toward the content of the propositional clause. In (3c) the adverb is a much more developed example of an 'epistemic (sentence) adverb,' expressing the speaker's involvement. Here, "in my reason" (underlined) indicates that the statement is based on John III's own reasoning. Occurring with a conditional clause, the adverb emphasizes the speaker's confident prediction with the assumption that the conditions are satisfied.

(3) a. Though I write right ***certeynly***, if ye loke hem lightly and see hem seld thei shall sone be forgete. (0770167)[1]

b. And as for ȝoure breteren, tei wylle I knowe ***certeynly*** laboren all tat in hem lyeth for ȝow. (0300014)

c. [B]ut in my reason, and (=if) my lord Chamberleyn wold send my lady a letter wyth some preuy tokyn betwyx theym, and allso to meue my lord of Norffolk when he comyth to the perlement, ***serteynly*** Caster is yours. (3540052)

3.2.2. Scale based on syntax

To avoid a subjective classification when examining the subjectivity of each adverb, I classified the grammatical environment of the adverbs according to the syntactic features as shown in (4). After considering those scales there, I classified the adverbs.

(4) a. manner adverb: occurs before or after a verb to modify it, and occurs with emphatic adverbs (e.g. *right*, *more*, etc.)

b. intermediate adverb: expresses the speaker's attitude toward the propositional content of the clause, and is usually used with an epistemic verb with a *that*-clause [2] (e.g. I know *verily* that ...), although it is syntactically a manner adverb.

c. epistemic (sentence) adverb: occurs at the beginning or in the final part of the sentence, modifies the whole sentence, and is used with the verb *be* when located within the sentence (see (3c) above).

3.3. Points to check based on the strata in the sentences

To investigate to what extent the adverbs have developed their grammatical unity and subjectivity, I have established the points to check according to the three strata in the sentences according to Sawada (1993: 207). Although these three strata in a sentence are usually expressed at once, I will consider the points to check in each stratum as shown below (3.3.1-3.3.3).

3.3.1. Stratum of proposition

Positions of adverbs, person of the subjects, self-controllability of the verbs (self-controllable / not self-controllable) in the scope of adverbs, and types of the clauses including the adverbs

3.3.2. Stratum of modality

Whether or not the adverbs co-occur with modal auxiliaries and / or epistemic verbs

3.3.3. Stratum of pragmatic force

Social relationships (between addressers and addressees)

4. Results of my investigation based on the points to check listed in 3.3.

In this paper I will chiefly focus on the four representative adverbs in Italics in Table 1, because the frequency of their occurrence is comparatively greater than that of the others and they have some noteworthy features. I have picked up these adverbs: *peradventure* is used as an epistemic adverb; *plainly* is mainly used as a manner adverb; *truly* is used both as a manner and an epistemic adverb; *verily* is used as an 'intermediate adverb,' which is much more frequently used in this way than any other ones.

Table 1

	manner	intermediate	epistemic	total
certainly	8	2	4	14
clearly	21	2	4	27
credibly	5	2	0	7
evidently	1	0	0	1
faithfully	38	0	0	1
forsooth	0	0	3	3
iwis	0	0	7	7
justly	0	0	1	1
needs [3]	0	0	42	42
openly	13	0	0	13
parde	0	0	1	1
peradvanture	***0***	***0***	***31***	***31***
percase (per case)	0	0	9	9
plainly	***78***	***2***	***4***	***84***
readily	12	0	0	12
really	1	0	0	1
reasonably	19	0	2	21
sickerly	0	0	1	1
sooth	1	0	1	2
surely	16	1	1	18
truly	***35***	***0***	***28***	***63***
utterly	15	1	2	18
verily	***78***	***35***	***6***	***119***
witterly (= clearly)	3	0	0	3
total	344	45	148	537

4.1. Stratum of proposition

4.1.1. Positions

First, I will focus on the positions in which the adverbs occur. Here, 'initial position' includes the beginning of the clause.

All 31 examples of *peradventure* in the text are epistemic adverbs wherever they occur as seen in the Table 2. Although examples of *truly* in the initial position are epistemic ones, there are many examples of a manner adverb in the medial position (33/63 (52%)) as seen in the Table 3. It is certain that the adverbs occurring in the initial position tend to be epistemic adverbs as many previous studies have pointed out (Quirk et al. 517, Brinton 111, etc.). An example of epistemic *peradventure* in the medial position and an example of epistemic *truly* in the initial position are cited in (5) and (6).

Table 2 ***peradventure***

	initial	medial	final	total
manner	0	0	0	0
intermediate	0	0	0	0
epistemic	18(100)	12(100)	1(100)	31
total	18(100)	12(100)	1(100)	31

Table 3 ***truly***

	initial	medial	final	total
manner	0	33(97)	2(40)	35
intermediate	0	0	0	0
epistemic	24(100)	1(3)	3(60)	27
total	24(100)	34(100)	5(100)	63

(5) My maister your husbond wole ***parauenture*** blame vs all if this mater be not applied, for he may not of reson do so largely heryn by his myght. (7160017)

(6) And ***truly*** my moder dede here devere ryth feythfully þer-jn, as myn cosyn Clere xal tellyn Zw qhan þat he spekyth wyth Zw. (1280034)

As shown in Tables 4 and 5, many examples of *plainly* (78/84 (93%)) and *verily* (115/119 (97%)) occurring in the medial position are seen. Moreover, they are different from each other in terms of the ratio of 'intermediate' (*plainly*: 2 (3%); *verily*: 35 (30%)). This is what we cannot characterize the adverbs only from the viewpoint of their positions. However, comparing each semantic range of *plainly* and *verily* in the *OED*, we can find the difference between them. *Plainly* expresses both sheer manner and the speaker's subjective meanings (*OED s.v. plainly* (1 and 3)), but *verily* is more expressive of the speaker's subjectivity collocating with verbs of believing, thinking, etc. rather than sheer manner (*OED s.v. verily*). In (7) and (8) I have cited each example of manner plainly and verily, which are in the medial position.

Table 4 ***plainly***

	initial	medial	final	total
manner	0	76(97)	2(67)	78
intermediate	0	2(3)	0	2
epistemic	3(100)	0	1(33)	4
total	3(100)	78(100)	3(100)	84

Table 5 ***verily***

	initial	medial	final	total
manner	0	77(67)	1(50)	78
intermediate	0	35(30)	0	35
epistemic	2(100)	3(3)	1(50)	6
total	2(100)	115(100)	2(100)	119

(7) I supose ***veryly*** þat it schall be so nye Estern er euer my lord come to London þat I schal not moue come home to yow be-for Estern. (3210028)

(8) [A]nd þerfore he seyd ***playnly*** þat I shulde lese my hede. (6920033)

4.1.2. Person of the subjects

Next, I will focus on the person of the subjects in the scope of the adverbs.

Most examples (23/31 (74%)) of *peradventure* occur with the third person subjects and they are all epistemic adverbs. An example is cited in (9). On the other hand, although the ratio of the third person subject is very high (67/84 (80%)), *plainly* tends to be used as a manner adverb (62/67 (93%)). An instance is given in (10).

(9) ***Paraventure*** he may amitte the Dukes presentacion and leve myn, in which case I and Ser Thomas Howes must take an accion ayens the Duc and the Bisshop and the prest, or ellis I shuld lese the patronage. (0770107)

(10) The seyd Colyn, berere here-off, can tell yow more ***playnlye*** of myne aunsuers. (5550034)

As seen in Table 6, *truly* tends to be an epistemic adverb occurring with a first person subject, but on the other hand, it tends to be a manner adverb occurring with a third person subject. The typical examples in each case are cited in (11a) and (11b). We can safely say that *truly* increases the speaker's subjectivity when occurring with the first person subject.[4]

Table 6 ***truly***

	1st person	2nd person	3rd person	total
manner	5(24)	6(100)	24(67)	35
intermediate	0	0	0	0
epistemic	16(76)	0	12(33)	28
total	21(100)	6(100)	36(100)	63

(11) a. As touchyng my Maister Clementes letters, Halle is in-to his cuntré. And de la Rruer hath bothe his letter and Halles letter, but ***truly*** I coude not yet haue answer of hym. (5670039)

b. And if he hathe nought do well, nor wyll nought amend, prey hym that he wyll ***trewly*** belassch hym tyl he wyll amend. (0280004)

4.1.3. Verbs (self-controllable / not self-controllable)

Next, I classify the verbs in the scope of the adverb into two groups with regard to their self-controllability.[5] Here, I will focus on *plainly* and *verily*.

As seen in Table 7, occurring with the self-controllable verbs (67/84 (80%)), *plainly* tends to indicate the subject's manner (65/67 (97%)). Most examples of *plainly* as manner adverbs here (32/65 (49%)) occur with the verb *say* (underlined) as cited in (12).

Table 7 ***plainly***

	self-controllable	not self-controllable	total
manner	65(97)	13(76)	78
intermediate	0	2(12)	2
epistemic	2(3)	2(12)	4
total	67(100)	17(100)	84

(12) He seyde to me ryght ***pleynly*** that þe jugis dedenot ther-in as thei owght to do. (1920084)

The ratio of *verily* with not self-controllable verbs is the highest of the four adverbs (*peradventure*: 16/31 (52%), *plainly*: 17/84 (20%), *truly*: 26/63 (41%), *verily*: 85/119 (71%)). In Table 8 *verily* is more often an intermediate adverb when occurring with not self-controllable verbs (26/35 (74%)) than with self-controllable ones (9/35(26%)). An instance with a 'not self-controllable' verb is indicated in (13).

Table 8 ***verily***

	self-controllable	not self-controllable	total
manner	24(71)	54(63)	78
intermediate	9(26)	26(31)	35
epistemic	1(3)	5(6)	6
total	34(100)	85(100)	119

(13) [A]nd I knowe *verely* he owyth you ryght gode wyll. (1810004)

4.1.4. Clauses including the adverbs

Next, the types of the clauses including the adverbs I am investigating will be considered. I have picked up the five well-used clauses as seen in the tables. I have added a column for independent clauses ('ø') in the tables.

There are many examples of *peradventure* (19/31 (61%)) and *verily* (61/119 (51%)) used in independent clauses. It is safe to say that they can be independently used with no epistemic clauses.

Ten examples of *plainly* out of 84 (12%) occur in manner *as*-clauses and they are all manner adverbs as seen in Table 9. The ratio of *plainly* in manner *as*-clauses is the highest of all four adverbs. Moreover, in manner *as*-clauses all the adverbs (including *plainly*) in the whole text tend to be used as manner adverbs (23/24 (96%)). An instance of *plainly* is cited in (14).

Table 9 ***plainly***

	**for*	*if*	*think* that, etc	*say* that, etc	manner *as*	ø	**total
manner	7(78)	1(100)	0	4(80)	10(100)	48(98)	78
intermediate	0	0	0	0	0	0	2
epistemic	2(22)	0	0	1(20)	0	1(2)	4
total	9(100)	1(100)	0	5(100)	10(100)	49(100)	84

(*'*for*' as a coordinating conjunction. **The 'total' numbers at the right end include the numbers of the examples in other clauses.)

(14) Plese yow to wete þat Charlis Nowell, with odir, hath in þis cuntré

mad many riot and savtis, and among othir he and v of his felachip set vp-on me and to of my seruantis at þe Chathedrall church of Norwich, he smyting at me whilis on of his felaws held myn armis at my bak as the berer herof shall more ***playnly*** inform yow. (0430006)

Eleven out of 63 examples (17%) of *truly* occur in the coordinating *for*-clauses and they are all epistemic adverbs as shown in Table 10. In this circumstance the adverb behaves as an epistemic adverb both when the subject is the first person (as in (15a)) and when it is the third person (as in (15b)).

Table 10 ***truly***

	**for*	*if*	*think* that, etc	*say* that, etc	manner *as*	ø	**total
manner	0	2(100)	1(100)	0	0	13(46)	35
intermediate	0	0	0	0	0	15(54)	0
epistemic	11(100)	0	0	0	0	0	28
total	11(100)	2(100)	1(100)	0	0	28(100)	63

(*'*for*' as a coordinating conjunction. **The 'total' numbers at the right end include the numbers of the examples in other clauses.)

(15) a. Sire, I beseche bethe not displesed, for ***truly*** and (= if) I woste to haue yowr heuy maystirship þer-for I had leuer it had bene on-þoght. (6240027)

b. Ser, I pray you wyth all myn hert hold me excusyd that I wryte thus homly and briefly on-to you, for ***truly*** conable (= covenable) space suffycyd me nowt. (4390034)

4.2. Stratum of modality

4.2.1. Modal auxiliaries.

Comparing the four adverbs with each other, I have found that the ratio of 'with modal auxiliaries' is higher than that of 'without modal auxiliaries' only in the examples of *peradventure* (*peradventure*: 20/35(65%); *plainly*: 20/84(24%); *truly*: 18/63(29%); *verily*: 16/119(13%)). Occurring with modal auxiliaries, *peradventure* is most frequently used as an epistemic adverb of the four (*peradventure*: 20/20(100%); *plainly*: 3/20(15%); *truly*: 8/18(49%); *verily*: 3/16(19%)). An example is cited in (16). From the viewpoint of 'harmonic,' it is safe to say that *peradventure* has developed its speaker-oriented epistemic meaning the most fully of the four.[6]

(16) Ser, I besech you be good master to Fox wyff if ye may, how be it he

is nowight, but ***paraventur*** he <u>may</u> amend. (8550024)

4.2.2. Epistemic verbs

Next, I will focus on the co-occurring verbs expressing the speaker's inference about nominal clauses such as 'I think (that) …' Here I will pick up *verily*, because the ratio of the adverb occurring with such verbs is the highest of the four adverbs (*peradventure*: 0/31 (0%), *plainly*: 7/84 (8%), *truly*: 2/63 (3%), *verily*: 66/119 (55%)).

As seen in Table 11 concerning *verily*, the largest number of examples (66 examples) co-occurs with epistemic verbs with *that*-clauses, and half of these (33 examples) are intermediate indicating the speaker's attitude about *that*-clauses. Here we can recognize that the relationship between epistemic verbs and intermediate *verily* is by far the strongest of the four (*peradventure*: 0/0(0%); *plainly*: 0/7(0%); *truly*: 1/2(50%); *verily*: 33/66(50%)). I have cited an example in (17).

Table 11 ***verily***

	with ep. verb with *that* cl.	with non-ep. verb[7] with *that* cl.	without *that*-cl.	total
manner	33(50)	4(100)	41(76)	78
intermediate	33(50)	0	2(4)	35
epistemic	0	0	6(11)	6
total	66(100)	4(100)	54(100)	119

(17) As for the todyr þat ye desyiryd I scholde meue to of the same mater, me semyth he is to yonge to take ony swhyche thyngys vp-on hym, and also I <u>knowe</u> ***veryly*** þat he schall neuer loue feythfully the todyr man that ye desyiryd þat he schuld do for when he rem[em]bryth the tyme þat is paste; (1540014)

4.3. Stratum of pragmatic force

Finally in (18) I have cited two examples of epistemic *truly* expressing the relationship between the addressers and the addressees although it is difficult to show the ratios with quantifiable data. Here both examples have highly developed the speakers' subjectivity. I have cited an example in (18a) from the beginning of a letter from Henry Windsor (who is "one of the corps of agents" (Gies 114) of John Fastolf) to John Paston I. In this example Windsor is praising John Paston I because in the following part of this letter he has to beg John Paston I "not to let Fastolf hear of an error Windsor had made in handling the case of Thomas Fastolf's wardship" (ibid.). Here *truly* emphasizes Windsor's modest attitude used with the underlined politeness markers "ser," "I dar sey," and "shuld." In (18b), used with the underlined familiar form of address "cosyn," and functioning as an epistemic adverb inserted in front of propositions, *truly* is drawing the addressee's attention to what the addresser Sir John Heveningham is stating.

(18) a. For ***truly***, ser, I dar sey I shuld haue had as speciall and as gode a maister of you as any pour man, as I am. (6460010)

b. I haue as moche as I may to gader myn owune lyfflode, and ***truli***, cosyn, I can not gadere that well. (6510008)

5. Conclusion

In the discussion above, I have investigated the adverbs, especially *peradventure*, *plainly*, *truly*, and *verily*, with special regard to the points in 3.3 based on each stratum such as proposition, modality, and pragmatic force. I will sum up my results as follows.

First, concerning the stratum of proposition, I have found that the adverbs cannot be described only from the viewpoint of their positions. Therefore, I have focused on several other points in the scope of the adverbs. First, I found that *truly* tends to be an epistemic adverb when it occurs with a first person subject and it tends to be a manner adverb when it occurs with a third person subject. Then, concerning the self-controllability of verbs, *plainly* tends to act as a manner adverb co-occurring with a self-controllable verb, and *verily* tends to act as an intermediate one co-occurring with a verb which is not self-controllable. Thirdly, concerning the clauses which include adverbs, *truly* tends to be an epistemic adverb in the coordinate *for*-clause. On the other hand, *plainly* tends to be a manner adverb in the manner *as*-clause.

Secondly, I focused on the stratum of modality. Considering the four adverbs, I have found that the ratio of occurrences 'with modal auxiliary' exceeds that of occurrences 'without modal auxiliary' only in the examples of *peradventure*. Here, I have recognized a strong relationship between modal auxiliary verbs and epistemic *peradventure*. I have also found that *verily* co-occurs with epistemic verbs much more frequently than the other three, and in such a case it indicates the speaker's supposition about the propositional content of the *that*-clause.

Thirdly and finally, concerning the stratum of pragmatic force, I have illustrated a few examples of epistemic *truly* expressing speech acts of confirmation in the contexts involving human relationships. Here, the examples have shown us that the speech acts of confirmation reinforce the speakers' subjectivity.

Through the above examination, I have made clear some features of the language in the *Paston Letters* as regards the four representative adverbs such as *peradventure*, *plainly*, *truly*, and *verily* with a special focus on the grammaticalization and subjectification of each adverb.

Notes

* This article is a revised version of a paper read at the 19th Congress of the Japan Society for Medieval English Studies held at Tokyo University of Foreign Studies on 13th and 14th December 2003.

1 077: letter number, 0: letter distinction (putting A, B… if there are letters of the same numbers), 167: the line number of *certainly*

2 In this paper '*that*-clause(s)' refers to the nominal clauses with or without *that*.

3 Here I regard the adverb *needs* as an epistemic adverb since it modifies *must* indicating the speaker's attitude toward the proposition.

4 This tendency opposes those of modal auxiliaries. Modal auxiliaries tend to express a root (objective) sense with the first person subject and an epistemic (subjective) sense with the third person subject.

5 I regard the verbs denoting the actions which can be operated by the subjects such as *go*, *come*, *write*, etc. as 'self-controllable'; on the other hand, I regard the stative verbs such as *be*, *know*, *seem*, etc. and those that are in the passive voice as 'not self-controllable.'

6 This is a controversial point. There are two standpoints concerning the co-occurrence of adverbs with modal expressions: the one is that only modal expressions express modal meanings if they are used, and the other is that "two harmonic forms are said to be mutually reinforcing" (Coates 45). I adopt the latter view in this paper.

7 'Non-epistemic verb' here indicates the verbs other than the epistemic verbs, which cannot include the speraker's subjectivity (e.g. *say*, *tell*, etc.).

References

Brinton L. J. (1996) *Pragmatic Markers in English*. Berlin and New York: Mouton de Gruyter.

Coates, J. (1983) *The Semantics of the Modal Auxiliaries*. London and Canberra: Croom Helm.

Gies, F. and J. Gies (1998) *A Medieval Family: The Pastons of Fifteenth-Century England*. New York: Harper Collins.

Hopper, P. J. and E. C. Traugott (1993) *Grammaticalization*. Cambridge: Cambridge UP.

Kurath, H., M. K. Sherman, and E. L. Robert, eds. (1952-2000) *Middle English Dictionary*. Ann Arbor: University of Michigan Press.

Quirk, R., S. Greenbaum, G. Leech, and J. Svartvik (1972) *A Grammer of Comtemporary English*. London: Longman.

Sawada, H. (1993) *Shiten to Shukan-sei: Nichi-eigo Ho-jodoshi no Bunseki* (*Viewpoint and Subjectivity: Studies in English and Japanese Auxiliaries*), Tokyo: Hitsuji-shobo.
Simpson, J. A. and E. S. C. Weiner, eds. (1989) *The Oxford English Dictionary*. 2nd ed. Oxford: Clarendon.
Swan, T. (1988) *Sentence Adverbials in English: A Syntactic and Diachronic Investigation*. Oslo: Novus.
Traugott, E. C. (1972) *A History of English Syntax: A Transformational Approach to the History of English Sentence Structure*. New York: Holt, Rinehart and Winston.

The Subjunctive in Deloney

KAZUKO MATSUURA

1. Introduction

The purpose of this paper is to examine what kinds of the subjunctive are allowed to appear in early Modern English (henceforth early ModE) period. In present-day English (henceforth PE), as is stated in Brook (1973: 133), it is commonly acknowledged that the subjunctive has survived vestigially only in several independent sentences to express a wish and a few fixed phrases, such as *God bless you!* In the Old English period, the subjunctive was expressed by inflectional verb endings, but in the course of time, it was gradually replaced by indicatives and the use of auxiliaries due to the decay of distinctive inflectional endings. Barber (1976: 172) points out that in early ModE, with regard to the verb *to be*, we find *be* in all persons the present subjunctive, *were* the preterit subjunctive. Concerning other verbs except *to be*, the subjunctive is distinctive in only two forms: the second person singular, *thou* which has the inflection *-est* after the verb, and the third person singular of the present tense.

Furthermore, Mustanoja (1960: 452) divides the subjunctive into two forms: inflectional subjunctive and periphrastic subjunctive. The former stands for "the simple verb form (I be, I were)" and the latter "periphrastic form (I may be, he would come)".

Judging from the above, there were three subjunctive forms in early ModE period: A. Inflectional subjunctive, B. Periphrastic subjunctive, C. Indicative, which is mainly used today and D. Others, which is less distinctive as to the subjunctive-indicative borderline. Periphrastic subjunctive falls into two kinds of auxiliaries. According to Blake (2002: 89), one is modal auxiliary like *will* and *shall* and the other is non-modal auxiliary like *have* and *do*. To sum up, we would like to deal with the subjunctive in which (1) with the verbs *to be*, in the present tense the subjunctive is *be* while *were* in the preterite. In the case of preterite subjunctive, it is possible to make a distinction only in the 1st person singular, the second person singular, 'thou' and the 3rd person singular. (2) with other verbs, we regard the 2nd person singular, 'thou' and the third person singular as the present subjunctive. In the case of the preterite subjunctive, it is less clear-cut except for the 2nd person singular, 'thou'.

What we wish to show in this paper is the ratio of four morphological forms we have given above and to clarify what kind of conjunction leads to subjunctive form in early ModE. The two prose works used here are "*The Pleasant History of Iacke of Newberrie*" and "*The Pleasant History of Thomas of Reading*" of Thomas Deloney. Visser (1963-73), who paid much attention to subjunctive verb form, subdivided the subjunctive from Old English to Modern English into the following syntactical units in which, in the first place, he classified them into independent units and dependent units. The latter involves nominal clauses, adjective clauses and adverbial clauses. We support his approach because my concentration will be mainly on the verb form, namely morphologically. He is only concerned with present subjunctive of the 2nd person singular 'thou' and the third person singular. We would like to deal with all the persons, treating ambiguous ones as others. Furthermore, we adopt the classification of Blake (2002) particularly in the adverbial clauses so that we can focus on the conjunctions in early ME because Visser includes the conjunctions of Old English and Middle English.

2. Independent units

2.1. Apodosis

What we would like to pick up here is inflectional subjunctive and periphrastic subjunctive that are often used.

A. Inflectional subjunctive

The following is a notable example of preterite subjunctive used in the apodosis. There are seven other examples.

(1) *It were* happy for England (said the Queene) if in euerie market Towne there were Iybbet to hang vp curres of that kinde, (25)

Besides *if*-clause, *to*-infinitive illustrates condition. We find two other examples.

(2) I tell thee wife, *it were* as vndecent for vs to goe like Londoners as it is for Londoners to goe like courtiers. (238)

We see that the subjunctive was the only way in the case of *it were better/best* even though the subject was changed into others. According to Visser (811), this phrase was often used in early ModE. There are other two instances.

(3) And the man said, he knew not *what were best* to be done. (258)

B. Periphrastic subjunctive
There are many cases where some modal auxiliaries are used as often as today. Examples of this kind are one hundred thirteen.

(4) *they would put* the burden on their consciences, if they deale vniustly with them, (217)

2.2. Wish
We find two types of subjunctive, inflectional subjunctive and periphrastic subjunctive.
A. Inflectional subjunctive
2.2.1. *God send*
There are various fixed expressions. We find thirteen other examples.

(5) *God send* euerlasting ioyes. (246)

B. Periphrastic subjunctive
Today, we find that modal auxiliary, especially *may* is used in the similar cases. However, we have only two instances.

(6) *May it please* your Maiesty to vnderstand, that hee which rideth formost there, is called Iacke of Newbery, (24)

3. Dependent units

3.1. Nominal clause
A. Inflectional subjunctive
3.1.1. Clauses introduced by *if or whether*
We have four instances.

(7) And so going into the Kitchen, hee *asked* his wife *if it were* not dinner time. (230)

B. Periphrastic subjunctive
Examples of this kind are twelve.

(8) They had not sitten long, but in comes a noise of Musitians in tawny coates, who (putting off their caps) *asked if they would haue* any musicke. (10)

C. Indicative

This is the only example of indicative. In the case of 'thou', we notice 'thou' take the inflection *-est* in the auxiliary's ending.

(9) go wife (quoth he) vnto my neighbours, and *see if thou canst* get any of them to be my baile. (269)

D. Others
There are six examples in which we cannot distinguish subjunctive or indicative.

(10) The King presently perusing it, *asked if they were* all Clothiers? (44)

3.1.2. *I would to God*

A. Inflectional subjunctive
According to the OED, "I would to God" means a wish (s.v. *will*, *v.* 36). This phrase can be seen four times and two of them are inflectional subjunctive. Here we only deal with it.

(11) *I would to God he were* cleare of all other mens debts, so that I gaue him mine to begin the world againe. (58)

3.1.3. *Think*

A. Inflectional subjunctive
It was common to use indicative or auxiliary after the verb 'think'. However, we have two examples of the inflectional subjunctive.

(12) Now alas, good soule (quoth *Ienny*) I *think he be* the kindest young man in the world. (224)

The verb "trow" has the same meaning of 'think' in the OED (s.v. *trow*, *v.* 4).

(13) gud faith I *tro the men be* wood. (244)

3.1.4. *Look*

A. Inflectional subjunctive
There are two examples where imperative construction is used.

(14) *looke thou goe* to bed to thy fellowes, for with mee thou shalt not lye to night. (18)

3.2. Adjective clause

3.2.1. Relative pronoun

A. Inflectional subjunctive
Clauses introduced by relative pronoun hardly take the subjunctive. We find only two examples.

(15) Ione on the other side that well perceiued his passions, did as it were

triumph ouer him, as *one that were* bondslaue to her beauty, (47)

3.3. Adverbial clause

Blake classifies roughly into temporal and causal conjunctions, conditional clauses, result or consecutive clauses, final clauses, concessive clauses and clauses expressing comparison. We would like to focus on some subjunctive clauses that are peculiar to early ME.

3.3.1. Conditional clauses

The occurrence of the subjunctive is frequently in the *if*-clause. We have plenty of examples to illustrate how the subjunctive is used. Therefore, let us devote a little more space to examining *if*-clause because it will be our main concern in this paper. For the present, it may be useful to look more closely at some of the more important features of the subjunctive in terms of each personal pronoun.

3.3.1.1. *If*

(i) First personal pronoun

A. Inflectional subjunctive

In the first person singular, 'I', we find two pure subjunctive morphologically. One of them is used the conjunction 'so', which represents condition 'if' in the OED (s.v. *so*, *conj*. 26). There is no example of the clear subjunctive in the first person plural, 'we'.

(16) Well (quoth shee) I perceiue thy consent is quickly got to any, hauing no care how I am matcht *so I be* matcht: (6)

B. Periphrastic subjunctive

I have ten other examples, including the first person plural.

(17) Deare friends, consider that our Trade will maintain vs, *if we will vphold* it: (44)

D. Others

In the first person, it is difficult to distinguish between indicative and subjunctive. We have eight examples in 'I' while we have one example in 'we'.

(18) *If I heare* of her comming to London, I will send you word, or perhaps come selfe: (65)

(ii) Second personal pronoun

A. Inflectional subjunctive

We have two kinds of second person, namely 'you' and 'thou'. As to the former, we realize that the subjunctive always appears in *be*-verb. There are four.

(19) Well (quoth their husbands) *if you be* so head-strong, we will tame you: (217)

On the other hand, we find that 'thou' takes the inflection, -est, even in the auxiliary except for the four instances such as:

(20) and *if thou chance* to haue any sute in Court, make account the Queene will bee thy friend, and would to God the King had many such Clothiers. (24)

As to 'periphrastic subjunctive', in 'you', there are sixteen examples as well as in the first person pronoun. Meanwhile, we have no example in 'thou'.

C. Indicative

In 'you', it is impossible to distinguish whether indicative or subjunctive. However, it is manifest in 'thou', including various auxiliaries. We have twelve instances.

(21) and *if thou wilt* haue my fauour, thou must be wise and circumspect, (219)

As to 'others', we have twenty-one examples of this kind. Most of them are in 'you'.

(iii) Third personal pronoun

A. Inflectional subjunctive

Interestingly, we realize that most examples take the subjunctive. There are thirty-eight examples in the third person singular. However, in plural, there are two examples in which it is clear only in the present subjunctive, *be*. As to *be*-verb, we cannot find any indicative. Examples of this kind are eleven.

(22) *If it be* not performed, the fault is yours, (245)

Taking a look at other verbs but *be*-verb, we find that almost all the examples are subjunctive. There are twenty-three examples.

(23) but *if shee come* any more in my house, she were as good no. (57)

With regard to 'periphrastic subjunctive', we find twenty-two instances as often as in the inflectional subjunctive. As to 'indicative', we have only two examples.

D. Others

We have ten examples in which some of them are considered as subjunctive semantically, judging from the context such as:

(24) and *if she washt* him but a band, he would giue her an Angell: (49)

3.3.1.2. *Except*

A. Inflectional subjunctive

'Except' also introduces condition. We find one example.

(25) *except you be* good fellowes, therefore if you will go with vs, we will bestow the Ale vpon you. (235)

We have one example each in 'indicative' and 'others' and two in 'modal'.

2.3.2. Concessive clauses

In early ModE, we often see the subjunctive in the concessive clauses, unlike present-day English. Let us show each conjunction in detail.

3.3.2.1. *Though, although*

A. Inflectional subjunctive

In 'though', we find the subjunctive overwhelms more than indicative. Above all, the point I stress is that *be*-verb takes no indicative form. We have twenty-two examples. As to other verbs besides *be*-verb, we have only two examples. In 'although', all we can see is in *be*-verb.

(26) He pierst his braine, and broke the bone, *though he were* fifty foote of length. (31)

With regard to 'periphrastic subjunctive', we have five instances of this kind.

C. Indicative

'Although' takes the indicative in *be*-verb, though we have no example in 'though'. We have two examples. With respect to other verbs, both 'though' and 'although' take the indicative and there are six examples.

(27) *Although it becommeth* not mee your seruant to pry into your secrets, nor to bee busie about matters of your loue: (5)

D. Others

We have twelve indistinguishable examples.

(28) The fellow seeing the King (in asking that question) to bend his browes, *though he knew not* what he was, yet being abasht, he answered thus: (215)

3.3.2.2. *Albeit, notwithstanding*

Both of them have no clear subjunctive. As to 'periphrastic subjunctive', in the former we have four examples and in the latter we have two.

C. Indicative

We have three examples in 'albeit' while we have two in 'notwithstanding'. Both of them tend to take indicative in *be*-verb.

(29) he promised that he would, *notwithstanding Cole was not satisfied*: (257)

As to 'others', each of them have two examples.

3.3.2.3. *Whatsoever, wheresoever, whosoever, howsoever*

A. Inflectional subjunctive

Here we only deal with inflectional subjunctive. We notice four examples of subjunctive, though we have three examples each in 'indicative' and 'others'. No example of periphrastic subjunctive is found.

(30) I am pleased *howsoeuer it bee*. (11)

3.3.3. Temporal conjunctions

3.3.3.1. *Till, until*

A. Inflectional subjunctive

With regard to the former, we have seven instances, though we have no instance of the latter.

(31) Wee pardon the maids life, and grant her libertie, but let her not passe, *till she see* her louers eies put out, (265)

As to 'periphrastic subjunctive', we find three instances only in 'till'.

C. Indicative

We have eleven examples in 'till', though the following one is the only example in 'until'.

(32) And why? because we know her not, *vntill miserie doth make* her manifest. (222)

As to 'others', we have seventeen examples in all.

3.3.3.2. *Ere, before*

A. Inflectional subjunctive

We have three examples both in 'ere' and 'before'.

(33) If I did lacke as many of my teeth (quoth the old woman) as you lacke points of good husbandry, I doubt I should starue *before it were long*. (13)

With regard to 'periphrastic subjunctive', we have twelve examples of this kind. As to 'indicative', we find two examples only in 'before'. What is more, with respect to 'others', we find eleven examples.

4. Conclusion

So far we have outlined the subjunctive used in early ME, focusing on the verb form.

A close look at independent units reveals that the subjunctive was used even in the apodosis, which is no longer used though there are few. At the same time, it is clear that the periphrastic subjunctive, in other words, some modal auxiliaries, which are common today, took the place of the subjunctive. In the fixed expressions like 'wish', by contrast, the subjunctive is predominant over the periphrastic subjunctive, 'may'.

In dependent units, we recognize from nominal clause that the subjunctive was used in the clauses introduced by 'if' or 'whether' after the verbs like 'ask' or 'see' though we find many instances of the periphrastic subjunctive. We further see the phrase 'I would to God', which is often used in early ME, tended to take the subjunctive. Other verbs such as 'think' and 'look' occasionally take the subjunctive when there is strong doubt. Moreover, we should not overlook that the subjunctive was used in adjective clause.

With respect to adverbial clauses, in *if*-clause we have examined in terms of each personal pronoun. In the first person, it is hard to draw the line between subjunctive and indicative. As to the second person, what has to be noticed is that 'thou' takes the inflectional ending, -est even in the auxiliaries. Regarding the third person, the point we would like to emphasize is that the subjunctive tended to be used. Interestingly enough, we furthermore found the subjunctive in concessive clauses and temporal clauses, which are hardly seen today.

It is concluded that the inflectional subjunctive was still dominant even though the periphrastic subjunctive and indicative gradually gained their strength in those days. It also turned out that each conjunction had a certain tendency whether to take subjunctive or not.

Acknowledgements

I would like to express my sincere appreciation to Professor Toshiro Tanaka and Professor Akiyuki Jimura for giving me valuable advice. I am also grateful to Mr. Jason Cox, my colleague at Kurashiki Sakuyo University, who kindly read my draft and improved my English. My thanks are due to the members of English Research Association of Hiroshima as well, who gave me helpful suggestions. However, any remaining inadequacies are, of course, all my own.

Text

Deloney, T. (1912) *The Works of Thomas Deloney*. Ed. Francis Oscar Mann. Oxford: The Clarendon Press.

References

Abbott, E. A. (1870) *A Shakespearian Grammar*. 3rd.ed. London: Macmillan; reprinted New York: Dover.

Barber, C. (1976) *Early Modern English*. London: André Deutsch.

Blake, N. F. (2002) *A Grammar of Shakespeare's Language*. London: Palgrave.

Brook, G. L. (1958) *A History of the English Language*. London: André Deutsch.

Dahl, T. (1951) *Linguistic Studies in Some Elizabethan Writings I. An Inquiry into Aspects of the Language of Thomas Deloney*. Aarhus: Universitetsforlaget.

Fridén, G. (1958) *Studies on the Tenses of the English Verb from Chaucer to Shakespeare*. Trans. Matsunami Tamotsu. Eigogaku Library 34. Tokyo: Kenkyusha.

James, F. (1986) *Semantics of the English Subjunctive*. Vancouver: University of British Columbia.

Jespersen, O. (1949) *A Modern English Grammar on Historical Principles*. Part VII. London: George Allen & Unwin.

Lycan, W. G. (2001) *Real Conditionals*. Oxford: Clarendon Press.

Mustanoja, T. F. (1960) *A Middle English Syntax*. Part I. Helsinki: Société Néophilologique.

Quirk, R., et al. (1985) *A Comprehensive Grammar of the English Language*. London: Longman.

Quirk, R. (1999) *Grammar of Spoken and Written English*. London: Longman.

Rissanen, M. (2000) "Syntax." In Roger Lass (ed.), *The Cambridge History of the English Language*, Vol. III: 1476-1776, 187-326. Cambridge: Cambridge University Press.

Simpson, J.A. and E.S.C. Weiner, (eds.) (1989) *The Oxford English Dictionary*. 2nd ed. Oxford: Clarendon Press.

Ukaji, M. (2000) *Eigoshi*. Tokyo: Kaitakusha.

Visser, F. Th. (1963-73) *An Historical Syntax of the English Language*. Three Parts, Four Vols. Leiden: E. J. Brill.

A Cognitive Observation on Metaphors in E. Spenser's *Amoretti*

MASARU KOSAKO

1. The Aim of this Essay

This essay describes from a cognitive point of view advocated by Steen (1994) how conceptual metaphors and linguistic metaphors are structured in the *Amoretti*, how they interact with each other in the contexts of discourse, and how some of them are foregrounded with some structural and textual implications. We may be able to simplify the discourse in the sonnets into three contexts. A first is when the poet-lover admires the lady for her attractive attributes, beauties and virtues. A second is when he desperately complains of her coldness and stubbornness. A third is when he negotiates with her for attaining her love by means of ironical comments on her inhuman qualities. It is, however, hardly possible for us to single out each context of discourse, because they are often blended or overlapped with each other.

2. Spenser's Sonnets

Edmund Spenser (1552?-1599) married Elizabeth Boyle probably on 11 June 1594. The *Amoretti* (1595), which is a sequence of 89 sonnets, is recognized as his tribute to her.[1] A great variety of metaphors enable the poet-lover to admire her in effective ways for the inward virtues and outward beauties, and at the same time complain of his hardship in attaining her love.

Deneef (1982) discusses Petrarchan, neo-Platonic, Ovidian, and Christian perspectives in the metaphors of the *Amoretti*, but not in terms of cognitive operation proposed by Steen.

3. Cognitive Approaches to Metaphor

Cognitive investigation has presented new findings to various fields of science. The trend has not been exceptional in literary studies, particularly in the research of metaphor. According to Steen, the so-called 'cognitive turn' in metaphor research took place at the end of the 1970s with not a few landmark publications. Steen tries to redress the balance between the research into the structure of metaphorical concept on the one hand and the way it is processed in the actual usage on the other. The balance is, in other words, the equilibrium between metaphor as an idea in discourse (i.e. conceptual metaphor) and metaphor as a kind of expression (i.e. linguistic metaphor). Conventional conceptual metaphors are stored as conceptual units in the mind, which constitute the structure of metaphor as cognition or conceptualization. The verbal manifestations of conceptual metaphor, on the other hand, are dependent on, or derived from, the conceptual metaphor. The interaction of these two kinds of information structures during processing, or on-going individual cognition, is considered by Steen to be the most interesting target for metaphor research.

Steen sets up the following essential aspects of metaphor research: metaphor as conceptual structure, metaphor as linguistic structure, and metaphor as analogical processing. Conceptual metaphor and linguistic metaphor are regarded as two kinds of information structures. The understanding of the on-going metaphor process is shaped by means of analogizing. He adds to these three a discourse context, all of which are the on-going aspects in the actual process of understanding metaphor.

He pays attention to how writers use metaphor in poetry to achieve a special effect: i.e. how they intend to foreground a particular metaphor. Poets do this by means of four strategies: the extension, elaboration, questioning, and composing of conceptual metaphors. This kind of functional approach leads to consider the structural and textual implications of metaphor. These cognitive operations will reveal that literary metaphors are novel (by way of extension and elaboration), critical (by way of questioning), and complex (by way of composing).

We will show conceptual metaphors in capital letters, and linguistic metaphors by underlines.

4. LOVE AFFAIR IS WARFARE

The hardship for the poet-lover to attain her love is very often processed with the conceptual metaphor, LOVE AFFAIR IS WARFARE.[2] The Sonnet XII abounds with linguistic metaphors which are extended from the concept of warfare: '<u>make a truce</u>'[3], '<u>entertaine termes</u>', '<u>enemies</u>', 'disarmed', 'ambush', 'brunt', 'yeeld my selfe into their hands', 'captiuing', and 'cruell bands'.

4.1. THE LOVER'S SUING IS THE SIEGE

The conceptual metaphor of warfare sub-categorizes THE LOVER'S SUING IS THE SIEGE. The Sonnet XIV is full of linguistic metaphors interacting with the concept of siege: her castle 'needeth greater might/ then those small forts which ye (i.e. the lover) were wont belay:/ such haughty mynds enur'd to hardy fight,/ disdayne to yield vnto the first assay.' The poet-lover encourages himself to bring all the forces and 'lay incessant battery to her heart'.

4.2. THE LADY IS THE WARRIOR

The warfare metaphor sub-categorizes another conceptual metaphor, SHE IS THE WARRIOR. In the sonnet XI, his efforts of suing are shown with the following linguistic metaphors: 'Dayly when I do seeke and sew for peace,/ And hostages doe offer for my truth:/ she cruell warriour doth her selfe addresse/ to battell, and the weary war renew'th' (XI).

The warrior metaphor has analogy with she is the foe: 'in hand my tunelesse harp I take,/ then doe I more augment my foes despight' (XLIIII).

It is extended to another linguistic metaphor, the lady's countenance is a banner(V).

4.3. THE LADY'S SIGHT IS THE ARROW

The warrior metaphor co-relates with THE LADY'S SIGHT IS THE ARROW: The sweet eye-glaunces, that like arrowes glide (XVII); seeing my hart through launched euery where/ with thousand arrows, which your eies have shot:/Yet shoot ye sharpely still, and spare me not (LVII); her fayre eyes vnwares doe worke in mee:/ that death out of theyr shiny beames doe dart (XXIV); Fayre eyes, the myrrour of my mazed hart,/ …the which both lyfe and death forth from you dart/ into the obiect of your mighty view? (VII).

The adjective 'mazed' above is an extended metaphor in the sense that his 'mazed' state is caused by the arrows from her eyes. The 'mazed' metaphor is elaborated to another metaphor: her eyes are the mirror of the lover's heart.[4] The metaphor is interpreted to signify that the lady's heart is not moved, but that it simply reflects back the lover's dazed heart with no sympathy for him.

4.4. THE LADY IS THE VICTOR

The lady is recognized as victor when the poet-lover is willing to be her thrall. There must, however, be a contention between the lover and the lady to decide which should be the victor, i.e. bearer of the bay. The victor metaphor coheres with the following linguistic metaphors: the conquest, her great triumph, blaze trump of fame, decke her head with glorious bayes, her victorious prayse (XXIX).

The Sonnet LXIX has the victor's trophy focused: i.e. 'What trophee then shall I most fit deuize,/ in which I may record the memory/ of my loues conquest, peerelesse beauties prise' (LXIX).

4.5. THE LADY IS THE TYRANESS

The victor metaphor co-relates with THE LADY IS THE TYRANESS, when she will not respond to his suing, but rather despises him. The conceptual metaphor underlies the linguistic metaphors which are used in his complaint of her cruelty: 'loe myne humbled hart before her poure:/ the whiles her foot she in my necke doth place,/ and tread my life downe in the lowly floure' (XX); 'torment me thus with cruelty,/to proue your powre'(XXV); the similar processing is seen in the Sonnets XXXVI, XLI, XLII, XLIII, and X.

The lover's mental state of captivity is reflected even in the poet's book: 'Happy ye leaues when as those lilly hands,/ …shall handle you and hold in loues soft bands,/ like captiues trembling at the victors sight' (I).

The victor and tyraness metaphors, which are co-relating with each other, are contrasted with THE LOVER IS THE CAPTIVE; 'Bring my selfe captyued here in care,/ My hart, whom none with seruile bands can tye,/ but the fayre tresses of your golden hayre,/ breaking his prison forth to you doth fly' (LXXIII); 'But since ye deignd so goodly to relent/ to me your thrall' (LXXXII); 'I goe lyke one that hauing lost the field,/ is prisoner led away with heauy hart' (LII).

The captive metaphor carries analogy with THE POET IS A BIRD; he is likened to Mauis (=thrush)(LXXXV) and the Culuer (=dove) (LXXXVIII).

It is interesting to note that the poet-lover takes the role of the female dove mate, for it is natural to interpret that the female dove mate refers to the lady: 'sits mourning for the absence of her mate:/ and in her songs sends many a wishfull vow,/ for his returne that seemes to linger late' (LXXXIX). This metaphor may be pointed out to be foregrounded by the conversion of his usual captive situation into hers, composing THE LADY IS THE CAPTIVE, in spite of the fact that she has behaved as victor and tyraness towards the poet-lover. See how the analogy is extended; 'Sweet be the bands, the which true loue doth tye,/...the gentle birde feeles no captiuity/ within her cage' (LXV); 'I ioy to see in your drawen work,/ Your selfe vnto the Bee ye doe compare;/ and me vnto the Spyder that doth lurke, in close awayt to catch her vnaware' (LXXI).

5. THE LADY IS A PLANT

Complaining of her unmoved stubbornness, the poet-lover has the analogy that the inhuman lady is a plant. Even when he praises her bodily beauties, we notice that he does not simply praise her beauty but that he ironically hints on her inhuman apathy.

5.1. SHE IS A TREE

She is likened to a 'durefull(=lasting) oak tree' (VI). The oak's condition that the 'sap is not yet dride' is associated with her not being ready to get the lover's 'kindling fyre', although once it burns, he hopes, it will disperse 'great heat' and the flames will reach high to heaven.

5.2. SHE IS A FLOWER

The lily metaphor for her hands is already cited in 4.5. Her hands' whiteness, fairness, and perhaps their scent are focused in the metaphor. Her other bodily parts have also the analogy with flowers: her lips are 'gillyflowers; her cheeks are 'roses'; her eyes are 'pinks'; her brows are 'bellamoures' (LXI); 'the rose in her red cheeks appeares' (LXXXI); her bosom is 'a strawberry bed'; her neck is 'a group of 'columbines'; her breasts are again 'lillies'; her nipples are 'jasmines', concluding that 'Such fragrant flowers doe giue most odorous smell,/ But her sweet odour did them all excel' (LXIIII); her nipples are also likened to 'early fruit in May'(LXXVI) , and her breasts are 'golden apples' (LXXVII).

6. THE LADY IS A BEAST

Her cruelty triggers the analogy with the beast, the metaphor of which is co-related with the victor and entrapper metaphors.

6.1. She is a panther

The lady is likened to the panther which 'knowing that his spotted hyde/ Doth please all beasts, but that his looks them fray,/ within a bush his dreadfull head doth hide,/ to let them gaze whylest he on them may pray (LIII).

6.2. She is a tiger

She is a 'cruell and vnkind' tiger 'that with greediness/ hunts after bloud, when he by chance doth find/ a feeble beast, doth felly him oppresse (LVI).

6.3. She is a deer

The lady is likened to a deer, while the lover is to a huntsman in the Sonnet LXVII: 'when I all weary had the chace forsooke,/ the gentle deare returned the selfe-same way,/…Strange thing me seemd to see a beast so wyld/ so goodly wonne with her owne will beguyld.'

The poet-lover is also processed as a young fawne (=fallow deer) 'that late hath lost the hynd' (LXXVIII). This metaphor is foregrounded in the sense that she and he are of the coupling species, contrary to most other metaphors which represent her and him confronting more or less.

7. THE LADY IS AN ENTRAPPER

The lady is recognized as an entrapper, who, attracting the victim, captures and gives pain to him: the poet tells his eyes to pay attention to 'that guileful net of her golden hair: 'in which if euer ye entrapped are,/ out of her bands ye be no meanes shall get' (XXXVII); her glorious beauty is 'a bayt, such wretches to beguile' (XLI); her smiling looks are hooks, which 'theyr bayts doe hyde'(XLVII); 'her louely hew' is the sweet allurement to 'entrap the beholder' (XXXI).

8. THE LADY IS A STONE

Her stubborn heart is desperately or perhaps ironically likened to a stone: 'harder growes the harder she is smit,/…What then remaines but I to ashes burne,/ and she to stones at length all frosen turne?' (XXXII); 'if nor mirth nor mone,/ she is no woman, but a senseless stone' (LIIII). The poet ironically sees 'that fairest ymages/ Of hardest Marble', whose famous monuments do not fade in her 'stubborne hart' (LI).

8.1. HER BODILY PARTS ARE JEWELRY

The poet admires the richness of the lady's bodily parts with jewelry metaphors. However, we may easily associate these metaphors with the ironical stone metaphor: 'if Saphyres, loe her eies be Saphyres plaine,/ if Rubies, loe hir lips be Rubies sound:/ if Pearles, hir teeth be pearles both pure and round;/ if Yuorie, her forhead yuory weene;/ if Gold, her locks are finest gold on ground;/ if siluer, her faire hands are siluer sheene, concluding that her mind, the fairest of all these things, is 'adornd with virtues manifold' (XV); 'But fairest she, when so she doth display,/ the gate with pearles and rubyes richly dight:/ through which her words so wise do make their way' (LXXXI); her chest is 'a goodly table of pure yvory:/...Mongst which there in a siluer dish did ly/ twoo golden apples of vnualewd price' (LXXVII).

9. LOVE AFFAIR IS TRADE

The metaphor of jewelry as trading goods interacts with the metaphor of trade, through which the trader-poet tries to purchase her goods, i.e. her love and her immortality, etc: 'this verse, that neuer shall expyre,/ shall to you purchas with her(=its) thankles paine' (XXVII); 'The happy purchase of my glorious spoile,/ gotten at last with labour and long toyle' (LXIX); 'Fayre bosome fraught with virtues riches tresure' (LXXVI); 'Fayre when her brest lyke a rich laden barke,/ with pretious merchandize she forth doth lay' (LXXXI).

9.1. She is a miser-trader

She is a miser-trader who will not declare the time of payment, so that the lover-trader has to waste his money, being uncertain of the possibility to get money or lose it: 'How long shall this lyke dying lyfe endure,/ And know no end of her owne mysery:/ but wast and weare away in termes vnsure,/ twixt feare and hope depending doubtfully' (XXV).

10. THE LADY IS NATURAL PHENOMENA

Her cold and annoying response carries analogy with natural phenomena with similar qualities.

10.1. HER WRATH IS THE STORM

Her wrath gets an analogy with storms: 'that when a dreadfull storme away is flit,/...So my storme beaten hart likewise is cheared,/ with that sunshine when cloudy looks are cleared' (XL); 'and all these stormes ...shall turne to caulmes and timely cleare away' (LXII); 'After long stormes and tempests sad assay' (LXIII); similar instances are found in the Sonnets VIII, XXXVIII, XLI, and LXIII.

The storm metaphor includes the ship metaphor, in which the ship-lover is afflicted by the storm-love: 'against which a ship of succour desolate,/ doth suffer wreck both of her selfe and goods./ That ship, that tree, and that same beast am I,/ whom ye doe wreck, doe ruine, and destroy' (LVI).

The ship metaphor has the displaced metaphor foregrounded, i.e. it is not he but she that is likened to a ship: 'Thrise happie she.../ that like a steddy ship doth strongly part/ the raging waues and keepes her course aright' (LIX). It co-relates with the deer metaphor in the sense that both she and he are put in the same situation.

The storm metaphor is extended to HER EYES HAVE THE LIGHTNING: 'but when ye lowre, or looke on me askew,/ then doe I die, as one with lightning fyred' (VII); 'the beame of light, whom mortal eyes admire' (LXI); similar instances are in the Sonnets LXVI, VII, and LXXXI.

10.2. She is ice, while he is fire

The lady is: 'lyke to yse, and I to fyre;/ how comes it then that this her cold so great/ is not dissolu'd through my so hot desyre,/ ...Or how comes it that my exceeding heat/ is not delayed by her hart frosen cold:/...What more miraculous thing may be told/ that fire which all thing melts, should harden yse:/ and yse which is congeald with sencelesse cold,/ should kindle fyre by wonderfull deuyse?' (XXX).

10.3. She is a bubble

The poet appeals to the lady, suggesting that 'All flesh is frayle, and all her strength vnstayd,/ like a vaine bubble blowen vp with ayre' (LVIII).

10.4. She is dross

The poet-lover persuades her not to be proud of her glory: 'Faire proud now tell me why should faire be proud,/ Sith all worlds glorie is but drosse vncleane:/...That goodly Idoll now so gay beseene,/ shall doffe her fleshes borowd fayre attire' (XXVII).

11. THE LADY IS A HEAVENLY BEING

The poet-lover admires the lady for her charms and virtues, making various use of metaphor which ranges from earthly things to celestial beings. The heaven ascent is called platonic: 'But that same lofty countenance seemes to scorne/ base thing, and thinke how she to heauen may clime:/ treading downe earth as lothsome and forlorne,/ that hinders heauenly thoughts with drossy slime' (XIII); 'Within my hart, though hardly it can shew/ thing so diuine to vew of earthly eye,/ the fayre Idea of your celestial hew,/ and euery part remaines immortally'(XLV); similar metaphors are seen in the Sonnets LV, LXXVI, LXXIX, LXXX, and LXXXV.

11.1. HER EYES ARE STARS

The lady's eyes shine like stars in the praising context of discourse, although her eyes have already been discussed in the warfare and natural phenomena contexts: 'Dark is the world, where your light shined neuer' (VIII); 'The souerayne beauty.../ the light whereof hath kindled heauenly fyre,/ in my fraile spirit by her from basenesse raysed./ That being now with her huge brightnesse dazed, /...but looking still on her I stand amazed,/ at wondrous sight of so celestiall hew' (III); similar metaphors are found in the Sonnets LXXXI, LXXXVIII and LXXXIX.

In the Sonnet XI, the poet declares that he cannot compare the lady's eyes to stars or the sun, because her eyes have purer sight than the stars and the sun does not shine by night. The poet further goes to sing that her eyes are 'likest to the Maker selfe'.

11.2. THE LADY IS A MYTHOLOGICAL BEING

11.2.1. She is an angel

'And happy rymes bath'd in the sacred brooke,/ of Helicon whence she deriued is,/ when ye behold that Angels blessed looke,/ my soules long lacked foode, my heauens blis (I); goe visit her in her chast bowre of rest,/ accompanyde with angelick delightes' (LXXXIIII); similar instances are seen in the Sonnets XVII and LXI.

11.2.2. CUPID IS PRESENT IN HER SIGHT

The lady's eyes sometimes encourage the lover to continue his suing: 'I mote perceiue how in her glauncing sight,/ legions of loues with little wings did fly' (XVI); 'New yeare...calling forth out of sad Winters night,/ fresh loue, that long hath slept in cheerless bower:/ wils him awake, and soone about him dight/ his wanton wings and darts of deadly power' (IIII).

11.2.3. She is a *Penelope*

Penelope in the Greek mythology makes a web all day, and disentangles the same at night to deceive her wooers. However, the lover-wooer weaves and spins in the Sonnet XXIII.

11.2.4. She is a *Pandora*

She is a *Pandora* who was created by *Jove* as a result of his wrath at *Prometheus* and his desire to have revenge on man. In the Sonnet XXIV, she is a scourge for the lover's faults (See Variorum, 428).

11.2.5. She is a *Daphne*, whereas he is a *Phaebus*

The poet-lover is likened to *Phaebus*, who bears the laurel badge, while the lady is a proud *Daphne*, who will be transformed into a laurel tree for scorning *Phaebus*'s lovely fire. The lover's chase of her is alluded in *Phaebus*'s chase of *Daphne* in the sonnet XXVIII.

11.2.6. THE LADY IS A SAINT

The saint metaphors are as follows: 'therefore, I lykewise on so holy day,/ for my sweet Saynt some seruice fit will find./ Her temple fayre is built within my mind,/ in which her glorious ymage placed is,/ on which my thoughts doo day and night attend/ lyke sacred priests that neuer thinke amisse./ There I to her as th'author of my blisse,/ will builde an altar to appease her yre:/and on the same my hart will sacrifise,/ burning in flames of pure and chast desyre:/ The which vouchsafe O goddesse to accept,/ amongst thy deerest relicks to be kept' (XXII).[5] Similar instances are in the Sonnets LXXXIIII and LXI.

12. Concluding Remarks

We have described how conceptual metaphors are structured, interacting to each other, and how conceptual metaphors appear as linguistic metaphors, having structural and textual implications fore-grounded. We can illustrate how metaphors in the *Amoretti* are structured, and how they are interacting with each other, as follows:

- LOVE AFFAIR IS WARFARE
  - THE LOVER'S SUING IS THE SIEGE
  - THE LADY IS THE WARRIOR – foe
    - Her countenance is a banner
    - THE LADY'S SIGHT IS THE ARROW
      - Her eye-beams dart
  - THE LADY IS THE VICTOR – TYRANESS – CAPTIVE
  - THE LOVER IS THE CAPTIVE – BIRD – mauis – culuer
- THE LADY IS A PLANT – TREE – FLOWER – lily, etc
- THE LADY IS A BEAST – panther – tiger – deer
  - He is a young fallow deer
- THE LADY IS AN ENTRAPPER
  - Her hair is the net of snare
  - Her glorious beauty is the bait
  - Her smiling looks are hooks
- LOVE AFFAIR IS TRADE
  - She is a miser
- THE LADY IS A STONE – JEWELRY – ruby – pearl – etc.
- THE LADY IS NATURAL PHENOMENON
  - HER WRATH IS THE STORM – LIGHTENING
    - The lover is a ship afflicted by the storm

The lady is a ship
She is ice – bubble – dross
THE LADY IS A HEAVENLY BEING
HER EYES ARE STARS
THE LADY IS A MYTHOLOGICAL BEING
She is an angel – *Pandora* – *Penelope* –*Daphne* – saint
CUPID IS IN HER SIGHT

Notes

1 Cf. Hamilton (1990), "Amoretti".

2 According to Renwick (Variorum, 423), the warfare conceit derives from Ovid (*Amores* 1.9) and inspires innumerable sonnets.

3 OED: *truce* =A suspension of hostilities for a specified period between armies at war.

4 Renwick (Variorum 422) does not quite understand this line, saying that it seems a reversal of a common conceit.

5 Erskine (Variorum, 428) notes that 'it is typical…of Spenser that instead of likening his mistress to a goddess, as had been the honored custom of sonneteers, he refers to her always as his saint; the very term indicates the spiritual rather than the physical excellence that he admires.'

Texts

Sélincourt, E. de, ed. (1966, 1910) *Spenser's Minor Poems*. Oxford: The Clarendon Press.

Osgood, C. G. & Lotspeich, H. G., ed. (1966, 1947), *The Works of Edmund Spenser, The Minor Poems*, A Variorum Edition Vol. 8, Part Two. The Johns Hopkins Press.

References

Deneef, A. L. (1982) *Spenser and the Motives of Metaphor*. Duke Univ. Press.

Hamilton, A. C., gen. ed. (1990) "Amoretti" in *The Spenser Encyclopedia*. Univ. of Toronto Press.

Steen, G. (1994) *Understanding Metaphor in Literature: An Empirical Approach*. Longman.

Well as a discourse marker in *The Taming of the Shrew*: A preliminary sketch

SHIGENOBU FUAMI

1. Introduction

The present paper gives a preliminary sketch of the use of *well* as a discourse marker in Shakespeare's *The Taming of the Shrew*, a play where marker *well* is not used very often but where a textual consideration of the use of marker *well* is still left to be done.

The Taming of the Shrew is the title of the play which appeared in the 1623 First Folio (F1). Prior to the First Folio text, three Quarto texts (Qq) were published under the title of *The Taming of a Shrew*: the first Quarto text in 1594 (Q1), the second Quarto in 1596 (Q2) and the third Quarto in 1607 (Q3). The second and the third Quarto texts are reprints with a few typographical corrections or alterations of the first.

The frequency of marker *well* in the present play is not so great as in comedies such as *The Merry Wives of Windsor* and *Much Ado About Nothing*, which can be regarded as reflecting Elizabethan everyday speech more faithfully, but it is closer to that in the Q1 text of *Henry V* – a play where marker *well* does not occur very frequently, but which provides us with typical examples of use closely connected with textual matters (Fuami 1997: 239).

2. Colloquial or textual?

It is reported that marker *well* is 'virtually restricted to spoken language, where it is one of the most frequent words' (Svartvik 1980: 169). On the other hand, the frequency of *well* as a marker in written English depends largely on text type (Fuami 1997: 163-4).

I have shown elsewhere that the use and nature of marker *well* in Shakespearean plays can be better understood by taking into consideration both colloquialism and textual matters. This can be clearly shown using texts of the three plays: *Much Ado* (ADO), *The Merry Wives* (WIV) and *Henry V* (H5), as follows.

Table 1

Play	Text	Occurrences of marker *well*	
ADO	Q/F_1	31	Colloquialism causes higher frequency than in other Shakespearean plays
WIV	Q_1	43	
WIV	F_1	34	
H5	Q_1	18	Textual reasons cause higher frequency in Q_1 texts
H5	F_1	8	

(Fuami 1997: 173)

This table shows that the greater frequency of marker *well* in *Much Ado* and *The Merry Wives* is connected with simulated everyday situations recurring in both plays, while the more frequent use of marker *well* in the Q_1 texts of *The Merry Wives* and *Henry V* than in the F_1 texts reflects a use closely connected with textual matters.

To what extent in the *Shrew* play is marker *well* used to represent colloquial language or because of textual constraints (e.g. to link otherwise incomplete sections of text)? One may reasonably surmise that it can be better understood textually as shown in the following table showing results of present work on other plays of Shakespeare.

Table 2

Play	Text	Occurrences of marker *well*	
ADO	Q/F_1	31	Colloquialism causes higher frequency than in other Shakespearean plays
WIV	Q_1	43	
WIV	F_1	34	
H5	Q_1	18	Textual reasons cause higher frequency in Q_1 texts
H5	F_1	8	
SHR, A	Q_1	16	(?)
SHR, The	F_1	14	

The textual genealogy of *A/The Shrew*, however, does not seem to be so simple as to allow us to accept this conclusion without question. The point here is that marker *well* occurs more frequently in the Q1 texts of *The Merry Wives* and *Henry V* than in the F1 texts, and that the same pattern of frequency can also be seen between the texts of *A Shrew* and *The Shrew*, although the discrepancy is not so great as in the other two plays. The number of occurrences of marker *well* in the *Shrew* play may simply reflect the colloquial nature of the play, or, as in other Shakespearean plays which exist in 'bad' quartos, may be connected to some extent with how the play texts were brought into existence.

The number of occurrences of marker *well* can give a slightly different impression when it is considered in relation to the text length. The F1 version of the *Shrew* play is almost twice the length of that of the Q1: F1 has 2,659 lines as against Q1's 1,542. One might therefore expect that the total number of occurrences of discourse marker *well* in F1 would be almost twice as great as in Q1, but the actual count of occurrences in each text shows that the total number of occurrences of discourse marker *well* in each of these two texts is not proportional to the length of the text, and in fact the number of occurrences decreases slightly in the longer version: 14 instances in F1 and 16 instances in Q1.

Table 3

	Q *A Shrew*	F *The Shrew*
Length of text (number of lines)	1,542	2,659
Occurrences of *well*	16	14

This imbalance in the frequency of marker *well* between Q and F is of the same pattern as was the case for the two versions of both *The Merry Wives* and *Henry V*, as shown in the following table.

Table 4

	A/The Shrew		*Henry V*		*The Merry Wives*	
	Q1	F1	Q1	F1	Q1	F1
Length of text (number of lines)	1,542	2,659	1,622	3,085	1,500	2,700
Occurrences of *well*	16	14	18	8	43	34

It may readily be surmised that the imbalance in the frequency of marker *well* between the Q *Shrew* and the F *Shrew* reflects the nature of each version of the play as is the case in the other two plays, although the imbalance is not so great. The question, however, arises here again whether individual instances of marker *well* in the play actually reflect the colloquial nature of the play, or a usage of the marker resulting from how the play text was transmitted. The imbalance in the frequency of marker *well* in the *Shrew* play does not seem to be great enough to suggest textual reasons, as was the case in *Henry V* and *The Merry Wives*.

3. Spelling variation

Spelling variations of marker *well* are <well> and <wel> (including one instance of <vvel> in Q2). In this section I include Q2 and Q3 separately because they differ significantly in spelling from both Q1 and F1 as shown in the following table.

Table 5

	A Shrew			*The Shrew*
	Q1	Q2	Q3	F1
<well>	13	1	6	12
<wel>	3	14	10	2
<vvel>	0	1	0	0
Total	16	16	16	14

In both Q1 and F1 the spelling <well> is basically established. In the Q2 and Q3 texts, on the other hand, the form <wel> is more freely used: it occurs almost regularly in Q2; and often, though less regularly, in Q3.

The form <wel> is often used for line-justification in Early Modern texts: one of the letter *l*s is taken away so that the utterance involving the word *well* can be squeezed into the horizontal space on the page. It is more than likely that the use of the shortened form <wel> in Q1 is due to the need to justify the line because there is no horizontal space left on the page for the utterance which includes the word. The two instances of <wel> in F1 occur in unjustified lines; that is, where there is enough horizontal space left in the right-hand margin on the page; they must have happened to occur with a single *l*. The choice between single or double *l* in Q2-3 is more or less arbitrary: the form with a single *l* is freely used in unjustified lines. This arbitrariness in Q2-3 can also be observed in the choice of the spellings <well> or <wel> for the word *well* acting as an adjective or an adverb with lexical meaning, as shown in the following table.

Table 6

	A Shrew			*The Shrew*
	Q1	Q2	Q3	F1
<well>	27	12	16	65
<wel>	3	18	14	9
Total	30	30	30	74

4. Punctuation

The punctuation following marker *well* varies slightly among the earliest extant texts of the *Shrew* play, but does not vary so much as between the two versions (Q1 and F1) of *The Merry Wives of Windsor*. (Spelling variations are ignored in the following table.)

Table 7

	A Shrew			*The Shrew*
	Q1	Q2	Q3	F1
well (with no punctuation)	13	13	10	7
well, (with comma)	2	2	5	7
well: (with colon)	1	1	1	0
Total	16	16	16	14

The Q1's punctuation following marker *well* is faithfully reproduced in Q2: thirteen instances of marker *well* out of the total sixteen are followed by no punctuation marks, two are followed by a comma, and only one is followed by a colon. Q3 is slightly different from Q1-2: three instances of *well* with no punctuation following in Q1-2 are reproduced with a comma in Q3. Unlike these 'bad' or shorter versions, the F1 *Shrew* shows a preference for the use of a comma after marker *well* as in other Shakespearean F1 texts, although half of the total fourteen instances are followed by no punctuation. The F1's stronger preference for a comma after marker *well* is more clearly shown in *The Merry*

Wives and *Henry V* as in the following table.

Table 8

	The Merry Wives Q1	F1	*Henry V* Q1	F1
well (with no punctualtion)	32	1	13	2
well, (with comma)	11	25	5	6
others	0	8	0	0
Total	43	34	18	8

(cf. Fuami 1997: 179, 208)

When marker *well* is followed by a form of address, the punctuation varies: usually it is put after the address form or there is no punctuation at all even after the address form. The following table shows how marker *well* is punctuated when it is followed by an address form in the *Shrew* texts.

Table 9

	A Shrew Q1	Q2	Q3	*The Shrew* F1
well + address form (with no punctuation)	6	3	0	1
Cf. *well:* + address form	1	1	0	0
well + address form: (with colon)	1	1	0	0
well + address form, (with comma)	1	4	8	3
Cf. *well,* + address form, (with comma)	1	1	1	0
well: + address form, (with comma)	0	0	1	0
Total	10	10	10	4

The Q1's punctuation immediately after marker *well* is faithfully reproduced in Q2 as mentioned above. When the marker is followed by an address form, however, punctuation following the address form shows a slight variation between these two texts: Q2 puts a comma after the address form in three out of the six instances when Q1 had the combination '*well* + address form' with no punctuation following either marker *well* or the address form. Q3 differs from both of these two earlier texts: it puts a comma after address forms regularly. As mentioned earlier, F1 shows a preference for a comma after the marker, but when it is followed by an address form, a comma is deferred until after the address form except for one instance which is followed by no punctuation at all.

Spelling and punctuation variations may not be regarded as relevant in examining the use of the discourse marker *well* in Shakespeare. They may be ascribed to someone else who may have been mechanically responsible for production of the texts.* The purpose here is to describe the details of similarities and differences among the earliest extant texts. It is hoped that detailed textual information will contribute to better understanding of the use of *well* as a discourse marker in Shakespearean texts.

5. Collocation

In present-day spoken English, the marker *well* often collocates with a form of *say* or *think, you know, you see, I mean, look, really, then, so, no, yes* (Svartvik 1980:170). These collocations are not found in the *Shrew* texts. The only conspicuous collocation is with forms of address, as has already been shown in the above table of punctuation — ten out of the total sixteen instances of marker *well* in the Q1 *Shrew* text (62.5%) are collocated with a form of address, and four out of the F1's fourteen (28.6%). The collocation with forms of address seems to occur more frequently in 'bad' quarto texts than in First Folio texts as is the case in *The Merry Wives* and *Henry V*, although the Q1 text of *Henry V* is lower in frequency than the F1 *Shrew* text as is clear in the following table.

Table 10

Play	Text	Number of occurrences of marker *well*	Collocations with address forms	Percentage (%)
SHR,A	Q1	16	10	62.5
WIV	Q1	43	15	34.9
SHR,The	F1	14	4	28.6
H5	Q1	18	2	11.1
WIV	F1	34	1	2.9
H5	F1	8	0	0

It is not clear yet whether the higher frequency in the Q1 *Shrew* text is due to the textual nature of the version or reflects the colloquial nature of the language used in the play. The '*well* + address form' collocation may reflect the colloquial nature of the language, but it can be more closely connected with the speaker's attitude, or degree of politeness or intimacy intended in the utterance. In play text, forms of address can also be used for the purpose of making explicit to whom the speech is directed. They act as important keys to understanding the 'relationship between characters' both generally and at specific moments of high tension (Blake 2002: 283). This function may be why the '*well* + address form' combination occurs more frequently in 'bad' quarto texts; it can help simply to keep up apparent coherence between conversational or addresser-addressee gaps which may have arisen because of deficiencies in the text as transmitted. In *Much Ado about Nothing,* a play in which marker *well* occurs thirty-one times probably because everyday conversational situations recur as often as in *The Merry Wives*, the '*well* + address form' collocation occurs only six times (19.4%). These statistical results may suggest a textual rather than colloquial language reason for the collocation in Shakespearean texts.

6. Location of *well*

The discourse marker *well* can occur initially at the beginning of a new turn (i.e. after speaker-switch) and non-initially embedded in a single speaker's speech. Classifying the instances of marker *well* in the *Shrew* texts according to where in the utterance they occur, initially or non-initially, we get the following table.

Table 11

	A Shrew (Qq)	*The Shrew* (F1)
Initial	12	10
Non-initial	4	4
Total	16	14

In both texts marker *well* occurs more often initially than non-initially. The marker *well* in non-initial position occurs in the Qq text as often as in F1 (four times each). The difference, though slight, in the total number of occurrences of the marker between these two texts results from a difference in the number of occurrences of marker *well* used in initial position.

The location of marker *well* in the *Shrew* play resembles that in *The Merry Wives* and *Henry V*.

Table 12

	Merry Wives		*H5*		*A Shrew*	*The Shrew*
	Q1	F1	Q1	F1	Qq	F1
Initial	32	23	16	6	12	10
Non-initial	11	11	2	2	4	4
Total	43	34	18	8	16	14

It is interesting to note here that marker *well* occurs more often initially than non-initially in both *The Merry Wives* and *Henry V*, as in the *Shrew* play, and that the number of occurrences of marker *well* in non-initial position remains the same between the Q1 and F1 texts of both plays, in which the greater difference in the total number of occurrences of marker *well* between Q1 and F1 comes from a difference in frequency of use in the initial position.

This fact seems to be important when we examine the functions of marker *well* in Shakespearean texts. Although marker *well* in contemporary spoken English is reported to occur with equal frequency both initially and non-initially (Svartvik 1980: 169), the marker in Shakespearean texts more often takes initial position. If the higher frequency in Q1 reflected a colloquial style, then marker *well*, one might think, must occur equally often both in initial and non-initial positions as in contemporary English. This, however, is not the case. One can imagine that marker *well* used initially works effectively in connecting as an adjacent pair such speeches or speech groups as would lack conversational or logical sequence to some degree without some connecting particle intervening between them. One can also imagine that it is mainly for such textual reasons that initial marker *well* occurs frequently in Q1.

7. Conclusion

I have given a preliminary sketch of the discourse marker *well* as it actually occurs in the *Shrew* play, and posed the question of whether it is a reflection of colloquial style of the language used in the play or of textual constraints on the earliest extant texts. Statistically, it has both similarities to and differences from the use of the marker in *The Merry Wives, Henry V* and *Much Ado.*

It is not yet clear whether the use of marker *well* in the *Shrew* texts supports or refutes the idea of the use of marker *well* in Shakespearean texts which is demonstrated in the table 2 above. We need further discussion of how the play was transmitted through the earliest extant texts, and have to examine individual instances of marker *well* left on the page of earliest extant texts accordingly. Further examination of the use of *well* as a discourse marker in the *Shrew* texts will be necessary to elucidate this matter.

Notes

* Punctuation can come to the fore when *well* triggers syntactic ambiguity and raises an interpretative problem as to whether *well* acts as a discourse marker or an adverb. For detailed analysis of specific instances, see Blake (2002: 293) and Fuami (1998: 5-8).

References

Blake, N. F. (2002) *A Grammar of Shakespeare's Language.* Basingstoke: Palgrave.

A Facsimile Series of Shakespeare Quartos: Containing all the pre-Folio editions in which are included the Griggs-Praetorius facsimiles. Issued under the supervision of T. Otsuka. Tokyo: Nan'un-do, 1975.

The First Folio of Shakespeare: The Norton Facsimile. Prepared by Charlton Hinman. London & New York: Paul Hamlyn, 1968.

Fuami, S. (1997) *Essays on Shakespeare's Language: Language, Discourse and Text.* Kyoto: Apollon-sha.

Fuami, S. (1998) '*Well* as a discourse marker in *Much Ado About Nothing*', *Ohtani Women's University Studies in English Language and Literature,* 25: 1-22.

Svartvik, J. (1980) '*Well* in Conversation', *Studies in English Linguistics for Randolph Quirk.* Eds. S. Greenbaum, G. Leech & J. Svartvik. London: Longman, 167-177.

The Grammaticalization of *I tell you* in Shakespeare

HIROJI FUKUMOTO

1. Introduction

In Present-day English, the construction *I tell you* is used to introduce a suggestion or emphasize a statement when occurring idiomatically. OED (s.v. *tell* 9) offers this definition: "To assert positively to; to assure (a person). Often *parenthetically* in expressions of emphasis." Examples of such usage from OALD are:

(1) a. I'll tell you what,–let's stay in instead.
b. I'm telling you, that's exactly what she said.
c. It isn't cheap, I can tell you!

The purpose of this paper is to describe in which circumstances *I tell you* occurs in Shakespeare from syntactic and semantic viewpoints and to investigate to what degree the grammaticalization of this phrase is progressing. I would also like to discuss the problem of the choice of 2nd person pronouns, *you* and *thee*, when they collocate with *I tell* and to examine the relationship between the choice of pronouns and the degree of grammaticalization.

2. Syntactic analysis

First of all, I will examine which complements follow *I tell you* from a syntactic viewpoint. Table 1 demonstrates the frequency of the syntactic patterns which come after *I tell you*.

Table 1 The frequency of the complement of *I tell*

I tell you	I tell you +O	I tell you +ADV	I tell you +PP	Total
30	151	25	2	208

As seen in Table 1, there are a total of 208 examples of *I tell you* in Shakespeare. Out of them, there are 30 instances in SVO pattern, where *I tell you* occurs by itself or parenthetically. I find 151 examples

in SVOO pattern, where *I tell you* is followed by an object. This type is the most frequent in Shakespeare (72.6%). *I tell you* appears before an adverbial phrase and a prepositional phrase, 25 times and twice respectively.
I will look at the examples of *I tell you* according to each complement pattern.

2.1. I tell you

I will begin with the examples where *I tell you* occurs by itself or parenthetically. There are only 5 examples where *I tell you* occurs as a full sentence by itself. In this type, *I tell you* is used to draw the addressee's attention and the proposition is expressed in the sentence that follows. *Tell* is used as a verb of saying and, needless to say, semantic bleaching does not occur.

(2) a. Why, I'll tell you. (Per 2.1.99)[1]

b. I will tell you. (AC 2.2.190)

c. I'll tell thee. (KL 1.4.296)

There are instances where *I tell you* appears in the mid position parenthetically as in (3). This type is found 15 times in Shakespeare. In (3a) and (3b), the idiomatic expression intervenes between a subject and a verb and is used to emphasize the proposition. Examples with brackets are also seen as in (3c) and (3d). In this parenthetical type, *I tell you* can be deleted grammatically and therefore can be regarded as a kind of intensifier. It is reasonable to say that semantic bleaching occurs in this type.

(3) a. The King, I can tell you, looks for us all, we must away all night. (1H44.2.56-7)

b. the Duchess, I tell you, expects performance of your promises. (2H6 1.4.1-2)

c. she's as fartuous a civil modest wife, and one (I tell you) that will not miss you morning nor evening prayer, as any is in Windsor, (MW 2.2.97-9)

d. I shall be with her (I may tell you) by her own appointment; (MW 2.2.261-2)

Finally, there are 10 examples in which *I tell you* comes in final position. The construction collocates with an auxiliary *can* 7 out of 10 examples. That is, I find that the collocation *I can tell you* is overwhelmingly found in the final position. In this type, *I can tell you* is used to strongly emphasize the preceding statement.

(4) a. He's one of the flowers of Troy, I can tell you. (TC 1.2.186-7)

b. Nay, you shall find no boy's play here, I can tell you. (1H4 5.4.75-6)

c. 'Tis in request, I can tell you. (WT 4.4.290-1)

When *I tell you* occurs by itself, it is used most frequently in mid or final positions. Because it is used to emphasize the statement parenthetically, it seems that the idiomaticization[2] of this phrase is progressing.

2.2. I tell you + O

In this section I will deal with the SVOO pattern, where *I tell you* is followed by an object. There are some examples in which *I tell you* is followed by a noun as in (5). However, this type is not so popular in Shakespeare.

(5) a. I will tell thee wonders. (LL 1.2.139)

b. I can tell you strange news that you yet dreamt not of. (MA 1.2.3-5)

c. I'll tell you my dream. (MW 3.3.161)

There are two examples in which *one thing* follows *I tell you* as in (6a) and (6b). When *I tell you* occurs with *one thing*, the phrase becomes a kind of idiomatic expression and plays the role of an attention-getter.

(6) a. But I can tell you one thing, my lord, and which I hear from common rumors, now Lord Timon's happy hours are done and past, (Tim 3.2.4-6)

b. I will tell you a thing, but you shall let it dwell darkly with you. (AW 4.3.10-11)

There are cases where a demonstrative pronoun or an interrogative word comes after *I tell you.* These expressions can often be regarded as a kind of set phrase. Some of them are used idiomatically even in Present-day English. Table 2 shows the frequency of the demonstratives and interrogative words after *I tell you.*

Table 2 The distribution of demonstratives and interrogatives

this	that	what	why	when	Total
2	5	17	2	1	27

From the table above, the examples of *I tell you this* are seen twice. The demonstrative *this* is used anaphorically and refers to the content of the statement that follows. It is noteworthy that a colon occurs after *I tell you this* exclusively in Shakespeare.

(7) a. I tell you this: Caesar through Syria Intends his journey,... (AC 5.2.200-1)

b. First, I must tell thee this: Desdemona is directly in love with him. (Oth 2.1.218-9)

Along with *this*, *that* is found five times after *I tell you* and cataphorically refers to the statement that precedes it as in (8). *I can tell you that* is sometimes added after the proposition in the final position as in (8a) and (8b), while it is put in brackets as in (8c). This expression seems to be used to emphasize the statement.

(8) a. He's a good fellow, I can tell you that; (KL 5.3.285)

b. All the water in Wye cannot wash your Majesty's Welsh plood out of your pody, I can tell you that. (H5 4.7.106-8)

c. As I perceiv'd it (I must tell you that) Before my daughter told me– (Ham 2.2.133-4)

I will now proceed to the examples in which interrogative words come after *I tell you. What* is the most frequent after *I tell you* in Shakespeare—17 times in all. In OALD, *I tell you what* is defined as "used to introduce a suggestion." In (9a) and (9b), a pause is placed by using a comma after *I tell you.* In (9c) and (9d), a vocative is inserted between *I tell you what* and the following sentence. It is possible that *I tell you what* is regarded as an independent word in these examples and so any word may be inserted after the expression parenthetically. In (9e) and (9f), an imperative sentence appears after *I tell you what.* As mentioned above, *I tell you what* is followed by declaratives, imperatives and vocatives. This means that this phrase is rather fixed and grammaticalized. This confirms that the grammaticalization is progressing.

(9) a. I'll tell you what, I think it is our way, (R3 1.1.78)

b. I'll tell you what, my cousin Buckingham– (R3 3.1.89)

c. I tell thee what, Hal, if I tell thee a lie, spit in my face, call me horse. (1H4 2.4.193-4)

d. I tell thee what, Corporal Bardolph, I could tear her. (2H42.4.153-4)

e. I tell thee what: get thee to church a' Thursday, Or never after look me in the face. (RJ 3.5.161-2)

f. I'll tell thee what–yet go! (Cor 4.2.22)

As interrogative words other than *what*, there are two examples in which *I tell you* is followed by *why* and one example by *when*. Because there are few examples of these types in Shakespeare, they cannot be regarded as idiomatic expressions.

(10) a. eftsoons I'll tell thee why. (Per 5.1.255)

b. Right, sir, I'll tell you when, and you'll tell me wherefore. (CE 3.1.39)

Next, I will turn to the examples of an indirect question after *I tell you.* In (11a), an indirect question with *what* occurs after *I tell you.* In (11b), there is an example where an indirect question is placed before *I tell you.* In (11c), a vocative intervenes between *I tell you* and an indirect question.

(11) a. [I'll] tell you what you shall do. (Oth 2.3.314)

b. When and where and how We met, we woo'd, and made exchange of vow, I'll tell thee as we pass, (RJ 2.3.61-3)

c. I'll tell thee, Suffolk, why I am unmeet: (2H6 1.3.165)

Let me look at the examples of *that*-clauses. There are many examples of this type in Shakespeare. In (12a) and (12b), there are some examples where *I tell you* is followed directly by a *that*-clause. In (12c) and (12d), a comma is placed between *I tell you* and a *that*-clause. In (12e-h), a vocative follows *I tell you.* This means that *I tell you* is separated from the clause and the phrase becomes a set phrase and is grammaticalized.

(12) a. I tell you 'tis not very well. (Oth 4.2.196)

b. I'll tell thee thou dost evil. (KL 1.1.166)

c. And I'll tell you, he hath a fair daughter, and to-morrow is her birthday, (Per 2.1.107-9)

d. I tell you, he that can lay hold of her Shall have the chinks. (RJ 1.5.116-7)

e. I tell thee, Kate, 'twas burnt and dried away, (TS 4.1.170)

f. I tell thee, Litio, this is wonderful. (TS 4.2.15)

g. I'll tell thee, Diomed, This brave shall oft make thee to hide thy head. (TC 4.4.136-7)

h. I'll tell you, Cardinal, I should judge now unhappily. (H8 1.4.88-9)

2.3. I tell you + ADV

There are 25 examples where *I tell you* is followed by an adverbial phrase. Here *tell* functions as a verb of saying and the semantic bleaching does not occur.

(13) a. I'll tell you straight. (KL 5.3.280)

b. I'll tell you true, I'll call to you. (Tim 1.2.217)

c. For I must tell you friendly in your ear, (AY 3.5.59)

2.4. I tell you +PP

There are only 2 examples where *tell* is used as an intransitive and *I tell you* is followed by an *of*-phrase.

(14) a. I'll tell you largely of fair Hero's death. (MA 5.4.69)

b. My master knows not of your being here, and hath threat'ned to put me into everlasting liberty if I tell you of it, (MW 3.3.29-31)

3. Semantic analysis

In this section, I will deal with the examples of *I tell you* from a semantic perspective. *Tell* is originally a verb of saying and has the meaning "say, have a word." When the collocation *I tell you* comes to be used frequently, the phrase becomes fixed and comes to be used as an idiomatic expression. This process is called idiomaticization. According to OED (s.v. *tell* 9), the first citation of *I tell you* is dated 1440. In Shakespeare, this phrase is found in idiomatic usage. In this instance, the meaning of the sentence does not change even when the phrase is omitted. Then the meaning of saying gets weaker and semantic bleaching occurs.

I will examine in which circumstances semantic bleaching occurs. There are three cases in Shakespeare. First, it occurs when *I tell you* is followed by a clause, and a vocative is inserted between *I tell you* and a *that*-clause as in (15). In this type, even if *I tell you* is omitted, the meaning of the sentence does not change. It seems that the phrase is used for emphasis or introducing a conversation. Therefore, I assume that semantic bleaching occurs.

(15) a. I tell thee, Kate, 'twas burnt and dried away, (TS 4.1.170)

b. I tell thee, Litio, this is wonderful. (TS 4.2.15)

c. I'll tell thee, Diomed, This brave shall oft make thee to hide thy head. (TC 4.4.136-7)

d. I'll tell you, Cardinal, I should judge now unhappily. (H8 1.4.88-9)

Second, this type is found when *I tell you* is parenthetically put in a sentence as in (16). In (16a) and (16b), *I tell you* occurs between a subject and a verb. It seems that the idiomatic expression emphasizes the statement. In (16c) and (16d), *I tell you* is placed within brackets.

(16) a. The King, I can tell you, looks for us all, we must away all night. (1H4 4.2.56-7)

b. the Duchess, I tell you, expects performance of your promises. (2H6 1.4.1-2)

c. she's as fartuous a civil modest wife, and one (I tell you) that will not miss you morning nor evening prayer, as any is in Windsor, (MW 2.2.97-9)

d. I shall be with her (I may tell you) by her own appointment; (MW 2.2.261-2)

Third, *I tell you* is used for emphasis when it is placed in final position. In this case, *I tell you* is often accompanied by an auxiliary *can* as seen in 2.1.

(17) a. He's one of the flowers of Troy, I can tell you. (TC1.2.186-7)

b. Nay, you shall find no boy's play here, I can tell you. (1H4 5.4.75-6)

c. 'Tis in request, I can tell you. (WT 4.4.290-1)

4. The Choice between *you* and *thee*

In this section I would like to focus attention on the problem of the choice of pronouns. In Early Modern English, there were 2 types of second person pronouns, *you* and *thou*, and they were differentiated semantically and stylistically according to their particular function. Barber (1997: 153) points out that "In the middle of the Early Modern period, *You* was the polite form used by inferiors to superiors: by servants to their master or mistress,... On the other hand, *Thou* was used for addressing a social inferior: by a master to a servant,..." This rule holds for each objective case, *you* and *thee*. Therefore, the 2 types, *I tell you* and *I tell thee*, are found in Shakespeare. Table 3 shows the frequency of the pronouns which follow *I tell*.

Table 3 The frequency of the pronouns after *I tell*

you	thee	ye	others
123	80	3	2

According to this table, *you* is the most frequent pronoun after *I tell* 123 times, whereas *thee* occurs 80 times. As Barber remarks, *you* is often used to speak to a superior person. Therefore, I find that *I tell you* often occurs with *sir, my lord* and *captain* as in (18).

(18) a. Right, sir, I'll tell you when, and you'll tell me wherefore. (CE 3.1.39)

b. My lord, I'll tell you what: If my young lord your son have not the day, Upon mine honor, for a silken point I'll give my barony. (2H4 1.1.51-4)

c. I tell you what, Captain Gower: I do perceive he is not the man he would gladly make show to the world he is. (H5 3.6.82-4)

On the other hand, *I tell thee* is used with a vocative to speak to an inferior person as in (19).

(19) a. I tell thee, Litio, this is wonderful. (TS 4.2.15)

b. I'll tell thee, Diomed, This brave shall oft make thee to hide thy head. (TC 4.4.136-7)

c. I'll tell thee, Hubert, half my power this night, Passing these flats, are taken by the tide– (KJ 5.6.39-40)

I also find two examples of the second person plural pronoun *ye* which follows *I tell*.

(20) a. As I walk thither, I'll tell ye more. (H8 4.1.116-7)

b. Lascivious Edward, and thou perjur'd George, And thou misshapen Dick, I tell ye all I am your better, traitors as ye are, (3H6 5.5.34-6)

Then there are cases where honorific titles, such as *your majesty* and *your worship*, are used instead of *you* as in (21).

(21) a. I can tell your Majesty, the Duke is a prave man. (H5 3.6.95-6)

b. and I will tell your worship more of the wart the next time. (MW 1.4.159)

7. Conclusion

I have examined the examples of *I tell you* in Shakespeare. From a syntactic viewpoint, I found that the *I tell you* + O type is the most frequent (72.6%) in Shakespeare. Of them, there are some idiomatic expressions which are seen in Present-day English. For example, *I tell you* occurs with demonstratives and interrogative words, such as *this*, *that*, *what, why* and *when.* In Shakespeare *I tell you what* is particularly frequent 17 times. I can say that *I tell you what* is a rather fixed phrase in Shakespeare.

From a semantic viewpoint, it is concluded that there are three types where the meaning of *I tell you* gets weaker when the expression is used to introduce a suggestion or emphasize a statement. First, semantic bleaching occurs when *I tell you* is followed by a clause, and a vocative is inserted between *I tell you* and the *that*-clause. The second type is found when *I tell you* is parenthetically put in a sentence, particularly between a subject and a verb. Lastly, *I (can) tell you* is used for emphasis when it is placed in final position.

As for the choice between *you* and *thee*, *I tell you* occurs more frequently than *I tell thee* and is used to speak to a superior person with words which denote respect, while *I tell thee* often appears with a vocative, particularly a first name. Because the idiomatic usage occurs with both pronouns, it seems reasonable to conclude that the choice of the pronouns bears little relation to the degree of the grammaticalization that occurs.

Notes

1 The numerals in the citation refer to the act, the scene, and the line. The abbreviated titles are from Blake (2002).

2 For this, see Akimoto (2002) Chapter 2.

Text

Shakespeare, William. *The Riverside Shakespeare.* 2nd edition by G. B. Evans. Boston, Houghton Mifflin Company, 1997.

References

Aijmer, K. (2002) *English Discourse Particles: Evidence from a corpus*,

Amsterdam, John Benjamins.
Akimoto, M. (ed.) (2001) *Bunpouka—kenkyu to kadai*, Tokyo, Eichosha.
Akimoto, M. (2002) *Grammaticalization and Idiomatization*, Tokyo, Hituji syobo.
Andersen, G. (2001) *Pragmatic markers and Sociolinguistic variation*, Amsterdam, John Benjamins.
Blake, N. F. (2002) *A Grammar of Shakespeare's Language*, New York, Palgrave.
Brinton, L.J. (1996) *Pragmatic markers in English. Grammaticalization and discourse functions,* Berlin & New York, Mouton de Gruyter.
Brinton, L. (2002a) "The development of *(I) say*: grammaticalization, pragmaticalization, or lexicalization?" Paper presented at Aoyama Gakuin University.
Brinton, L. (2002b) "The development of pragmatic markers in English" Paper presented at Aoyama Gakuin University.
Brinton, L. (2002c) "Historical Pragmatics and the Diachronic Study of Pragmatic markers: a Reassessment" Paper presented at the 12th International Conference on English Historical Linguistics at Glasgow University.
Fischer, O., A. Rosenbach and D. Stein (2000) *Pathways of change: grammaticalization in English,* Amsterdam, John Benjamins.
Hopper, P.J. (1991) "On some principles of grammaticalization" In E.C.Traugott, and B. Heine (eds.). *Approaches to grammaticalizatin* Vol.1, 17-35.
Hopper, P.J. and E.C. Traugott. (1993) *Grammaticalization*, Cambridge, Cambridge University Press.
Jucker, A. H. (2002) "Discourse markers in Early Modern English." In R. Watts and P. Trudgill (eds.) *Alternative Histories of English*, London and New York, Routledge. 210-30.
Jucker, A. H. and Y. Ziv (eds). (1998) *Discourse markers. Descriptions and theory,* Amsterdam/Philadelphia, John Benjamins.
OALD=*Oxford Advanced Learner's Dictionary*. 6th edition (2000) Oxford, Oxford University Press.
OED=*The Oxford English Dictionary*. (1989) 2nd ed. Simpson J. A. and E.S.C. Weiner (eds.) 20 vols. Oxford, Clarendon Press.
Schiffrin, D., D. Tannen and H. E. Hamilton. (2001) *The Handbook of Discourse Analysis,* Oxford, Blackwell.
Schmidt, A. (1902) *Shakespeare Lexicon and Quotation Dictionary*. 3rd edn. 2 vols. New York, Dover Publications.
Sweetser, E. E. (1990) *From Etymology to Pragmatics: Metaphorical and Cultural Aspects of Semantic Structure*, Cambridge, Cambridge University Press.
Traugott, E. C. (1982) "From propositional to textual and expressive meanings: some semantic-pragmatic aspects of grammaticalization" In W. P. Lehmann and Y. Malkiel (eds.) *Perspectives on Historical Linguistics*, 245-271.
Traugott, E. C. (1989) "On the rise of epistemic meanings in English: An example of subjectification in semantic change" *Language* 65 (1), 31-55.
Traugott, E. C. (1995a) "Subjectification in grammaticalisation" In D. Stein and S. Wright. (eds.) *Subjectivity and subjectivisation*. Cambridge, Cambridge

University Press. 31-54.
Traugott, E. C. (1995b) "The role of the development of discourse markers in a theory of grammaticalization" Paper presented at the 12th International Conference on Historical Linguistics at Manchester University.
Traugott, E. C. (2000) "*Promise* and *pray*- parentheticals" Paper presented at the 11th International Conference on English Historical Linguistics, Santiago de Compostela, Spain.
Traugott, E. C. and B. Heine (eds.)(1991) *Approaches to grammaticalization* 2 vols. Amsterdam/Philadelphia, John Benjamins.

Be-perfect and *Have*-perfect in John Evelyn's *Diary*

AKEMI SASAKI

1. Introduction

The purpose of this study is to examine the distribution of *be* and *have* with mutative intransitive verbs in the seventeenth century.

The perfect and pluperfect aspect expressing action itself rather than the result of an action, is formed with the auxiliary *have* and a past participle of a verb. In Old English, however, the auxiliaries *be* and *have* were used to form the perfect and pluperfect: *be* was regularly used with intransitive verbs, whereas the use of *have* was restricted to transitive verbs. As time moved on, *have* gradually extended the sphere of its use to the intransitives. By the Early Modern English period, all the transitives and almost all the intransitives were construed with *have*, though the *be*-construction held the advantage with the mutative verbs (= verbs denoting some kind of change, like *come*, *go*, *become*, and *grow*). This tendency continued down to the late Modern English period and then in Present-day English *have*-perfect was perfectly established, as can best be summarised in the following quotation:

> In the eighteenth century *have* gains ground steadily at the expense of *be*, although even at the end of the century *be* is the more common auxiliary with intransitives. The final establishment of *have* as the auxiliary of the (plu)perfect takes place in the early nineteenth century.
> (*The Cambridge History of the English Language*: 215)

Certainly a large number of studies have been made on the rivalry between the auxiliaries before now, but little attention has been given to seventeenth-century English. Therefore I will gather the data from the diary of John Evelyn (1620-1706) and investigate how he employs *be*-perfect and *have*-perfect.

2. *Be*-perfect and *have*-perfect in Evelyn's *Diary*

This section shows the distribution of *be* and *have* with mutative intransitive verbs in Evelyn's *Diary*. There are 32 kinds of intransitive verbs forming the (plu)perfect constructions and *be*-perfect and *have*-perfect are used in the ratio of 143 to 62. The use of *be* amounts to 70 percent and overwhelmingly prevail over *have*. However, not every intransitive takes *be* more frequently than *have*; some verbs are conjugated only with *have*.

Now the following will examine the *be*-perfect and *have*-perfect with each verb by giving examples from Evelyn's *Diary*. At the same time, I would like to take account of the tendency of other periods, especially of the 18th and 19th centuries. Concerning these centuries, Rydén & Brorström (1987) supply the exhaustive data and useful information, to which frequent references will be made.

2.1. Verbs taking only *be*-construction

There are eight mutative verbs taking exclusively *be* to form the (plu)perfect: *advance, become, end, hurry, land, mount, retire, settle*.

2.1.1. *advance* (7 exx.)

(1) After we *were advanc'd* into this noble, and altogether wonderfull Crypta...(175)

Until the 18th century, there are few instances of *have* with *advance* in the preceding studies. Neither Söderlind(1951) nor Ando(1976) gives any. Visser quotes the earliest example of *have* from Defoe (1725). Rydén & Brorström (1987:34-35) shows that the *have* ratios in the 18th and 19th centuries are 36% and 7%, respectively. Even in the 19th century, *be* is the dominant auxiliary. One of the reasons for the absence of *have* in ME and EMod.E may be that *advance* was not used intransitively in ME. *OED*'s earliest citation of the intransitive use is dated 1513. From this viewpoint, it is quite natural that Evelyn does not use *have*.

2.1.2. *become* (5 exx.)

(2) It seems he traveld in search of Iewels, & *was become* extremely rich. (689)

Jespersen's comment helps account for the *be* perfect predominance in Evelyn: *is become* is practically universal in the 18th and the beginning of the 19th c.(*MEG* IV. 3.5(1)).

2.1.3. *end* (3 exx.)

(3) I purposely went to the Bourse (*after* the sermons *were ended*) to see their Dog-market ... (27)

(4) *When* the Anatomie Lectures (which was in the Mornings) *were ended*, I went to see cures don in the Hospotals ... (241)

End can be used both intransitively and transitively. When this kind of verb conjugates with *be*, it is sometimes difficult to discern the meaning: the *be* + past participle combination can be taken as both a perfect and a passive. But the examples (3) and (4) prove to be definitely pluperfect constructions when we direct our attention to *after* and *when*, on the grounds that in this period the conception of time was more strict and the use of the (plu)perfect was frequent in clauses beginning with *after* and *when*.

2.1.4. *hurry* (1 ex.)

(5) Roterdam, whither we *were hurried* in lesse than an houre ... (20)

2.1.5. *land* (4 exx.)

(6) Fresh reports of the Pr: *being landed* somewher about Portsmouth or Ile of Wight (892)

2.1.6. *mount* (1 ex.)

(7) ... it being to be applying to discharge the debt of the nation, which *was* now *mounted* to a prodigious arrear: (1054)

2.1.7. *retire* (3 exx.)

(8) I went to visite Dr. Tenison at Kensington whither he *was retired* to refresh after he had ben sik of the small-pox. (769)

According to Rydén & Brorström (1987: 149-150) the verb *retire* itself does not come into use until the 16th century and *be*-perfect is evidently potential even in the first half of the 19th century.

2.1.8. *settle* (1 ex.)

(9) After I *was* somewhat *settled* there in my formalities ... I added as benefactor to the Library of the Coll: these Books following: (11-12)

2.2. Verbs taking only *have*-construction

There are 10 kinds of verbs taking only *have* in the (plu)perfect construction: *appear, climb, escape, drop, happen, repair, ride, slip, stir, travel.*

2.2.1. *appear* (1 ex.)

(10) God knows what this had produc'd if the spots *had* not *appeard* (264)

In Fridén's materials (1948:102) before 1900, there is only one *be*-construction with *appear* in Shakespeare.

2.2.2. *climb* (1 ex.)

(11) We rod next morning by Monte Pientio ... till we *had climed* to the Inn at Radicofany (114)

2.2.3. *escape* (3 exx.)

(12) one Ferguson who *had escaped* beyond sea ... (745)

Since Rydén & Brorström (1987:85) suggests that the "marked regression of *be* with *escape* in the 18th century ... was obviously completed early in the 19th" century, it is clear that *escape* was commonly construed with *have* from an early period.

2.2.4. *drop* (1 ex.)

(13) I was constrain'd to keepe my Chamber, imagining that my very eyes would *have droped* out (263)

2.2.5. *happen* (5 exx.)

(14) It being in England this yeare one of the most severe frosts that *had happn'd* of many yeares, he told me (763)

Evelyn invariably uses *have* with *happen*, as Rydén & Brorström (1987:121) have numerous examples of *have* in their data. For the present, it may be useful to look more closely at the sentence pattern where *have* appears. Rydén & Brorström (1987) go on to say that certainly *be* is still in use in the latter half of the 17th century, but it appears only once in the type "*there + be + happened*". I have two examples with *be* from Bunyan quoted below, both of which have the construction "*it + be + happened to* someone".

(15) *it is happened unto thee* as to other weak men, who medding with things too high for them, do suddenly fall in thy distractions (Bunyan, *The Pilgrim's Progress* 154)

(16) *it is happened to him* according to the true Proverb, The Dog is turned to his Vomit again, and the Sow that was Washed to her wallowing in the mire (Bunyan, *The Pilgrim's Progress* 194)

It can be supposed that *be* tends to appear in the sentence pattern with zero subject and *have* in the other patterns. Looking at quotations from Evelyn in detail from this point of view, this rule applies to Evelyn's case.

2.2.6. *repair* (1 ex.)

(17) it is the usual place of publique Execution, who suffer here, for any capital crime, tho committed in another Country, by which Law, divers fugitives have ben put to death, who *have repaird* hither for protection (233)

2.2.7. *ride* (1 ex.)

(18) ... *having* after dinner *rid* about that vast levall, pested with heate & swarmes of Gnatts, we returnd over New-market-heath (542)

The *be*-construction with *ride* is also missing from examples in the 18th and 19th centuries collected by Rydén & Brorström (1987: 157).

2.2.8. *slip* (1 ex.)

(19) Thus Davids feete *had* once well nigh *slip'd.* (294)

OED's last citation with *be* is dated 1730.

2.2.9. *stir* (1 ex.)

(20) Our Doctor Preached at Deptford (nor *had* that good man *stirred* from his charge) on 2: Heb:1: (482)

2.2.10. *travel* (7 exx.)

(21) I went to visite Sir J. Chardin that French gent, who *had* 3 times *travelled* into Persia by Land ... (762-763)

Travel is often used in the senses "to go" and "to move", as well as "to journey". In the examples where *travel* bears a similar meaning to *go*, it is more likely that the *be*-perfect appears. However, there is not a single example with *be* in Evelyn, *have*-perfect might have already become established with *travel* at least in the 17th century.

2.3. Verbs taking both *be*-construction and *have*-construction

This section considers the rest of the verbs discussed above, namely the verbs which are combined with both auxiliaries. The frequency of use is as follows:

(a) *be*-perfect is predominant: *arrive, come, enter, get, go, meet, return.*

(b) *have*-perfect is predominant : *run, sit.*

(c) the ratio is almost even: *fall, pass, set, sink, turn.*

The ratios of *be* to *have* in each verb are given parenthetically next to the total number of the examples.

2.3.1. *arrive* (15 exx. / *be* 13 : *have* 2)

(22) I *am* this day *arived* to the 85 yeare of Age ... (1123)

(23) I *had* this day *arived* to my 72d yeare of Age... (960)

Evelyn uses predominantly *be* in the ratio of 13 to 2. The examples above have a similar meaning and sentence pattern. This is a good illustration of how Evelyn uses both auxiliaries with little distinction in meaning. From data furnished by Rydén & Brorström (1987: 44), the ratio of *be* remains high (88%) in the 18th century and falls sharply to less than 20 % from the moment the 19th century opens. Apparently there is a reversal of *be* and *have* during the opening decade of the 19th century.

2.3.2. *come* (34 exx. / 31:3)

(24) I met with my old friend Mr. Tho: Henshaw, who *was* then newly *come* out of Spaine (101)

(25) ... a suddaine, & unexpected thing (when every body believed the first marriage, would *have come* to nothing:) (674)

2.3.3. *enter* (12 exx. / 9:3)

(26) the Queens Almoner who *was* now *entered* upon the sole Regal Government during her husbands Absence (925)

(27) I was to meete that most ingenious and learned Gent: Sir: Geo: Wheeler, ... who being a knight of a very faire estate & young *had* now newly *entred* into holy Orders (762)

Rydén & Brorström (1987:82) suggests that in the 18th century the general predominance of *be* continues, but by the end of the century *be* suddenly goes out of use. It is fair to say that the *be*-perfect is favoured in the days of Evelyn.

2.3.4. *fall* (11 exx. / 6:5)

(28) I had the un-wellcome newes of my sonns *being falln* ill of the Small-pox (616)

(29) we could not passe admiring at the Great Church ..., it shewing so beautiful after a shoure *has fall'n* (208)

Fall often takes *have* in Evelyn, as Visser (1976:2058) comments that *have* is "extremely frequent throughout the ME period". But considering that *fall* can be freely conjugated with *have* already in the 17th century, the frequency seems to be comparatively low. Are there any reasons why *be* is positively used? The following may be of some help in answering this question: in four examples of *be*-perfect out of six, *fall* is used in the idiomatic phrase *fall ill*; in three examples of *have*-perfect out of five, its subject is the rain or the shower.

2.3.5. *get* (13 exx. / 11:2)

(30) One of the first things I went to see after I *was gotten* abroad, was the Towne-house, fairly built of stone. (265)

(31) Twas now also reported that Col: Kirke *had gotten* into Lond: Derry

with supplies (911)

2.3.6. *go* (28 exx. / 20:8)

(32) I turn'd my head the Contrary way til the Coach *was gon* past it … (745)

(33) we enter a vast Cave, in which *having gon* about two hundred paces, we passe a narrow Entry (180)

2.3.7. *meet* (10 exx. / 6:4)

(34) The Ceremony was (after the Cardinals & Princes *were met* in the Consistory) in the Popes Chapell … (135)

(35) 'til now I *had met* with no Phanatical Preachers, but going this day to our Church, I was surprizd to see a Tradesman … (333)

2.3.8. *pass* (7 exx. / 4:3)

(36) Our Charter *being* now *passed* under the Broad-Seale (442)

(37) *Having* now *pass'd* neere three weeked at Euston, to my greate Satisfaction, with much difficulty he sufferd me to looke homewards. (641)

Söderlind (1951: 53) says *be* declines as early as the 17th century.

2.3.9. *return* (10 exx. / 9:1)

(38) I returned to my home, being two daies after my Wife &c *was returned* from Tunbridge, where they had ben… (713)

(39) I return'd, *having return'd* my Visites to the L: Chamberlain, Sir Ste: Fox and other my kind friends. (721)

Evelyn exhibits a marked preference for *be*, which is in agreement with Rydén & Brorström (1987: 151-154): in the 18th century *be* has still a distinct ascendancy, but in the 19th century *be* declines on average from 83% to 28%.

2.3.10. *run* (4 exx. / 1:3)

(40) There was one of their ships fired, suspected as don by the Enemie, she *being run* on ground … (512)

(41) Thus *having run* thro the most memorable buildings & Curiositys of this noble Citty (110)

According to Fridén (1948:97ff) and *OED* (s.v. *run*, *v*. B. I.), until the 16th century *be* maintains a superior position, while *have* is also repeatedly used by various authors; when the 18th century comes, *have* becomes predominant and at the same time *be* is frequently employed.

That is to say, down to the 19th century, there is a long rivalry between the two. Evelyn's usage takes on the characteristics of the 18th century.

2.3.11. *set* (3 exx. / 1:2)

(42) The weather now *was set* in to an absolute Thaw & raine, but the Thames still hard. (767)

(43) Mr. Mat had the stables which indeede are very faire, *having set* out the Walkes in the park, & Gardens (464)

The example (42) is the first citation in *OED* (s.v. *set*, v^1. 146 e).

2.3.12. *sit* (5 exx. / 1 : 4)

(44) The King *being sate* under gold & pearle, made a glorious shew (449)

(45) Was the Long Parliament (which now *had sate* ever-since his Majesties restaurantion) disolv'd by perswasion of the L: Tressurer ...(663)

Rydén & Brorström (1987: 168) suggests that the simple verb *sit* is invariably construed with *have* from the 18th century on. It may be said that Evelyn's usage goes with the tendency of the times.

2.3.13. *sink* (3 exx. / 2 : 1)

(46) There was about this time brought into the Downed, a vast treasure which after 45 yeares *being sunk* in a Spanish galioon (867)

(47) This subterranean Grott, leads quite through to Cuma, but is in some places obstructed by the Earth which *has sunk* in (180)

2.3.14. *turn* (4 exx. / 2 : 2)

(48) he began to speake Latine, and make his Apology in so good a style, that their derision *was turn'd* to admiration ... (56)

(49) after we *had turn'd* about & considerd the goodly Prospect towards the Sea, and Citty ... (171)

3. Comparison with other writers

This section will deal with the comparison with other authors in different periods to make further investigation of Evelyn's usage. The table given below shows the frequency of *have* from the 14th century to the 19th century in relation to 10 verbs. Though Evelyn uses 32 kinds of intransitive verbs in the (plu)perfect construction, some of them appear only once. Such verbs are excluded from the observation in this section, because it seems too extreme to analyse data with a single example. In addition, there are some verbs about which we cannot get enough data for some periods from preceding studies. Accordingly 10 verbs were picked out and are shown in the table below.

The data on Chaucer, the 15th century and Shakespeare are derived from Fridén(1948); the data on Pepys are from Nakamura(1986); the data on the 18th and 19th centuries are from Rydén & Brorström (1987).

Table Frequency of *have*-perfect (%)

	Chaucer	15c.	Shakes.	Pepys	Evelyn	18c.	19c.
arrive	0		12	0	13	12	82
become	0	0	4	0	0	20	80
come	5	12	13	7	9	18	79
enter		31		0	25	29	100
fall	13	9	29	16	45	55	93
go	18	28	9	11	29	21	56
pass		19		80	43	73	86
return				6	10	17	73
run		48		47	75	45	72
turn				0	50	30	65
Total	10	18	11	12	30	26	72

First, this table shows that Evelyn prefers *have* in the ratio of 30%, compared with the authors of other periods. It is natural that the 17th century has a higher frequency than before, but even when compared with his contemporary, Pepys, Evelyn displays a far higher frequency in every verb except for *pass*. In many verbs, Evelyn's figures are close to those of the 18th century and as for *run* and *turn* he shows greater frequency.

Next, a close look at the transition of each verb reveals some interesting points. As for the verbs such as *arrive* and *become*, where the use of *have* had not established by the 18th century, the frequency of *have* remarkably increases. On the other hand, as for the verbs such as *go*, *run* and *turn*, where *have* was already in general use at earlier period, its frequency goes up gradually with the course of the times but even in the 19th century remains not so high.

4. Final remarks

In conclusion, the following two features can be pointed out from what has been said above: (1) Evelyn, the 17th-century diarist, frequently uses the *have*-perfect with many kinds of intransitive verbs, though the *be*-perfect is still used commonly even in the 18th century. (2) Certainly Evelyn uses *have* with greater frequency than Pepys, another contemporary diarist, but he himself does not takes the lead in using *have*. He uses *be* with the verbs which had seldom been construed with *have* before Evelyn's period in accordance with the former usage. In contrast, with the verbs where the *have*-perfect was getting commoner by appearing in various authors, he makes extensive use of *have*.

Texts

John Evelyn (1959) *The Diary of John Evelyn.* (The Oxford Standard Authors). Ed. E. S. de Beer. London: Oxford University Press.

John Bunyan (1966) *Grace Abounding to the Chief of Sinners* and *The Pilgrim's Progress from this World to that which is to come.* Ed. Roger Sharrock. London: Oxford University Press.

References

Abbott, E. A. (1870) *A Shakespearian Grammar.* 3rd ed. London: Macmillan; reprinted New York: Dover (1966).

Ando, S. (1976) *A Descriptive Syntax of Christopher Marlowe's Language.* Tokyo: University of Tokyo.

Barber, C. (1976) *Early Modern English.* London: André Deutsch.

Baugh, A. C. and T. Cable. (1978) *A History of the English Language.* New Jersey: Prentice-Hall.

Brook, G. L. (1958) *A History of the English Language.* London: André Deutsch.

Fridén, G. (1948) *Studies on the Tenses of the English Verbs from Chaucer to Shakespeare.* Uppsala: Almqvist & Wiksell.

Görlach, M. (1991) *Introduction to Early Modern English.* Cambridge: Cambridge University Press.

Jespersen, O. (1931) *A Modern English Grammar on Historical Principles.* Part VI. London: George Allen & Unwin.

Lass, R. ed. (1999) *The Cambridge History of the English Language.* Vol. II. Cambridge: Cambridge University Press.

Mitchell, B. (1985) *Old English Syntax.* I-II. Oxford: Clarendon Press.

Mustanoja, T. F. (1960) *A Middle English Syntax.* I. Helsinki: Société Néophilologique.

Nakamura, F.(1986) "Auxiliary *Have* in Samuel Pepys's 'Diary', with Special Reference to Mutative Verbs: (1) A Statistical Study." *Studies in Modern English* 3: 23-51.

Otsuka, T. and F. Nakajima, ed. (1982) *The Kenkyusha Dictionary of English Linguistics and Philology.* Tokyo: Kenkyusha.

The Burns Text of *Tam Lin* Revisited

Seiichi Ikadatsu

Tam Lin (Child 39) is a well-known Scottish traditional ballad, full of ancient folklore.[1] Among the fourteen variants (though some of them are only fragments) collected in Francis J. Child's *The English and Scottish Popular Ballads* (hereafter *ESPB*) ,[2] version A, which is "communicated by Robert Burns," [3] has been said to be the finest. John D. Niles, for example, comments on the Burns text that this is the version of *Tam Lin* which is known to most readers today, as editors have been nearly unanimous in selecting it for their anthologies. [4]

Some thirty years ago, Emily B. Lyle worked on the various versions of *Tam Lin*, examining how Burns drew on other traditional sources when composing his text.[5] Several years later, Niles also made a close textual analysis between versions A and B,[6] showing some differences between Burns's style and the style of the traditional ballad.[7] As far as the folklore in *Tam Lin* is concerned, David Atkinson investigated the fairies' tradition and revival in his recent paper.[8]

In the present paper, with special reference to Niles' analysis, I will re-examine the Burns text in the light of the language and style of the traditional ballad, hoping to elucidate what kind of literary artistry Burns has displayed in his text and to what extent he has succeeded in reproducing a traditional ballad text.[9]

The first example of Burns's self-conscious literary artistry is seen at the very beginning of the story (italics mine):

> O I forbid you, maidens a'
> That wear *gowd* on your *hair* (A, 1)

> I FORBID ye, maidens a'
> That wear *goud* on your *gear* (B, 1)

Burns here altered the original "gear" into "hair" at the cost of the alliterative effect of the /g/ sound :goud—gear.

Lexical alteration can be seen again in the next stanza (italics mine):

> Either their *rings*, or green mantles, (A, 2)

> Either their *things* or green mantles, (B, 2)

Niles states, "From a purely aesthetic point of view, each change is felicitous in that it helps to call up an image of a flesh-and-blood young woman, complete with rings and flowing hair."[10] His comment makes sense if we assume that the text will be read closely by literate-minded readers. It is questionable, however, whether or not these simple lexical changes would have made any differences among the audience sitting at the oral performances.

"Thick" in B (13) is changed into "meek" as follows (italics mine):

> Out then spak her father dear
> And he spak *meek and mild*; (A, 13)

This is the reverse case of the above first example and if we take into account the alliterative effect of "meek and mild," Burns's emendation might be reasonable. It is still arguable that the change of single word like this could be cause for her father to be transformed into a completely different character.[11]

Let's move on to the second type of change. Burns adds a new word "Ance" (=once) which is not seen in B (9) (italics mine):

> And out then cam the fair Janet,
> *Ance* the flower amang them a'; (A, 9)

In B, the corresponding line reads, "She is the flower of them a'," which is a ballad commonplace[12] and always used to describe the characteristics of ballad heroines. By adding the simple word "Ance", Burns effectively describes the change Janet has suffered; "Janet was *but is no longer* the flower of them all; she is now *de*flowered."[13]

Addition is not limited to a single word. A new stanza not appearing in B is introduced here (italics mine):

> 'The steed that my true-love rides on
> Is lighter than the wind;
> Wi siller he is shod before,
> *Wi burning gowd behind* (A, 16)

The latter two lines of the stanza is also a commonplace for a horse in traditional ballads, mostly found in the variants of *Lord Thomas and Fair Annet* (Child 73) (italics mine).[14]

> The horse Fair Annet trade upon,
> He amblit like the wind;
> Wi siller he was shod before,
> *Wi burning gowd behind.* (A, 16)

Lyle maintains that Burns derived this stanza from other versions known to him from oral tradition,[15] while Niles suggests the possibility of Burns's borrowing it from the printed versions of other ballads.[16] Apart from the discussion of the origin of this stanza, there is wide agreement that this stanza evokes a strong association with supernatural world.[17]

So far, the textual difference between the two versions has not been so conspicuous. In the middle of text A, however, we come across an alliterative expression which proves Burns to be a literary poet (italics mine):

> I am sae *fair* and *fu* o *flesh*,
> I'm *feard* it be myself. (A, 24)

The most typical example of highly intentional use of alliteration, which may show the handling of a professional poet, is seen in the following stanzas in text A (italics mine):

> 'But the night is *Halloween*, lady,
> The morn is *Hallowday*;
> Then *win* me, *win* me, an ye *will*
> For *weel* I *wat* ye may.
>
> 'Just at the *mirk and midnight* hour
> The fairy folk will ride,
> And they that wad their true-love win,
> At Miles Cross they maun bide.' (A, 25-26)
>
> 'The night it is gude Halloween,
> The fairie folk to ride,
> And they that wad their true-loue win,
> At Miles Cross they maun bide.' (B, 24)

Niles comments on these stanzas that Burns's lines betray their literary origin in the way that they exploit the device of alliteration....Alliteration and repetition occur commonly in traditional texts too, of course, but scarcely in such an artful fashion as here. [18] It is also interesting to note that stanza 24 of B is expanded into two stanzas in A (25-26) to elaborate the scene and to make the atmosphere more suitable for the night when an unusual event is going to happen.[19]

Tam Lin's metamorphoses in B (31-32), to "a greyhound," and "a red het gad o iron" are changed in A (32-34), into "a bear," "a lion," "a burning gleed," respectively. Niles ascribes these changes to "Burns's desire to magnify terror."[20] It should also be noticed here that in B (30-33), the same sentence pattern is simply repeated four times in the first line of each stanza (italics mine):

> 'They'll turn me in thy arms, lady,

An adder and a snake; (B, 30)

On the other hand, in A, this pattern is slightly changed at the third, fourth and fifth stanza as follows:

'*Again they'll turn me in your arms*
To a red het gaud of airn; (A, 33)

'*And last they'll turn me in your arms*
Into the burning gleed; (A, 34)

'*And then I'll be your ain tru-love,*
I'll turn a naked knight; (A, 35)

Here the adverbial phrases, "Again," "And last," and "And then" are added at the front of the first lines of each stanza. It may be safely asserted that the addition of these words makes the lines sound more explanatory or commentary, which therefore causes the style of the Burns text to look different from that of the authentic traditional ballad.

Burns's desire to highlight the romantic element also seems to be the cause of other changes[21] (italics mine):

'But how shall I thee ken, Thomas,
Or how shall I *thee* knaw, (B, 25)

Here, Jannet refers to Tam Lin simply as "thee" but the corresponding line in A reads "my true-love" (27). Likewise, "mother-naked man" (B, 33) is altered into "a naked knight"; (A, 35).

The addition of a detailed description of Tam Lin may be in line with this romanticism:

Cockt up shall my bonnet be,
And kaimed down shall my hair. (A, 30)

These lines, as Niles points out, will help us to call up an image of a young gallant who seems to be aware of his own good looks.[22] In B, on the contrary, the young man is never described physically. In typical ballad style, he is to be recognized solely by the anonymous tokens of a gloved hand and a gloveless hand.

The B text has a tendency to be formulaic and repetitive in its expression (italics mine):

'*The first company that passes by,*
Say na, and let them gae;
The next company that passes by,
Say na, and do right sae;
The third company that passes by,
Then I'll be ane o thae. (B, 26)

This six-line stanza containing phrasal repetition is a style peculiar to folk poetry[23] and therefore might have been very popular among the audience of those days. In A, however, this is compressed into a four-line stanza, giving a tense situation to the stanza:

> 'Oh first let pass the black, lady,
> And syne let pass the brown,
> But quickly run to the milk-white steed,
> Pu ye his rider down. (A, 28)

It may be asserted that as these two stanzas seem to reflect their different origins, they should be appreciated or evaluated in the light of the process of their creation and performance.

The most striking difference between the two versions can be seen in the following stanzas (italics mine):

> Gloomy, gloomy was the night,
> And eerie was the way,
> As fair Jenny in her green mantle
> To Miles Cross she did gae.
>
> About the middle o the night
> She heard the bridles ring;
> This lady was as glad at that
> As any earthly thing.
>
> First she let the black pass by,
> And syne she let the brown;
> But quickly she ran to the milk-white steed,
> And pu'd the rider down. (A, 36-38)
>
> *Jannet has kilted her green kirtle*
> *A little aboon her knee,*
> *And she has snooded her yellow hair*
> *A little aboon her bree,*
> And she is on to Miles Cross,
> As fast as she can hie.
>
> The first company that passed by,
> She said na, and let them gae;
> The next company that passed by,
> She said na, and did right sae;
> The third company that passed by,
> Then he was ane o thae.
>
> She hied her to the milk-white steed,
> And pu'd him quickly down;
> She cast her green kirtle owr him
> To keep him frae the rai:

Then she did all was orderd her,
And sae recoverd him. (B, 35-37)

The italicized four lines of stanza 35 of B is a ballad commonplace which denotes 'urgency' and indicates 'action under the influence of strong emotions.'[24] This formula has already appeared three times in A (3, 8 and 17) also. It might, therefore, have felt for Burns that if he repeat this formula here once again, the style would look too simple and artless. Instead, Burns gives an atmospheric description in A (36-37). With these two stanzas, Niles comments that unlike the author of B, Burns is concerned with the atmosphere, and he exploits atmosphere to the full.... In place of highly charged adjectives, "gloomy," "eerie," and "earthly," we find emotionally neutral ones, "green," "yellow," "first," "next," and "third" in B.[25]

In the A text, Burns describes not only Jannet's action, "To Miles Cross she did gae" and "She heard the bridles ring," but also her emotional reaction, "This lady was as glad at that." In contrast, we find only simple actions in B, such as "She said na and let them gae."[26] Stanza 36 of B, which is already mentioned above, is resumed here, describing the action which is just taking place in front of us. When we call to mind the fact that a primary concern of ballad poetry is to tell a story in a dramatic way, it is understandable that such poetry tends to avoid explanatory descriptions of scenes and characters. For example, Matthew Hodgart comments on the traditional ballad style as follows:

> "The story is told in sharp flashes, with a distinct scene or a separate passage of dialogue in each stanza. The singer dramatizes the action in the most emphatic manner he knows, omitting everything that is unnecessary to a swift climax"[27]

In light of these ballad characteristics, it seems that the style of B, which looks more simple and unsophisticated, is more appropriate for a traditional ballad than that of A.

At the end of the story, Burns shows his skill as a literary poet in describing the fury of the Queen of Fairies (italics mine):

Out then spak the Queen o Fairies,
And an angry woman was she:
'*Shame betide her ill-far'd face,*
And an ill death may she die,
For she's taen awa the boniest knight
In a' my companie. (A, 41)

Out than spak the Queen o Fairies,
Out o a bush of rye:

'Them that has gotten young Tom Line
Has the best knight in my company. (B, 39)

The Queen's anger is described vividly in the three italicized lines. We can easily imagine her growing resentment over the loss of "the boniest knight," while there is no mention of her inner feeling in B. It may be true for modern readers that text A looks more attractive than text B in that it has, as a narrative, profundity produced by the inclusion of 'a theme of female jealousy.' Niles comments on this point as follows;

> The song has burst beyond the bounds of a simple tale of rescue from the fairy troops; we are to imagine a contest of wits and will between two possessive women, with a handsome young man as the prize. For its human interest, Burns's text again far outstrips its source.[28]

I have so far made a textual comparison between two versions of *Tam Lin* with special reference to Nile's analysis. To take stock, the changes made by Burns may be grouped into the following seven categories: (1) The replacement of words for the artistic effect. (2) The replacement of sounds for alliterative effect. (3) The addition or omission of a word or phrase to make the lines more expressive. (4) Intentional avoidance of the commonplace for artistic effect. (5) An improvement to the story line. Burns pulls the story together at points where the narrative movement is aimless or confused. (6) The highlighting of romantic elements. (7) A fascination with atmosphere.

Taking all the above into consideration, it may be concluded that Burns tried not to reproduce a ballad with exactly the same style as the traditional one but, following the traditional convention, to compose a ballad to his own taste. In other words, he is not so much concerned about the authenticity of his text as he is concerned about its artistry as poetry. This may well be supported by the fact that most modern readers tend to more impressed with the artistry of Burns text than traditional B. Niles aptly comments on this point as follows:

> The contrast between A and B may be summed up in a single statement; the Burns text was composed for the eyes of the reading public, not for the ears of the untutored folk. Unlike most texts transcribed from oral tradition, it can be read as poetry. One can savor it line by line and can delight in its pattern of sound, its artful repetitions, its balanced structure.[29]

Let us here think about the relationship between the text transcribed from oral tradition and the text recreated by a literary poet. Some purists will stubbornly insist that the latter can never be called as an authentic traditional ballad. Others will refute them arguing that the Burns's way of composition should be accepted, though not so common, as one of the processes some traditional ballads have suffered by way of transmission. The case on both sides seems to be well-grounded and therefore it seems better to leave them to judge for themselves. It may be, however, safely asserted that though it can hardly be called an authentic traditional ballad, the Burns text clearly shows us how a literary poet worked on the traditional text to make it more attractive to a wider range of readers. We may, therefore, reasonably conclude that from the viewpoint of ballad scholars, Burns may be worth admiring not because his text is much better than the traditional one but because he attracted, through his text, people's attention to the romantic and supernatural world of traditional balladry.

Notes

* I should like to thank Dr. Trevor Sargent, Tottori University, for improving my English. Needless to say, any inadequacy is all mine.

1. "Few ballads carry forward so much ancient folklore as *Tam Lin*." (Albert B. Friedman ed., *The Viking Book of Folk-ballads of the English-Speaking World*, New York: The Viking Press, 1956, reissued, 1982, 41.)

2. In 5 Vols. (Boston and New York: 1882-98, reprint ed., New York: Dover, 1965)

3. "First appeared in Johnson's Museum, 423. No 411." (*ESPB*, Vol. I, 340.)

4. "A Traditional Ballad and Its Mask: *Tam Lin*." Patricia Conroy ed., *Ballads and Ballad Research*, Seattle: University of Washington, 1978, 147.

5. "The Burns Text of *Tam Lin*", *Scottish Studies*, Vol.15, Part I, 1971, 53-65. Dr Lyle, who is now an honorary fellow at the School of Literatures, Languages & Cultures (Celtic and Scottish Studies), Edinburgh University, was my advisor while I was staying at the School of Scottish Studies (the name of the Institute at that time), for two months in 2000. The title of present paper is named after her above paper to express my gratitude for her kind assistance and valuable advice to me. Her papers about *Tam Lin* includes; "The Ballad *Tam Lin* and Traditional Tales of Recovery from the Fairy Troop "(*Studies in Scottish Literature* 6, 1969, 98-102.), "The Opening of *Tam Lin*" (*Journal of American Folklore* Vol.83, No.327, 1970, 33-43.), "The Teind to Hell in *Tam Lin.*" (*Folklore* 81, 1970, 177-81.)

6. Glenriddell's MSS, vol. xi, No.17 (*ESPB*, vol. I, 343.)

7. *op.cit.*, 147-58.

8. "Expropriating the Fairies: *Tam Lin*, Tradition and Revival", Sigrid Rieuwerts and Helga Stein ed., *Bridging the Cultural Divide: Our Common Ballad Heritage*, Hildesheim: Georg Olms Verlarg, 2000, 30-48.

9. It has been one of the major issues among ballad scholars that what parts of version A have come down from oral tradition and what parts are Burns's own creation. Willa Muir, for example, concerning to the opening

stanzas (A, 1-2), comments as follows:

> It is Robert Burns's communicated version that contains the prefatory admonition, copied later by all the other versions except two from the North. I incline to think that it was due to Burns himself: its tone belongs to the second half of the eighteenth century rather than to earlier times. (*Living with Ballads*, London: The Hogarth Press, 1965, 136.)

10. *op.cit.*, 148.

11. "The same person who speaks *thick and milde* in (B, 13) speaks *meek and mil*d in A. *Thick and milde*: the words call to mind a voice choked with emotion, yet soft. The emotion is being kept under control. But *meek and mild*! The picture is changed utterly. The great Scots lord is transformed into an image of timidity, a pale elder who speaks soft syllables in the shadow of his domineering daughter." (Niles, *op.cit.*, 148-9).

12. Child lists many types of commonplaces in *ESPB* (Vol. IV, 474-5.). Another type of commonplaces are also seen in *Tam Lin*. To take an example:

> She had na pu'd a double rose
> A rose but only twa, (A, 5)

With the function of the girl's flower-picking formula, Flemming G. Andersen explains as follows:

> "As soon as the girl enters the wood which she feels herself drawn towards she starts picking flowers/pulling nut, etc., and this act summons the immediate presence of a young man, in a manner less than promising... In the ballad below formula serves as prelude to sexual assault upon the girl." (*Commonplace and Creativity*, Odense: Odense University Press, 1985, 116-7.)

13. Niles, *op.cit.* 148.

14. In *ESPB*, vol. V, 475.

15. *op.cit.*, 53-4.

16. *op.cit.*, 148-9.

17. On the significance of this stanza, Niles comments that Burns's addition of the "silver horse" stanza is the first evidence of his fascination with the ballad's supernatural side. (*op.cit.*, 150.)

18. *op.cit.*, 151.

19. We may call this type of change as "expansion."

20. *ibid.*

21. *op.cit.*, 152. cf. the emendation of *hair* and *rings* in A (1-2).

22. *ibid.*

23. See, for example, MacEdward Leach, *The Ballad Book*, New York: Harper & Brothers, 1955, 18.ff. (III, Ballad Style)

24. Andersen, *op.cit.*,

25. *op.cit.*,153.

26. *ibid.*

27. Matthew Hodgart ed., *The Faber Book of Ballads*, London: Faber and Faber, 1965, 13-4.

28. *op.cit.*,154.

29. *op.cit.*,155

Free Indirect Discourse in *Emma*

Eiko Tatsumoto

1. Introduction

As Jane Austen herself says, "I am going to take a heroine whom no one but myself will much like,"[1] the heroine Emma Woodhouse is self-centered and defective. Therefore, according to Mary Lascelles (1954: 214), "she [Jane Austen] wished her readers to share her feelings towards them," so that Kazuhiko Ohshima (1997: 227) states:

> ... most of the story is written from Emma's point of views, and the skill which makes readers see various events in the story through the heroine's consciousness ... allows them to feel Emma's deficiency or weak point to be their own experience unconsciously, ... so that their pushing away and disliking Emma causes them difficulty.

Similarly, Wayne C. Booth (1983: 245) says, "By showing most of the story through Emma's eyes, the author insures that we shall travel with Emma rather than stand against her." As David Lodge (1992: 6) argues, "we begin to hear the voice of Emma herself in the discourse, as well as the judicious, objective voice of the narrator," and with regard to Emma's viewpoint, Booth (1983: 245) concretely explains:

> The solution to the problem of maintaining sympathy despite almost crippling faults was primarily to use the heroine herself as a kind of narrator, though in third person [free indirect discourse][2], reporting on her own experience.

Jane Austen frequently uses free indirect discourse, FID, to present Emma's viewpoints in the story.

Regarding the idea that FID makes readers share Emma's viewpoints, no philological studies seem to have been made. Accordingly, the purpose of this paper is to consider philologically whether defective Emma's viewpoints [FID] really enable readers to close the distance between them and Emma and also allow them to have sympathy for Emma.

2. On the Use of FID

In this section, we will give an explanation of FID in order to understand it explicitly. In English, Otto Jespersen (1951) called the term 'represented speech.' In addition, several other names are used: free indirect speech [Randolph Quirk (1985), Roy Pascal (1977)], free indirect discourse [Brian McHale (1978)], and others. Kurokawa (1994: 277) mentions that "at present 'free indirect discourse' ... is frequently used."[3] In English literature, as Norman Page (1972: 124) points out, Jane Austen established FID in her novel. Quirk (1985: 1032) defines FID as follows:

> FREE INDIRECT SPEECH is used extensively to report speech or (particularly in fiction) the stream of thought. It is basically a form of indirect speech, but (a) the reporting clause is omitted (except when retained as a parenthetical clause, as in direct speech), and (b) the potentialities of direct-speech sentence structure are retained (for example, direct questions and exclamations, vocatives, tag questions, and interjections). It is therefore only the backshift of the verb, together with equivalent shifts in personal pronouns, demonstratives, and time and place references, that signals the fact that the words are being reported, rather than being in direct speech.

3. The Discourses in *Emma*

Before considering FID in detail, we need to examine discourses to fully recognise FID. Graham Hough (1970: 203-5) distinguishes five kinds of discourse in *Emma*:

1) The authorial voice,
2) Objective narrative,
3) Coloured narrative,
4) Free indirect style, and
5) Direct speech and dialogue

In respect to coloured narrative, Hough (1970: 204) observes: "This is a form into which the objective narrative, after a time, very commonly modulates. I mean by it narrative or reflection or observation more or less deeply coloured by a particular character's point of view." Thus, Yukiko Nakagawa (1983: 23) argues: "this can be interpreted as fragmentary free indirect speech." There are two kinds of FID in 4):

FID with quotation marks and without quotation marks. We will take these up as the subject of the examination.

4. An Examination of FID

In this section, we will examine whether readers actually sympathise with Emma by FID, specifically by the context of FID. We refer to Nakagawa (1983: 132, 142) regarding the subject of the examination and the pattern of frequency in it. The subject of the examination is FID without quotation marks, not FID with quotation marks. Nakagawa (1983: 142) states: "Since FID with quotation marks has quotation marks, it is obvious that readers recognize it as a character's voice; on the other hand FID without quotation marks contains both narration and a character's viewpoint." Moreover, the subject of the examination is not fragmentary FID, but sentential FID. The numbers listed in Table 1 are not the numbers of the sentences, but a succession of FID can be regarded as one occurrence. Passages not clearly identified as FID are not included in the frequency. It may not be an accurate frequency since the recognition of FID would differ, depending on the readers. Concerning this, Kurokawa (1994: 288), however, says: "we can say with fair certainty that the frequency means a general tendency or prospect."

Before coming to the context of FID, we must draw attention to the frequency in Table 1 in order to find the frequency of use of FID of Emma in the whole story.

Table 1 The Frequency of FID of Emma in *Emma*[4]

	Volume 1	Volume 2	Volume 3	Total
FID	47 (19.8%)	73 (30.8%)	117 (49.4%)	237 (100%)

As we can see from the above, the frequency of the use is gradually increasing from chapter 1 to chapter 3 since the presentation of "various events" and "experiences" through Emma's viewpoint is growing little by little. For instance, in Volumes 1, 2, and 3, the following are shown in the story: mainly, her selfish imagination, misunderstanding, resentment, surprise, repentance and reflection, reformation, consideration, and mental growth. Now, we shall look more carefully into FID. Jespersen (1951: 292) explains:

> Represented speech is more vivid on the whole than the first class of indirect speech. As it is nearer to direct speech, it retains some of its elements, especially those of an emotional nature, whether the emotion is expressed in intonation or in separate words like "Oh!", "Alas!", "Thank God!", etc.

Thus, in order to examine whether Emma's emotional nature of FID is really included, according to Quirk (1985: 1032), let us now attempt to extend the observation into the use of FID with exclamations or questions or interjections. The results are shown in Table 2.

Table 2 The Frequency in the Use of FID with Exclamations, Questions, or Interjections

	Volume 1	Volume 2	Volume 3	Total
Exclamation	4	10	26	40
Question	2	5	15	22
Interjection	0	0	3	3

Judging from Table 2, the frequency increases as the volumes progress. As we have concretely given an account of Emma's "various events" and "experiences" from her viewpoint in Table 1, we can find that Emma's emotional form of FID increases in Table 2 as the chapters progress. Therefore, the use of exclamations or questions or interjections in FID is proven to be a part of Emma's subjective views.

Let us now return to the real subject. We would like to focus attention on the context of FID, considering whether readers really sympathise with Emma by showing her FID expressing subjective viewpoints FID. McHale (1978: 267) observes:

> ... there are other indices of FID which are properly formal; for instance, cues in the immediate context, which Bally [Bally, Charles. "Figures de Pensée et Formes Linguistiques." *GRM* VI (1914): 410-12.] classified as early as 1914. According to his account ..., verbs (or other expressions) of speech or thought bear crucially upon the perceptibility of a sentence of FID when they appear in the context immediately preceding that sentence, or immediately following it, or both preceding and following it, ...

He also states Bally's idea about the context of FID. After this statement, however, in regard to Bally's idea, he (1978: 268) points out: "Bally's analysis is perhaps a little austere, limiting itself to only the most immediate and most obvious contextual cues," and he objects to the importance of the context. In contrast with McHale's opinion,

Junjirou Tanimura (1971: 92) says: "when clear reported verbs are used in the context preceding represented speech or following it ..., readers strongly ... feel the intervention of the author between characters and readers," and he gives attention to the context, observing the effect which readers are given by the context. Judging from his opinion, it is important to consider the context. Accordingly, referring to Pascal (1977: 26-7) and Tanimura (1971: 92, 94), we can divide the context into three categories: reported verbs preceding FID, following it, and both preceding and following it. We furthermore refer to Jespersen's idea (1951: 290) about reported verbs as follows:

> There are two kinds of indirect speech (indirect discourse), which I shall call *dependent* and *represented speech*. The former is generally made dependent on an immediately preceding verb, "he said (thought, hoped, etc.)" or "he asked (wondered, wanted to know, had no idea, etc.)," ....

To begin with, the following is the frequency of reported verbs preceding FID.

Table 3 The Frequency of Reported Verbs Preceding FID

	Volume 1	Volume 2	Volume 3	Total
say	0	0	0	0
think[5]	1	3	4	8
hope	0	2	1	3
ask	0	0	1	1
wonder	0	0	0	0
want to know	0	0	0	0
have no idea	0	0	0	0

With regard to FID with reported verbs preceding FID or following it, Tanimura (1971: 93) explains:

> ... these reported verbs have an element linking them with the author and the character extremely strongly, and readers are firmly conscious of the intervention of the author.

Therefore, he (1971: 97) mentions that readers' minds don't enter the character's subjective world [FID]. As we can see from Table 3, however, the frequency is small, representing only 5.1 per cent in Table 1. The following serves as an example:

(1) Of the lady, individually, *Emma thought* very little. *She was good enough for Mr. Elton, no doubt; accomplished enough for Highbury–*

handsome enough–to look plain, probably, by Harriet's side.
(163-4)[6]

In (1), the first sentence is the one preceding FID, which has a reported verb "Emma thought," and from the next sentence FID begins. Here, because of the reported verb readers don't enter the FID, Emma's objective viewpoints. Then, the following is the frequency of reported verbs following FID.

Table 4 The Frequency of Reported Verbs Following FID

	Volume 1	Volume 2	Volume 3	Total
say	0	1	0	1
think[7]	1	1	2	4
hope	0	2	1	3
ask	0	0	0	0
wonder	0	0	0	0
want to know	0	0	0	0
have no idea	0	0	0	0

As we have already explained in Table 3, readers do not enter Emma's world as there are reported verbs following FID. On the whole, however, the frequency of FID in Table 4 is 3.4 per cent. Here is an example:

(2) *Her manners too–and Mr. Elton's, were unpleasant towards Harriet. They were sneering and negligent. Emma hoped* it must rapidly work Harriet's cure; but the sensations which could prompt such behaviour sunk them both very much. (253)

In (2), the first and the second sentences are FID, and the third sentence has a reported verb "Emma hoped." Owing to the reported verb after FID, readers do not enter FID, Emma's world.

Finally, with regard to reported verbs both preceding FID and following it, which are used only once, Tanimura (1971: 94) observes: "when reported verbs ... are used in the sentences both preceding FID and following it, they make readers feel the presence of the author considerably." Thus, we can be fairly certain that it is hard for readers to share Emma's viewpoint with her, but the frequency of such constructions is very small.[8]

We have examined how many FIDs occur with exclamations, questions, or interjections in Table 2. Now let's examine, in Table 3 and 4, how many of the reported verbs occur preceding and following FIDs.

In this context, FID with exclamations are used two times out of forty, FID with questions occur three times out of twenty-two, and FID with interjections are not found at all. Therefore, FID with these three emotional expressions do not contain many reported verbs, so we have good grounds for thinking that readers not only are hardly conscious of the existence of the author through reported verbs, but they can also enter Emma's emotional nature showing Emma's subjective views.

Concerning the context of FID, Pascal (1977: 26) also points out "an introductory verb such as 'he stopped,' 'he was frightened'." According to Tanimura (1971: 97):

> ... when ... quasi-reported verbs or words scarcely having reported elements are used in sentences preceding FID or following it, readers have a gradually decreasing awareness of the author, ...

The introductory verbs, therefore, have a tendency to report less than reported verbs, so that it seems reasonable to suppose that we need only mention here the introductory verbs. As we can see from the results of Tables 3, 4 and so on above, Emma's points of view [FID] make readers enter Emma's subjective world because readers are hardly conscious of the intervention of the author.

In addition, referring to Pascal (1977: 26), we will go on to examine the frequency of direct speech containing an element of report in sentences preceding FID or following it, or both.

Table 5 The Frequency of direct speech preceding FID or following it

	Volume 1	Volume 2	Volume 3	Total
preceding[9]	3	5	0	8
following[10]	1	2	3	6

As we have seen in Tables 3 and 4, one may say that the use shown in Table 5 makes the author link with the character strongly, and readers are firmly conscious of the existence of the author. The frequency in Table 5, however, is only 5.9 per cent of the whole FID. Direct speech both preceding FID and following it is not used at all. The following is an example of direct speech preceding FID:

(3) "I certainly do forget to think of *her*," *said Emma*, "as having ever been any thing but my friend and my dearest friend."

He looked as if he fully understood and honoured such a sentiment. (180)

The first sentence is direct speech, and the next sentence is FID. Here, as the direct speech is shown before FID, readers don't enter the FID, Emma's objective viewpoint.

Just for information, direct *thought* preceding FID or following it, or both, is not used. Furthermore, in FID with direct speech preceding FID or following it, FID with exclamations or questions or interjections is found only four times (exclamations are used three times, questions once) in total.

5. Final Remarks

We have directed attention to the context in FID in order to examine whether Emma's points of view in the narrative, namely, FID make readers sympathise with Emma. In this context, representative reported verbs are not used very much, and readers are not conscious of the intervention of the author, so we have proven that readers' minds enter Emma's points of view. We therefore have reasonably concluded that readers accept Emma's subjective views and sympathise with the defective Emma. The conclusion was further supported since direct speech similar to reported verbs in the sentence preceding FID, or following it, is not used very much. Thus, we have proven Booth's, Lascelles's, and Ohshima's opinions on one side of philological studies.

Notes

1 J. E. Austen-Leigh, *Memoir of Jane Austen* (Oxford: Clarendon Press, 1926) 157.

2 The rest is omitted as FID. FID consists of the report of speech and the stream of thought. See Keizou Kurokawa, "Jane Austen no Shousetsu ni okeru Jiyuukansetsuwahou ni yoru Hatsuwa no Teiji," *Niigata Sangyo Daigaku Kiyou* 11 (1994): 277.

3 This time, we will examine without distinguishing speech and thought in FID since it is important to consider FID itself indicating with Emma's viewpoint. We will examine speech and thought individually on another occasion.

4 Volume 1 [Chapter 1 to 18], Volume 2 [Chapter 1 to 18], and Volume 3 [Chapter 1 to 19].

5 In the frequency, "made her ... think" and "she had been thinking of" are each included once, besides "she thought."

6 The text used is *Emma* (Oxford World's Classics, 1998), and the page references are to this edition. Italics are mine.

7 In the frequency, " ... to Emma to think" is included once.

8 As space is limited, we have limited reported verbs to examples of what

Jespersen (1951: 290) calls reported verbs. However, in relation to the reported verbs, we have further extended this category to include verbs [believe, consider, fancy, guess, imagine, suppose, wish] and examined the frequency of them in the sentence preceding FID or following it, or both preceding it and following it. This construction was used twenty-five times ("believe" was used six times, "consider" four times, "fancy" four times, "guess" once, "imagine" four times, "suppose" four times, "wish" two times) in total. The frequency percentage of 10.5 per cent is included in Table 1, so the use is small.

9 In the frequency of direct speech preceding FID, "moralized to herself" with quotation marks and "exclaimed" with it are each included once, in addition to quotation marks only and quotation marks with "said."

10 In the frequency of direct speech following FID, in addition to quotation marks only and quotation marks with "said," "added" with quotation marks and "continued" with it are each used once.

Text

Austen, J. (1980, rpt 1998) *Emma*. Ed. James Kinsley. The World's Classics. Oxford: Oxford niversity Press.

References

Austen-Leigh, J. E. (1926) *Memoir of Jane Austen*. Oxford: Clarendon Press.

Booth, W. C. (1983) *The Rhetoric of Fiction*. 2nd ed. Chicago and London: The University of Chicago Press.

Hough, G. (1970) "Narrative and Dialogue in Jane Austen." *Critical Quarterly* 12,201-29.

Jespersen, O. (1924, 1951) *The Philosophy of Grammar*. London: George Allen and Unwin.

Kurokawa, K. (1994) "Jane Austen no Shousetsu ni okeru Jiyuukansetsuwahou ni yoru Hatsuwa no Teiji." *Niigata Sangyo Daigaku Kiyou* 11, 275-95.

Lascelles, M. (1939, 1954) *Jane Austen and Her Art*. London: Oxford University Press.

Lodge, D. (1992) *The Art of Fiction*. London: Penguin. Rpt. of *The Independent on Sunday*, 1991-2.

McHale, B. (1978) "Free Indirect Discourse: A Survey of Recent Accounts." *PLT: A Journal for Descriptive Poetics and Theory of Literature* 3, 249-87.

Nakagawa, Y. (1983) *JiyuuKansetsuWahou–Eigo no Shousetsu ni miru Keitai to Kinou*. Kyoto: Aporonsha.

Ohshima, K.(1997) *Jane Austen "Sekaiichi Heibon na Daisakka" no Shouzou*. Tokyo: Chuo Koronsha.

Page, N. (1972) *The Language of Jane Austen.* Oxford: Basil Blackwell.

Pascal, R. (1977) *The Dual Voice: Free Indirect Speech and Its Functioning in the Nineteenth-Century European Novel*. Rowman and Littlefield: Manchester University Press.

Quirk, R., et al. (1985) *A Comprehensive Grammar of the English Language*. London and New York: Longman.
Tanimura, J. (1971) "Represented Speech no Ichi Kousatsu–Sakusha = Sakuchujinbutsu = Dokusha no Mondai–." *Buntairon Kenkyu* 17, 91-104.

The Reporting Clause in *Oliver Twist*: With Special Reference to the Reporting Clause of Sikes

MIYUKI NISHIO

1. Introduction

In the area of speech presentation, reported speech has been considered important, for it is useful in developing a story, defining character and the relationship between characters, and creating the sense of a background by supplying impressions of a society, its manner, and its concerns.(Carter and Nash, 1990: 90) Extensive descriptive work is being done on reported clauses, but only a few studies have so far been made on reporting clauses. Toyota (1993) studies the structure and function of the reporting clause and remarks that the reporting clause leaves much room for investigation. Yamaoka (1991) examines the style of the reporting clause in "The Killers" written by Hemingway. Kawai (1984) compares the verbs of saying in *The Vicar of Wakefield* with those in *Wuthering Heights* and concludes that the latter has more expressiveness and variety than the former. Wakimoto (1999) examines the structure and the function of the reporting clause in Fielding's *Joseph Andrews*, comparing it with other contemporary works. She points out, in her examination, that the verbs used in *JA* are more numerous and varied than those in other contemporary novels, and that the reporting clauses, including appropriate adverbs or adverbial phrases, contribute to the successful characterization by describing the character's inner mind. In Dickens's novels the reporting clauses also serve effectively as one of the methods of characterization.[1]

Page (1988: 28) asserts that theatrical elements are abundant in Dickens' works, and they play a significant part in his novels. In other words, describing the speaker's actions, manners of speaking, facial expression and voice may make the reader feel as if he were watching a drama in the theatre. Thus the reporting clauses function as stage directions as well as methods of individualizing the character.

This paper deals with *Oliver Twist* which was written in 1837, and it focuses on one of the characters, William Sikes, who is a man of strong physique and who gets easily provoked. The aim in this paper, therefore, is to show how Dickens depicts Sikes's personality and to individualize his character with regard to his reporting clauses.

In Section 1, the focus is on the variety of the speech presentation. Section 2 concentrates mainly on the structure of the reporting clause including Narrative Report of Speech Act (henceforth abbreviated as NRSA). Section 3 is devoted to the function of the reporting clause, that is, how the reporting clauses, especially adverbial adjuncts, are used in describing the character.

2. Structure

2.1. Variety of Reporting Formulae

Before proceeding to a more detailed discussion of the reporting clause, it is advisable to describe the objects of analysis. Yamaoka (1991) and Toyota (1993) deal with Direct Speech (hereafter abbreviated as DS), while Wakimoto (1999) researches Indirect Speech (henceforth abbreviated as IS) as well as DS. Leech and Short (1981:324) propose a model of speech and thought presentation which posits a continuum of categories along an axis representing degrees of the narrator's intervention.

Table 1 Cline of "interference" in report

<table>
<tr><td colspan="2">Narrator apparently
in total control
of report</td><td>Narrator apparently
in partial control
of report</td><td>Narrator apparently
not in control
of report at all</td></tr>
<tr><td>NRA</td><td colspan="2">Variety of speech presentation
NRSA → IS → FIS → DS</td><td>FDS</td></tr>
</table>

(*NRA: Narrative report of action, NRSA: Narrative report of speech act, FIS: Free indirect speech, FDS: Free direct speech)

According to this table, speech presentation is categorized into five types: NRSA, IS, FIS, DS and FDS. There is no reporting clause either in FIS or in FDS. In NRSA the reporter indicates that a speech act has taken place without giving any of the propositional content and without quoting any of the actual words. IS has the reporting clause, to which the reported clause is syntactically subordinated as a nominal *that*-clause. In DS the original utterance is introduced by a reporting clause which does not have any subordinate clause, and there is some expectation that the words are a close representation of the original utterance. As the main object of this paper is the reporting clause, IS and DS are dealt with in this paper. Though NRSA has no reporting tag, it is the subject of analysis as well.

2.2. Reporting Verbs

The table below shows the frequency of the reporting formulae: DS, IS and NRSA. NRSA are classified into three categories. In NRSA, a verb itself indicates that the speech act takes place, as in "The dog jumped from right to left, and from left to right: snapping, growling, and barking; the man, thrust and *swore*, and struck and *blasphemed*; . . ." (93, italics mine) while deverbative nouns such as *threat*, *promise*, *oath*, *imprecation* and so on are used as the markers of speech acts. Occasionally a verb is employed in combination with deverbative nouns as in "he muttered various curses on her awkwardness: . . . " (244).

Table 2 The Frequency of the Reporting Formulae

DS	IS	NRSA		
		Verb	Noun	V + N
208 (82.2%)	5 (2.0%)	18 (7.1%)	14 (5.5%)	8 (3.2%)

This table illustrates that the most frequent method of speech presentation in Sikes is DS, and that only five instances are used in IS. The variety of the verbs of saying used in DS, IS and NRSA is as follows:

Reporting verbs (DS): *add, answer, ask, continue, cry, demand, echo, exclaim, growl, inquire, interpose, murmur, mutter, observe, rejoin, repeat, reply, retort, return, roar, say, sneer, whisper.*

Reporting verbs (IS): *demand, ask, reply, remark, inquire.*

NRSA: *growl, swear, blaspheme, mutter, command, tell, bid, request, order, whisper, advise, utter, talk, shout, call,* etc.

The neutral verbs of saying such as *to say* and *to reply* are commonly used in Sikes' speech presentation. Besides the neutral and colourless reporting verbs which simply show the existence of utterances, there are found in Sikes' utterances the verbs such as *to growl*, *to rejoin*, *to inquire* and so on. These verbs, as they have expressiveness in themselves, can be described as follows: [to say + α]. *To growl*, for example, is defined, in *OED*, as "to utter or express with a growl or in a growling manner."[2] *To growl* is employed in NRSA as well as DS. *To rejoin* is defined in the *Longman Dictionary of Contemporary English* as "to say something in reply, especially rudely or angrily."[3] In this story *to growl* is used seven times and *to rejoin* ten times. These distinctive verbs contribute greatly to the characterization of Sikes. Furthermore, they are occasionally followed by adverbial adjuncts. These verbs and adverbial adjuncts serve as theatrical elements to individualize each character.

2.3. Reporting Adjuncts

Reporting clauses consist of two parts: verbs of saying and adverbial adjuncts. The latter are classified into seven categories in the light of their construction as seen in the table below.

Table 3 The Frequency of Reporting Adjuncts Used in DS, IS and NRSA

	DS	IS	NRSA	Total
Ø	38.0%	40%	67.5%	42.9%
Adv.	4.3%	20%	12.5%	6.0%
Adj.	0.5%	0	17.5%	3.2%
Clause	4.8%	0	0	3.6%
Part. phrase	31.3%	0	0	25.8%
Prep. phrase	8.7%	20%	2.5%	7.9%
Subject	3.4%	20%	0	3.2%
Multiple Occurrence	9.1%	0	0	7.5%

*Part.phr. : Participial phrase Prep.phr. : Prepositional phrase
*Total occurrences: DS 208 / IS 5 / NRSA 40 / total 252

In the speech presentation of Sikes, DS occurs with greater frequency than IS and NRSA. It is obvious from the table that adverbial adjuncts are more frequently used in DS. Furthermore, the following points can be deduced. First, no adverbial adjunct is employed in almost forty percent of DS, forty percent of IS and about seventy percent of NRSA. Secondly, in DS, participial and prepositional constructions are mainly used. Thirdly, adjectives are mainly used in NRSA. NRSA has, as mentioned above, three types of presentation and one of them is denoted by nouns, sometimes deverbative ones. Such nouns as *curse*, *threat*, and *oath* aryte accompanied by adjectives. Lastly, "subject" is mainly adopted in the reporting clauses of DS. "Subject" here means "elegant variation". According to Leech and Short (1981: 244), "elegant variation" is defined as "use of an alternative expression (not a pronoun or a substitute) as a replacement for an expression in the context." Sørensen (1984: 243) also states that elegant variation is used in order to avoid repetition. *Sikes* is adopted most frequently in this story, but sometimes such modes of address as *housebreaker*, *ruffian*, *murderer*, *robber* and so forth are used instead of Sikes. Koguchi (2001:10) mentions that the elegant variation given to the character provides a significant clue to identifying his nature and role. When Sikes first appears in the story, he is introduced as "this engaging ruffian"(77), "the ruffian"(77) and so on. After Sikes breaks into the house, he is called *robber*. In Chapter 47 Sikes commits a vicious murder, and *murderer* is then employed not only in the narrative but also in the reporting clause. Thus "elegant variation" is exploited in the reporting clause as well as adverbial adjuncts. As seen in table 3, "adjective" is used in the reporting clause. Most adjectives are embedded in a subject as "elegant variation".

Furthermore, Koguchi (2001: 21) points out that participant items[4] of the character are deliberately given to him according to the progress of the plot, not at random. In the reporting clause of Sikes, "elegant variation" changes with the development of the plot.

The adverbial adjuncts are divided, from a functional point of view, into the following eight groups: action, manner, countenance, tone, object, NRSA, time, and multiple occurrences. The phrases expressing action refer to the speaker's behaviour in speaking. Manner demonstrates in what way the speaker utters his words. Countenance evinces the speaker's facial expression such as laughter, weeping and so on. Tone shows whether the speaker's voice is loud or soft, high or low. Object implies the person to whom the speaker gives the utterance. Speech shows that in the reporting clause the utterances such as curse, oath and so on are employed especially with DS. The phrases denoting time indicate when the utterance takes place in conversations. "Multiple" here means that some of the categories mentioned above occur also in the reporting clause. The table below illustrates the frequency of each category.

Table 4 The Frequency of Each Category Used in Reporting Adjuncts

	DS	IS	NRSA
Action	72(57.6%)	0	0
Manner	14(11.2%)	2(100%)	10(77.0%)
Countenance	6(4.8%)	0	0
Tone	6(4.8%)	0	1(7.7%)
Object	1(0.8%)	0	0
Speech	6(4.8%)	0	0
Time	3(2.4%)	0	0
Multiple	12(9.6%)	0	0
Others	5(0.4%)	0	2(15.4%)

From the table above, two facts emerge. First, adverbial adjuncts implying the character's action are used most frequently, in addition, only in DS. The use of them not only gives the utterance dramatic effect but also helps readers particularly to visualize the bodily movement in the manner of a stage direction. Secondly, phrases denoting countenance and tone are mainly used in DS. For one thing, the contents of utterances are of great importance in IS and NRSA. One of the functions of DS, on the other hand, is to develop the story dramatically and make the reader feel as if he were watching scenes in a theatre. Therefore, facial and vocal expressions play a significant role making scenes realistic and dramatic.

3. Characterization

This section is devoted to designating how the reporting clause and NRSA contribute to the individualization of Sikes. In the reporting clauses used in Sikes's utterance, there are some noticeable expressions describing his personality: *to growl*, *fierce(ly)*, *impatiently*, *roughly*, *savage(ly)* and so forth.[5] Besides, NRSA frequently contains such nouns as *oath*, *curse*, *threat*, *blasphemy*. These words represent his hasty temper and aggressiveness. Dickens attempts to individualize the character by repeating synonymous expressions. Here I will consider especially the verb *to growl*.

From his first appearance in this story, Sikes is delineated by means of the verb of saying *to growl*. When he appears in the story for the first time, the narrator hides his identity from the reader, just saying "'Why, what the blazes is in the wind now!' growled a deep voice."(76) He is introduced in Chapter 13 as follows:

> The man who growled out these words, was a stoutly-built fellow of about five-and-thirty, in a black velveteen coat, very soiled drab breeches, lace-up half-boots, and grey cotton stockings, which enclosed a very bulky pair of legs, with large swelling calves; —the kind of legs, that in such costume, always look in an unfinished and incomplete state without a set of fetters to garnish them. He had a brown hat on his head, and a dirty belcher handkerchief round his neck: with the long frayed ends of which, he smeared the beer from his face as he spoke; disclosing, when he had done so, a broad heavy countenance with a beard of three days' growth: and two scowling eyes; one of which, displayed various particoloured symptoms of having been recently damaged by a blow. (76-7)

The verb *to growl* is embedded in the first sentence. *To growl*, including the noun *growl*, is used 34 times in this novel. The word collocates with Sikes 13 times, while it is adopted in describing his dog 12 times. He usually appears in the story with his dog. Calling his dog, he often growls to it as follows: "'Come in, d'ye hear?' growled this engaging ruffian."(77) The word, however, is not used in addressing the dog except in the line quoted above. Two instances are employed in bawling at Oliver in the following expressions: "Turning to Oliver, he roughly commanded him to take hold of Nancy's hand. 'Do you hear?' growled Sikes, as Oliver hesitated, and looked round." (97-8) and "'Now, then!' growled Sikes, as Oliver started up; 'half-past five! Look sharp, or you'll get no breakfast; for it's late as it is.'"(134) In the former citation, as Oliver does not obey Sikes's order at once, Sikes loses his patience with him and growls. Since even the first command to take hold of her hand is issued *roughly*, the reader can understand his annoyance. The reported speech "Do you hear?" also shows his irritation with Oliver. The latter indicates that Sikes gives Oliver a fright. Oliver does not wake up at five thirty in the morning, and Sikes then talks menacingly to him with the imperative sentence. It is intriguing that the reported speech collocating with *to growl* co-occurs with exclamation marks or is represented by interrogative sentences, which in most cases show his disgust and indignation, not his asking of a question.

Five of them are used in addressing Nancy:

(1) 'Well, then, keep quiet,' rejoined Sikes, with a growl like that he was accustomed to use when addressing his dog, 'or I'll quiet you for a good long time to come.'(103)

(2) ... Mr. William Sikes, awakening from a nap, drowsily growled forth an inquiry what time of night it was. (257)

(3) 'Oh! You've thought better of it, have you?' growled Sikes, marking the tear which trembled in her eye. (258)

(4) If she betrayed any agitation, when she presented herself to Mr. Sikes, he did not observe it; for merely inquiring if she had brought the money, and receiving a reply in the affirmative, he uttered a growl of satisfaction, . . . (266)

(5) 'Well, I suppose it is,' growled Sikes. (304)

Example (1) denotes that Sikes treats her like a dog. It is clear from Fagin's utterance: "If you want revenge on those that treat you like a dog—like a dog! worse than his dog, for he humours him sometime—come to me." (305) When Sikes addresses her, *to growl* goes with the reporting clause of Sikes. Garry Wills (1993: 604) also writes: "Dickens ranks Nancy's devotion to Sikes with that of his dog, which comes back and back to Sikes and even throws itself off the rooftop to follow him in death." In example (2) the verb *to growl* functions as NRSA with the deverbative noun *inquiry*. Because he wakes in a bad mood, he even growls in order to know the time. Sentence (3) also illustrates his bad temper. Though he is sick in bed, he calls her hard names. In example (4) *growl* is embedded as NRSA. In response to her, he just utters a growl of satisfaction because he seems to be entirely preoccupied with the idea of money. Sentence (5) is a conversation between Sikes and Fagin. They talk about Nancy. Here Sikes expresses displeasure over her: "I thought I had tamed her, but she's as bad as ever."(304) He complains that she does not obey his thought and cannot restrain his irritation.

His dog, of course, growls 12 times in this story. Saijo (1998: 93) suggests that his dog represents the ferocious and vicious features of Sikes. Dodger tells Oliver that his dog is fearful of nothing: "Won't he[the dog] growl at all, when he hears a fiddle playing!"(117) It is about to pounce on Oliver as follows:

> 'Give me the other,' said Sikes, seizing Oliver's unoccupied hand. 'Here, Bull's-eye!'
>
> The dog looked up, and growled.
>
> 'See here, boy!' said Sikes, putting his other hand to Oliver's throat; 'if he speaks ever so soft a word, hold him! D'ye mind?'
>
> The dog growled again; and licking his lips, eyed Oliver as if he were anxious to attach himself to his windpipe without delay. (98)

The dog waits for its chance to jump on Oliver. It growls twice in this scene so as to intimidate Oliver by threats. Both Sikes and his dog remain a threat to Oliver. As Saijo states above, his dog is ferociousness personified. *To growl* was originally used of an animal and is defined in *OED* as "to utter a low guttural sound, expressive of rising anger".[6] Applying it to Sikes contributes to individualizing him.

4. Conclusion

From what has been said above, I should like to draw three conclusions. First, reporting adjuncts are frequently accompanied by participial constructions, most of which represent the character's action and behaviour. They also function as stage directions. The second conclusion is that Dickens repeatedly uses synonymous expressions and attempts to individualize the character. In NRSA such nouns as *oath*, *curse*, *threat*, *blasphemy* and *imprecation* are adopted frequently, while in reporting clauses *fierce(ly)*, *impatiently*, *roughly* and *savage(ly)* are employed effectively. These words contribute to the characterization of Sikes. The reader can easily recognize that Sikes is so ill-tempered, ferocious and aggressive that he always abuses others. The third conclusion is that the verb of saying *to growl* plays an important part in this story. It collocates mainly with Sikes and his dog. As he treats Nancy as a dog, he often addresses Nancy by growling. Moreover, from considering the situations in which *to growl* is used, it emerges that the reported clause or the content of an utterance are indicated by imperative and interrogative sentences. Thus verbs of saying and reporting adjuncts contribute to individualizing the character.

Notes

* I would like to express my appreciation and thanks to David Vallins for reading the manuscript and improving my English. Of course I am solely responsible for any errors.

1 I have examined the reporting clause in *Great Expectations*. It is obvious from the examination that the reporting clause contributes to characterization. By classifying the words used in adverbial phrases, it emerges that Dickens gives synonymous expressions to one character skilfully and individualizes the character. Repetition of those expressions in describing a character contributes to description of the character's inner mind and disposition as well as characterization. Thus he embeds dramatic and theatrical elements not only in the reported clause but also in the reporting clause.

2 *OED*, s.v. *growl*, *v*[3]. 2.b.

3 *Longman Dictionary of Contemporary English*, s. v. *rejoin*, *v*. It also adds such explanation as "*to rejoin* means 'to answer showing disagreement'". Actually it emerges that the reported speech collocating with *to rejoin* frequently includes negative expressions and shows Sikes's disagreement and disapproval.

4 Koguchi (2001: 9) defines "participant items" as "the same referent with the characters' proper names, elegant variations, or personal pronouns."

5 The concordance is created by using the Project Gutenberg E-text of *Oliver Twist*. (http://gutenberg.net/index.html) From using this resource it emerges that it *fiercely* is used seven times in this story and four instances of it collocate with Sikes. *Impatiently* is employed four times in reporting clauses relating to Sikes. *Roughly* occurs five times in this story and four of them collocate with Sikes. *Savage* and *savagely* are adopted seven times and in three cases they are used with Sikes. Thus Dickens exploits synonymous expressions in order to individualize the character.

6 *OED*, s.v. *growl*, *v*[3]. 1.b.

Text

Dickens, C. (1966) *Oliver Twist*. Ed. Kathleen Tillotson. The Clarendon Press: Oxford.

References

Carter, R & W. Nash. (1990) *Seeing Through Language*, Basil Blackwell: Oxford.

Kawai, M. (1984) "Spoken English: Fact and Fiction," *Studies in Modern English*, 1, 62-69.

Kincaid, J. R. (1971) *Dickens and the Rhetoric of Laughter*, Clarendon Press: Oxford.

Koguchi, K. (2001) *The Language of Charles Dickens's "A Tale of Two Cities" From a Cohesive Point of View*, Research Institute for Language and Culture, Yasuda Women's University: Hiroshima.

Leech, G. N. & M. H. Short. (1981) *Style in Fiction*, Longman: London & New York.

Page, N. (1988) *Speech in the English Novel*, 2nd ed, Macmillan: London.

Quirk, R. (1961) "Some Observations on the Language of Dickens," *A Review of English Literature*, Vol. II, No.3, 19-28.

Saijo, T. (1998) *Dickens no Bungaku* (in Japanese), Eihousha: Tokyo.

Simpson, J. A. and E. S. C. Weiner, eds. (1989) *The Oxford English Dictionary*, 2nd ed, The Clarendon Press: Oxford.

Sørensen, K. (1985) *Charles Dickens: Linguistic Innovator*, Acta Jutlandica, 61. Humanities Series, 58. Arkona: Aarhus.

Sørensen, K. (1989) "Dickens on the Use of English," *English Studies*, Vol. 70, No.6, 551-559.

Toyota, M. (1993) "The Structure and Function of Reporting Clause," *Aspects of Modern English*, Eichousha: Tokyo, 561-75.

Wakimoto, K. (1999) "A Study of the Reporting Clause in Fielding's *Joseph Andrews*: With a Comparative Discussion of Several Contemporary Novels," *Studies in Modern English*, 15, 65-91.

Wills, G. (1993) "The Loves of *Oliver Twist*", *Oliver Twist*, Norton & Company: New York, 593-608.

Yamaoka, M. (1991) "Direct Speech ni okeru houkokusetsu no style"(in Japanese), *Studies in British and American Literature* 39, 77-92.

Yamamoto, T. (2003) *Growth and System of the Language of Dickens*, 3rd ed, Keisuisha: Hiroshima.

Dialectal Features of Stephen Blackpool's Pronunciation

OSAMU IMAHAYASHI

1. Introduction

In *Hard Times* Charles Dickens tried to describe regional dialect around Coketown, universally recognised as a fictitious name for Manchester, and created Stephen Blackpool, a power-loom operative at Mr Bounderby's mill. Dickens put some regional dialect to the mouth of Blackpool, whose name suggests its origin, so as to add some local colours to the novel. Manchester, located in south Lancashire, was one of the largest industrial cities in Victorian England and belonged to the area where West Midland dialect was spoken during the Middle English period.

Of all Dickens's works treating regional dialects, it may, however, be *Hard Times* that has been subject to the greatest criticism both by literary scholars and philologists. Robert Langton (1912: 208)[1] claims that "one of the least successful attempts in this or any of the books of Charles Dickens, is his rendering of the Lancashire dialect; the utterances put into the mouths of Stephen Blackpool, and others, in *Hard Times*, are very far from correct." L. K. Webb (1983: 78) also strictly comments that "his ear for dialect was poor; what he imagined to be the speech of Lancashire is the speech of nowhere, grating continually on the reader's inner ear." Humphry House (1950: 203-4) suggests that the cause of these caustic remarks is that "Dickens was writing of people and things quite outside the range of his own experience." G. L. Brook, philologist, also founder of the Lancashire Dialect Society points out that "Stephen Blackpool and Rachael, in *Hard Times*, speak with a strongly-marked regional dialect," and that "many of the features of this dialect can be paralleled in north-country speech today." He, however, avoids identifying the dialect with the Lancashire dialect, and argues that some of the linguistic features of the dialect "seem to be of doubtful authenticity."[2]

Edgar Johnson (1952) reveals that Dickens had paid a short visit to Manchester in Lancashire at least five times[3] before his visit to Preston in 1854, all of which took place between 1838 and 1848. Judging from these facts it is possible that he might have obtained some knowledge of the dialect around this area during his short visits, but neither in his letters nor writing records, can we find written evidence of his picking up any features of the dialect at all. Norman Page (1988: 67) describes in detail the main purpose of his visit to Preston early in 1854 and its influence upon his rendering of the dialect through the mouth of Stephen Blackpool as follows:

> Dickens began to write *Hard Times* early in 1854, visiting Preston at the same period in search of material. A by-product of the Preston visit was a *Household Words* article 'On Strikes', which contains evidence that his ears had been sensitive to the idiom and pronunciation, as well as to the content, of the Lancashire factory-workers' speech, for he reproduces in that article a speech by a Preston weaver which includes many of the forms which recur in the novel. Stephen's speech was created, then, with vivid impressions of the dialect of the Preston area fresh in the novelist's mind, though his knowledge of it was certainly limited.

Patricia Ingham (1986: 522) first demonstrates that Dickens's major source for the dialect used in *Hard Times* is from *A View of the Lancashire Dialect* by 'Tim Bobbin', the pseudonym of John Collier, first published in 1746.[4] Dickens owned a copy of the 1818 edition.[5] She argues that though the conversation between Tummus and Meary "must have been unintelligible to Dickens, it is evident that the Glossary was invaluable". Another source introduced by Ingham (1986: 523) is William Gaskell's *Two Lectures on the Lancashire Dialect*, published in 1854 in the fifth edition of his wife's *Mary Baton*.[6] She can find no striking correspondences between Blackpool's speech and Mr Gaskell's *Lectures*, and she regards them as "only of marginal use."

It is the aim of this paper to examine accuracy and consistency in Dickens's rendering the dialectal pronunciations of Stephen Blackpool considering the facts and illustrations offered by the dictionaries, letters and references mentioned below and to discuss whether the dialect intended by Dickens can be identified with the dialect employed in south Lancashire in the mid-nineteenth century. First of all we shall deal with the reduction of vowels and consonants.

2. Reduction of vowels and consonants

One of the most striking features of Stephen Blackpool's regional accents is the reduction of vowels and consonants. It is regarded as the most characteristic of Lancashire dialect. In this respect John Collier (1818: 4) illustrates thus:

> In general we speak quick and short; and cut of a great many letters, and even words by apostrophes; and sometimes sound two, three, or more words as one.

The reduction of the definite article to *th'* is constantly found in Stephen's speech. Brook (1970: 127) suggests that "in some northern dialects it is reduced to *th'* before vowels and to *t'* before consonants." In this novel we can find thirty-two examples (71 etc.)[7] of this deduced form before consonants and only one before a vowel (159). *EDG* (§312) informs us that the reduction exists in mid and south-east Lancashire, west-mid Stafford. In the conversation between Tummus and Meary, we can find many examples of this form, but in its glossary it is not listed at all. *DSL* lists this form of the definite article in the glossary.

As well as the case above, we often find a lot of examples of the reduction of the preposition *to* and the infinitive *to* to *t'*. The deduction of the infinitive *to* occurs sixteen times (65 etc.) and that of the preposition *to* appears thirteen times. *MEG* (§9.82) demonstrates that "in the 18th c. this elision became rarer, and has now disappeared." *OED* (s.v. *t'*[1]) stops recording examples of *t'* in 1746. Stanley Gerson (§7.17.4) concludes that "Dickens uses *t'* ... to indicate northern 'speech'."

In Blackpool's speech the loss of *d* occurs in the final position, and less frequently in the medial position. The loss of final *d* occurs fifty times as *an'* (73 etc.), and once as *an* (159) and *stan* (148). The loss of medial *d* sometimes occurs in *unnerstan'in* (273^{4x})[8] and *Gonnows* (71, 143), but the standard forms *understood* (74) and *understand* (161) are also found. *MEG* (§7.55) mentions that "*d* is very often dropped in *and*, thus regularly, but not exclusively, before consonants." *OED* (s.v. *and, conj.*[1]) records the spelling *an* for *and* from the thirteenth to seventeenth century, and *an'* as a dialectal form in the eighteenth and nineteenth century. It argues that "the final *d* has from early times been often dropped, as now universally in the dialects, and commonly in familiar speech." Gerson (1967: §24.7) suggests that "it will be noticed that Dickens uses *an'* mainly (and only consistently) in representations of northern 'speech'." He also informs us that /ən/ is recorded from Lancashire by K. G. Schilling (1906: §127) and by Hargreaves (1904: §62). According to *EDG* (§307), *an* is generally used in Scotland, Ireland and England, and *stan* occurs in Inverness, north-east Scotland, Ayr, Lothian, Edinburgh, Kirkcudbright, Ulster, north Northumberland, north and mid Cumberland, north Westmoreland, north-east Yorkshire, north-east, east-mid and south-east Lancashire, Isle of Man, north-east Derby, north-west Lincoln, east Man, north-east Derby, north-west Lincoln, east Oxford, Dorset, west Somerset, and Devon. *MW* and *DSL* record only the form *an*.

The loss of medial *l* is found in the speech produced by Blackpool. Examples are *a'toogether* (75), *awmost* (79), *awmust* (274), *faw'en* (151), *fawt*[9] (149), *gowd* (74), *owd* (72), towd (150, 159, 162), and *sma'est* (143). *EDG* (§253) comments that "medial *l* has often disappeared, especially in the combinations *ld*, *lf*, *lh*, *lk*, *ls*, and *lt*." According to *EDG* (§253), the loss of medial *l* occurs in *almost* in north Durham, south-west Yorkshire, mid Lancashire, south Cheshire, north Derby, Leicester, north Shropshire, north-west Oxford, mid Bucks, Hampshire, north-west and mid-east Wiltshire, and west Somerset; *gold* in west Forfar, west Perth, south Ayr, Lothian, Edinburgh, Peebles, south-east and south Northumberland, north Durham, mid Cumberland, north Westmoreland, Yorkshire, Lancashire, north-west Derby, north Lincoln, north-east and mid Shropshire, and east Suffolk; *hold* in Scotland, Northumberland, Durham, Cumberland, Westmoreland, Yorkshire, Lancashire, south Cheshire, Stafford, Derby, Nottingham, Lincoln, Leicester, north Worcester, east Hereford, south Norfolk, east and west Suffolk, Essex, north-east Kent, south Surrey, and west Sussex; *old* in west-mid Scotland, Northumberland, Durham, north Cumberland, north Westmoreland, Yorkshire, Lancashire, Cheshire, Flint, Denbigh, Stafford, Derby, Nottingham, Lincoln. Leicester, south-west Northampton, north Worcester, Shropshire, east Hereford, Bedford, south-east Hertford Cambridge, north-east and south Norfolk, east and west Suffolk, Essex, east Kent, south Surrey, and west Sussex; *told* in Orkney Isles, Lancashire, Cheshire, Flint, Denbigh, Stafford, Derby, Nottingham, north-west Lincoln, Leicester, west Worcester, mid and southeast Shropshire, north Bucks, north-east Norfolk, east and west Suffolk, Essex, and Sussex; and *fault* in Scotland, Antrim, Northumberland, south Durham, north and mid Cumberland, Westmoreland, Yorkshire, Lancashire, south Cheshire, north and west-mid Stafford, north and north-west Derby, south Lincoln, Leicester, south Warwick, north Worcester, mid Shropshire, north-west Oxford, north-east Norfolk, east Suffolk, Sussex, Wiltshire, and east Somerset. *MW* and *DSL* list *owd, howd, towd, fawt*. *MW* lists *gowd* and *fawn*.

EDG (§255) suggests that "final *l* has often disappeared after a guttural vowel, especially in Scotland, Ireland, north country, and north Midland dialects." We have a lot of examples of the disappearance of final *l* in Stephen's speech: *aw* (66 etc. 30 times), *faw* (73), *wa'* (143), *dreadfo'* (87), *faithfo'* (148), *fearfo'* (72, 88^{2x}, 147, 157), and *wishfo'* (88). *MW* records *faw*, *fo*, *fearfo*, and *DSL* lists *feerfo*. According to *EDG* (§255), the disappearance of final *l* is to be found in *all* in Scotland, Antrim, Northumberland, Durham, Cumberland, Westmoreland, Yorkshire, Lancashire, Cheshire, north Stafford, and Derby; *fall* in Scotland, Northumberland, south Durharn, north and mid Cumberland, Westmoreland, north-north-west and south-north-west Yorkshire, Lancashire, south Cheshire, north Stafford, north-east and north-west Derby, and north-east Shropshire; *full* in Shetland Isles, Orkney Isles, Scotland, Westmoreland, and south-east Lancashire; and *wall* in Scotland, Antrim, mid-east and south-east Northumberland, south Durham, north and mid Cumberland, Westmoreland, north-east, north-north-west and south-north-west Yorkshire, north, north-west, south-mid, south-east, south-west, mid-south and south Lancashire, south Cheshire, north Stafford, north and north-east and north-west Derby, and north-west Shropshire.

MEG (§2.424) points out that "*i'* was especially frequent in the 16th and 17th century before *th'* (*the*)" and that "at the present day *i' th'* survives only as a poetic archaism (apart from Scotch and some Northern dialects)." This combination is to be recognised in Stephen's speech: "*i' th'* papers" (73), and "*i' th'* road" (142). *EDG* (§271) suggests that the final *n* disappears in the preposition *in* in Scotland, north countries, north and west Midland, south Norfolk, and west Suffolk. Neither *MW* nor *DSL* lists *i'*.

The spelling with *ha'* and *o'* indicates the disappearance of /v/ in *have* and the preposition *of*. *OED* (s.v. *o'*, *prep.*[1]) says that "the contracted form is usual in the representation of dialectal or vulgar speech." *MEG* (§2.534) comments that "the preposition *of* often became *o'*; the writing *o* is found occasionally as early as 1300 ... but it does not become frequent till the 16th c."; and that "*have* was frequently *ha'* or *a'* in the infinitive this may be from ME *han*, but it is also found in the indicative." The loss of /v/ preceding a word beginning with a vowel occurs as the auxiliary *ha'* (148), the verb *ha'*(73) and the preposition *o'* (37 etc. 9 times). The loss of /v/ preceding a word beginning with a consonant occurs as the auxiliary *ha'* (64 etc. 71 times), the verb *ha'* (72 etc. 13 times) and the preposition *o'* (74 etc. 42 times).

MW and *DSL* lists *ha*, and with regard to the preposition *of* the former records *o'* and the latter *o*. *EDD* (s.v. *of*, *prep.*) suggests that the dialectal form *o* is to be found in Scotland, Wexford, Northumberland, east Durham, Cumberland, Westmoreland, north, east, and mid Yorkshire, Lancashire, Isle of Man, Derby, Lincoln, Warwick, west Worcester, Gloucester, Berks, west Somerset, and Cornwall. According to *EDG* (§279), "*v* has disappeared over an extensive area in *have*."

In Blackpool's speech the loss of medial /ð/ is seen in such forms as *wi'in* (272) and *wi'out* (88, 141, 151^{3x}, 159, 160, 272^{2x}). *EDD* (s.v. *within*, *prep.*) gives *wi'in* only in Surrey dialect. *EDD* (s.v. *without*, *prep.* and *conj.*) says that *wi'out* is to be found in Berks and Devon. Neither *MW* nor *DSL* gives *wi'in* or *wi'out* in their glossary.

Stephen uses *wi'* instead of *with*, which indicates the loss of final /ð/, thirteen times before vowels (74 etc.) and thirty-nine times before consonants (72 etc.). According to *EDG* (§317), *with* has generally become /wi/ in all dialects and /wi/ was formerly used in the dialects before a following consonants and /wiþ/, /wið/ before a following vowels. But most dialects now have /wi/ in both positions. *MW* does not list the form *wi'*. *EDG* ('Index,' s.v. *with*) suggests that *wi* is to be found in Shetland Isles, Orkney Isles, Caithness, Forfar, south Ayr, Edinburgh, Ulster, north and mid-east Northumberland, north Cumberland, north, west and south Westmoreland, Yorkshire, Lancashire, Isle of Man, Cheshire, north, west and south Stafford, north and northwest Derby, Nottingham, north, north-west and east Lincoln, Leicester, mid Northampton, east Warwick, north Worcester, Gloucester, north Oxford, mid Berks, east Hertford, south Norfolk, east Suffolk, Hampshire, west and north-west Wiltshire, Dorset, south Devon and west Cornwall.

In Stephen's speech we find the insertion of semi-vowel /j/ before a vowel which has become initial as a result of loss of *h* in the case of *year* (71, 74) instead of to *hear*. *EDG* ('Index,' s.v. *hear*) points out that /jiə(r)/ occurs in mid Yorkshire, south-east Lancashire, Gloucester, Dorset, and east Devon. This verbal form is listed only in *MW*.

3. Short Vowels

The use of /u/, spelt *oo*, instead of /ʌ/ is frequently found in the speech of Blackpool. Examples are:

> *aboove* (273), *amoong* (148^{4x}), *anoother* (151), *coom*, *pr.* (142, 146), *coom*, *pp.* (71 etc. 19 times), *cooms* (72, 88), *coompany* (155), *coop*

> (155), *coover* (274), *discoosed* (143), *doon*[10] (148), *droonken* (148), *oother* (273), *soom,* 'some' (142, 273), *soom*, 'sum' (151), *soombody* (274), *tooches* (273), *toother* (151), *t'oother* (74), and *yoong* (142, 273).

Alongside of these dialectal forms we sometimes encounter standard ones:

> *above* (73, 142, 151, 273), *among* (143^{2x}, 273), *another* (73, 74, 148^{3x}, 151^{2x}, 154, 159, 272, 273), *come* (present indicative 66, past participle 67), *coming* (73, 84), *done* (65, 89, 154, 159, 160, 273^{2x}), *young* (65, 71, 72, 154, 272).

EDG (§98) suggests that /ù/ is to be heard in Northumberland, Durham, Antrim, north, north-east, north-west, east-mid, south-east, south-mid and south Lancashire, Isle of Man, Cheshire, Flint, Denbigh, Stafford, Derby, Nottingham, Leicester, Northampton, Warwick, Worcester, Shropshire, Hereford, Gloucester, and Oxford. To represent the use of /u/ for /ʌ/, the spelling *u* instead of *ou* is sometimes employed in *MW* (*yunger*) and *DSL* (*yunger*, *yungster*). According to 'Index' of *EDG*, /ù/ in place of /ʌ/ occurs in /əbùv/ in south Lancashire, south Cheshire, north and north-east Derby, Leicester, north Worcester, and south-east Shropshire; /əmùŋ/ in south-west Yorkshire, east-mid and south Lancashire, Isle of Man, south Cheshire, north Stafford, north Derby, Leicester, mid Northampton, Warwick, and north Shropshire; /kùm/ in north, mid, south-west and south Lancashire, Isle of Man, south Cheshire, Flint, east-mid Stafford, east Derby, Nottingham, Leicester, mid Northampton, east, west and south Warwick, north-east and south-east Shropshire, and north-west Oxford; /kùp/ in Antrim, south-mid, south-east, south-west and south Lancashire, Isle of Man, Denbigh, north-west Derby, Leicester, mid and south-west Northampton, Warwick, north Worcester, Shropshire, west Oxford, and north Bucks; /kùvə(r)/ in south-west and south Lancashire, north-west Derby, and Leicester; /dùn/ in mid, south-mid, south-west and south Lancashire, Isle of Man, Cheshire, Flint, Denbigh, north, east-mid, west-mid and south Stafford, north Derby, Nottingham, Leicester, north-east and south-west Northampton, Warwick, north and south Worcester, Shropshire, north-west Oxford, and north Bucks; /drùŋkn/ in north-west, mid, south-west, mid-south and south Lancashire, Isle of Man, Cheshire, Flint, north, west-mid and south Stafford, Derby, Nottingham, Leicester, mid Northampton, east Warwick, south Worcester, north and south-east Shropshire, and north-west and west Oxford; /ùðə(r)/ in south-mid and south Lancashire, south Cheshire, Denbigh, north-west Derby, north

Leicester, Northampton, north and south-east Shropshire, and north and north-west Oxford; /sùm/ in Antrim, mid, south-east, south-west and south Lancashire, Isle of Man, Cheshire, Denbigh, east and west-mid Stafford, north-east, north-west, east and south Derby, Leicester, south-west Northampton, east and south Warwick, Worcester, north and north-east Shropshire, west and north-west Oxford, and north Bucks; /tùtʃ/ in Antrim, south-mid south-west Lancashire, Isle of Man, south Cheshire, north-west Derby, Leicester, and mid Northampton; /jùŋ/ in Antrim, south-east, mid-south and south Lancashire, Isle of Man, south Cheshire, Denbigh, north Leicester, north-east, mid and south-west Northampton, east and south Warwick, north and south Worcester, and north and south-east Shropshire. *EDD* (s.v. *company*, *sb*. and *v*.) suggests that /kùmpəni/ is found in Scotland, Yorkshire, Cheshire, Lincoln, Shropshire, East Anglia, Sussex, Dorset, Somerset, and Devon. *EDD* (s.v. *sum*, *sb*.[1] and *v*.) records that /sùm/ is used in Yorkshire, Lancashire, Derby, Nottingham, Leicester, Northampton, Warwick, Gloucester, Berks, Huntington, East Anglia, Kent, Somerset, and Devon.

The change of *o* to *u* in *awlung* for *along* is found in pp. 272 and 273. Brook (1970: 127) suggests that "this pronunciation is found in RP *among*, where it is generally thought to have been introduced from a regional dialect." Joseph and Elizabeth Wright (1924: §139) points out that "*o* became *u* before *ng* in the west Midland dialects during the ME. Period, and a few words from these dialects have crept into standard NE. with the regular change of *u* to *a*, as *among*, *monger*, *mongrel* which were formerly often spelled with *u*." *Awlung* is listed in both *MW* and *DSL*. We have one instance of the standard form *along* in Stephen's speech, "Not *along* of me." (71). As this standard form appears in the earlier issue of the weekly instalments, Dickens might not have had the enough knowledge of this dialectal form when he wrote the sixth weekly number of this novel in *Household Words*, published on 6 May 1854. Another reason why Dickens employed this form is that this standard form is most strongly stressed in the sentence.

The use of *o* in *monny* and *onny* instead of *many* and *any*(-) is frequently found in Blackpool's speech. Examples are *monny* (141, 142^{2x}, 148, 151, 154), *onny* (141^{2x}, 148, 150, 154, 156, 160, 272), *onnything* (162), and *onnyways* (162). Brook (1970: 127) remarks that "Stephen's *monny* is regularly from OE *monig* while his *onny*, also a common northern form, probably owes its stem-vowel to the analogy of *monny*." *EDD* (s.v. *many*, *adj*. and *sb*.) illustrates that *monny* is found in Scotland, west Yorkshire, Lancashire, Cheshire, and *EDG*

('Index,' s.v. *any*) suggests that /oni/ occurs in Yorkshire, south-mid, south Lancashire. *Monny* and *onny* are both listed in *MW* and *DSL*. In addition to them, *DSL* lists *onnyway* and *onnythin*.

OED (s.v. *well*, *adv*.) comments that "an early lengthening of the vowel is indicated by the ME. *weel* (*wiel*, *wele*, etc.), which appears in northern and Scottish texts from the 14th cent., and is still the current form in Scottish, northern, and north midland dialects."

> "I know *weel*" (142^{3x}, 152)
>
> "yo know *weel*" (154)
>
> "'tis as *weel* so ..." (159)

Both *MW* and *DSL* refer to the pronunciation of this adverb.

J. Wright (1892: §79) transcribes /wīl/ for the adverb well for the dialect of Windhill, but he (1892: §399) demonstrates that "when *well* begins the sentence we use /wel/, just as in literary English." Dickens observes this rule with one exception, "they loves as *well* as gentlefok loves theirs ..." (272):

> "*Well*! She went bad ..." (71)
>
> "*Well*, missus, I ha' seen the lady ..." (154)
>
> "'*Well well*' said he" (162)

4. Long vowels

Dickens uses the spelling with *owt* for either *aught* or *ought* to indicates the diphthong /au/ for the RP long vowel /ɔ:/. We have eight instances of *nowt* (71^{2x}, 146, 147, 148^{2x}, 151, 159) and five instances of *thowt* (89, 142, 156, 273, 274). *EDG* (§127) suggests that /au/ in *naught* is found in south Northumberland, north Durham, Westmoreland, north-west Yorkshire, and north-west, and south Lancashire; and that /au/ in *nought* in south-west and south Northumberland, north Durham, north Cumberland, Westmoreland, north-west Yorkshire, east-mid, south-east and south Lancashire, south Stafford, Gloucester, south Oxford, Sussex, and east Devon. *EDG* (§166) illustrates that /au/ in *thought* is heard in south-west Northumberland, north Durham, Westmoreland, and east-mid, south-east and south Lancashire. *Nowt* for *naught* is recorded in both *MW* and *DSL*, and *thowt* in *MW* only.

The spelling with *o* for *ou* in the second person pronoun in both nominative and accusative cases indicates the dialectal short vowel /ɔ/

for the RP long vowel /uː/. Blackpool employs *yo* (68 etc.) twenty-one times in the nominative, *yo* (71 etc.) twenty-two times in the accusative, and *yo'* (74) once in the accusative. According to *EDG* ('Index,' s.v. *you*), the dialectal pronunciation /jɔ/ is used in west Yorkshire, south Lancashire, south Cheshire, north-west Derby, and west Stafford. This second person pronoun is surely recorded in both *MW* and *DSL*.

5. Diphthongs

Blackpool utters /iə/ or /iːr/ instead of the RP diphthong /ɛə/ in such words as *theer* (141, 154), *wheer* (149, 150, 154), *elsewheer* (152), *wheerever* (143). *EDG* ('Index,' s.v. *there*) shows that /iə/ in *there* occurs in Durham, east, mid and west Cumberland, Westmoreland, north-east, mid, southeast, south-west and south Yorkshire, Lancashire, Cheshire, Flint, Denbigh, Stafford, Lincoln, Leicester, mid, south-west Northampton, Warwick, Worcester, Shropshire, Hereford, north, north-west and west Oxford, Berks, Buckingham, Bedford, south-east Hertford, south Norfolk, Essex, Dorset, and south Devon. *EDG* ('Index,' s.v. *where*) claims that /iə/ in *where* is to be heard in north Durham, north-east, south-north-west, east, mid, south-east, south-west and south Yorkshire, Lancashire, Cheshire, Flint, Denbigh, east, east-mid west-mid and south Stafford, Derby, Nottingham, Lincoln, Rutland, Leicester, Northampton, Warwick, north Worcester, Shropshire, east Hereford, north-west Oxford, Berks, Bedford, south-east Hertford, Huntingdon, east Suffolk, Essex, east and south-east Kent, Dorset, north-west Somerset, south-west and south Devon, and Cornwall. *DSL* records both *thee-er* and *wheer*, but *MW* lists neither of them.

The spelling *heer* indicates the vowel lengthening /iːr/ in place of the RP diphthong /iə/. Blackpool uses *heer* (142^{3x}, 143, 149, 151^{2x}, 273) eight times. *EDG* ('Index,' s.v. *here*) shows that the dialectal pronunciation /hiːr/ is employed in Shetland, Orkney Isles, Caithness, Inverness, north-east and south-north Scotland, west Forfar, east Perth, east-mid, west-mid and south-mid Scotland, Antrim, and mid-east and south-west Northumberland.

6. Consonants

Stephen employs the dialectal form *chilt* (74) instead of *child*. According to *EDG* (§302), OE. final *d* and medial *d* which has come to stand finally in the modern dialects have become *t* after *l*, *n*, *r* in monosyllables in Lancashire, Cheshire, north Stafford, and Derby, as /tʃàilt/ *child*, /fīlt/ *field*. This dialectal form is recorded in both *MW* and *DSL*.

Another dialectal form *brigg* in place of *bridge* is also employed by Blackpool (72). *OED* (s.v. *Bridge*, *n.*[1]) illustrates that "as in other OE. words in *-cg*, the northern dialect has retained hard /g/ against the palatalized /dʒ/ of the south." According to *EDG* ('Index,' s.v. *bridge*), *brig* is to be heard in Orkney Isles, Buchan, Aberdeen, west Forfar, east Perth, north Ayr, south-mid Scotland, Lothian, Antrim, mid-east and south Northumberland, Durham, north and mid Cumberland, Westmoreland, Yorkshire, Lancashire, north-east Derby, mid Nottingham. Lincoln, Leicester, mid Northampton, Bedford, Huntingdon, and east Anglia. This form is listed only in *MW*.

7. Concluding remarks

We have seen Dickens's phonetic representation of the dialect from the philological point of view. His accuracy of rendering the regional dialect is not so incomplete. Many of the dialectal pronunciations are to be found in *MW* and *DSL* and paralleled to the illustrations of the references used in this paper, but "some of them seem to be of doubtful authenticity", as Brook (1970: 125) mentions. According to the discussion above, the following phonetic descriptions are not to be recognised as Lancashire dialect: *anoother*, *discoosed*, *soombody*, *toother*/*t'oother*, *awlung*, *heer*, *Gonnows*, *a'toogether*, *faw'en*, *sma'es*, *wi'in*, and *wi'out*.

In the case of *weel* for *wel*, Dickens completely followed its dialectal usage except one example and used the standard form at the beginning of the sentence. We, however, find some inconsistencies of spellings representing dialectal pronunciations.

By using apostropes and phonetic spellings Dickens aimed at the verisimilitude with respect to representing Lancashire dialect. Due to some examples that are not to be recognized as Lancashire dialect and a few inconsistencies of spellings, the dialect Dickens tried to describe so as to add some local colours to *Hard Times* has been subject to the most caustic criticism by both literary and linguistic scholars.

In Blackpool's speech, in addition to dialectal features, there are many features of substandard English, as Brook (1970: 129) suggests. These linguistic features are important to understand the class to which Stephen belongs, but they are definitely beyond the scope of this present paper.

Notes

1 Numbers following publishing dates indicate page numbers from which quotations are extracted.

2 These quotations by G. L. Brook are extracted from his *The Language of Dickens*, 1970, p. 125.

3 Dickens's visits to Manchester occurred in early November 1838, mid-January 1839, early October 1843, early July 1847, and early June 1848.

4 G. L. Brook (1978: 193) illustrates this book thus: "The first edition of *A View of the Lancashire Dialect* was short but the author later added several episodes. The book belongs to the literature of low life and roguery. The two characters are Tummus and Meary, but Meary is clearly subordinate, as may be seen by her comparative taciturnity: she has 44 lines to Tummus's 320. The book was remarkably popular and had a good deal of influence on later Lancashire dialect authors; more than sixty editions have been published."

5 J. H. Stonehouse (1935) *Reprints of the Catalogues of the Libraries of Charles Dickens and W. M. Thackeray etc.*, p. 111.

6 In the post script of the letter dated 17 June 1854, Dickens wrote to Mrs Gaskell, "I have never thanked you for Mr. Gaskell's lectures, which I have read with uncommon pleasure. They are so sagacious and unaffected, and tell so much that is interesting." (*Let. VII*: 357)

7 All the quotations of *Hard Times* are taken from *The New Oxford Illustrated Dickens* edition, 1952.

8 Super-scripts with "x" following page numbers indicate the occurrence of the word in the same page.

9 *MEG* (§10.481) makes a historical sketch of this form.

10 Another dialectal form *dun* is to be found in p. 72.

Texts

Dickens, C. (1854) *Hard Times*. The New Oxford Illustrated Dickens Edition. Oxford University Press: Oxford, 1952.

Dickens, C. (1854) *Hard Times*. The Norton Critical Edition. The third edition. Edited by Fred Kaplan and Sylvère Monod. W. W. Norton & Co.: New York,2001.

Letters

Chapple, J. A. V. and A. Pollard, eds. (1966) *The Letters of Mrs. Gaskell*. Manchester University Press: Manchester.

Storey, G., K. Tillotson and A. Easson, eds. (1993) *The Letters of Charles Dickens*. Volume Seven 1853-1855. The Pilgrim Edition. The Clarendon Press: Oxford. (*Let. VII*)

References

Bamford, S. (1850) *Dialect of South Lancashire*. John Heywood: Manchester. (*DSL*)

Brilioth, B. (1913) *A Grammar of the Dialect of Lorton*. Uppsala University:

Uppsala.

Brook, G. L. (1963, 1978) *English Dialects*. The third edition, André Deutsch: London.

Brook, G. L. (1970) *The Language of Dickens*. André Deutsch: London.

Collier, J., 'Tim Bobbin'. (1818) *The Miscellaneous Works of Tim Bobbin, Esq.* T. and J. Allman: London / Wilson and Sons: York. (*MW*)

Dobson, E. J. (1957, 1968) *English Pronunciation 1500-1700*. 2 vols. The second edition. The Clarendon Press: Oxford.

Ellis, A. J. (1869-89) *On Early English Pronunciation*. 6 vols. Early English Text Society: London. Reprinted by Haskell House Publishers: New York, 1969.

Forster, J. (1872-4) *The Life of Charles Dickens*. 3 vols. Chapman & Hall: London.

Gaskell, The Rev. W. (1854) *Two Lectures on the Lancashire Dialect*. Chapman and Hall: London.

Gerson, S. (1967) *Sound and Symbol in the Dialogue of the Works of Charles Dickens*. Almqvist and Wiksell: Stockholm.

Hargreaves, A. (1904) *A Grammar of the Dialect of Adlington*. Carl Winter: Heidelberg.

Hedevind, B. (1967) *The Dialect of Dentdale in the West Riding of Yorkshire*. Studia Anglistica Upsaliensia 5. Uppsala University: Uppsala.

Hirooka, H. (1965) *Dialects in English Literature*. Shinozaki-Shorin: Tokyo.

House, H. (1941, 1942) *The Dickens World*. The second edition. Oxford University Press: London.

Ingham, P. (1986) "Dialect as 'Realism': *Hard Times* and the Industrial Novel." *The Review of English Studies* 37, 518-27.

Jespersen, O. (1909) *A Modern English Grammar on Historical Principles*. Vol. I. Reprinted by Meicho-Fukyukai: Tokyo, 1990. (*MEG*)

Johnson, E. (1952) *Charles Dickens: His Tragedy and Triumph*. 2 vols. Simon and Schuster: New York.

Langton, R. (1912) *Childhood and Youth of Charles Dickens*. Hutchinson and Co.: London.

Leavis, F. R. and Q. D. Leavis (1973) *Dickens the Novelist*. Chatto and Windus: London.

Melchers, G. (1978) "Mrs. Gaskell and Dialect". *Studies in English Philology, Linguistics and Literature: Presented to Alarik Rynell 7 March 1978*. Edited by Mats Rydén and Lennart A. Björk. Almqvist and Wiksell International: Stockholm. 112-124.

Nodal, J. H. and G. Milner. *A Glossary of the Lancashire Dialect*. Part I - Words from *A* to *Eysel* (1875). Part II - Words from *Ettle* to *Yoi* (1882) Alexander Ir. and Co.: Manchester / Trübner and Co.: London.

Orton, H. et al. eds. (1962-71) *The Survey of English Dialects*. 13 vols. E. J. Arnold & Son Ltd.: Leeds.

Page, N. (1970) "Convention and Consistency in Dickens's Cockney Dialect". *English Studies*. Vol. 51, No. 4. 339-344

Page, N. (1988) *Speech in the English Novel*. The second edition. Macmillan: London. First published by Longman: London, 1973.

Petyt, K. M. (1976) "The Dialect Speech in *Wuthering Heights*." Appendix VII to *Wuthering Heights*. The Clarendon Edition of the Novels of the Brontës. Edited by H. Marsden and I. Jack. The Clarendon Press: Oxford, 1976. 500-513.

Petyt, K. M. (1980) *The Study of Dialect: An introduction to dialectology.* André Deutsch: London.

Quirk, R. (1959) *Charles Dickens and Appropriate Language*. The University of Durham: Durham.

Quirk, R. (1961) "Some Observations on the Language of Dickens". *A Review of English Literature*. Vol. II. No. 3. 19-28.

Quirk, R. (1974) "Charles Dickens, Linguist". *The Linguist and the English Language*. Edward Arnold: London,

Schilling, K. G. (1906) *A Grammar of the Dialect of Oldham*. Dissertation. Darmstadt.

Simpson, J. and E. S. C. Weiner, eds. (2004) *The Oxford English Dictionary*. The second edition. CD-ROM, Version 3.1. Oxford University Press: Oxford. (*OED*)

Simpson, M. (1997) *The Companion to* Hard Times. (The Dickens Companions, No. 6). Series editors: Susan Shatto and David Paroissien. Greenwood Press: Connecticut.

Sørensen, K. (1985) *Charles Dickens: Linguistic Innovator*. Acta Jutlandica LXI, Humanistisk serie 58. Arkona: Aarhus.

Stonehouse, J. H. (1935) *Reprints of the Catalogues of the Libraries of Charles Dickens and W. M. Thackeray etc*. Piccadilly Fountain Press: London.

Wagner, T. (1999) "John Collier's 'Tummus and Meary': Distinguishing Features of 18th-Century Southeast Lancashire Dialect-Morphology," *Neuphilologische Mitteilungen*, 2 C. 191-205.

Wakelin, M. F. (1972) *English Dialects: An Introduction*. The Athlone Press: London.

Webb, L. K. (1983) *Charles Dickens*. Evergreen Lives. Tonsa: San Sebastian.

Wilson, A. (1970) *The World of Charles Dickens*. The Viking Press: New York.

Wright, J. ed. (1898-1905) *The English Dialect Dictionary*. 5 vols. Henry Frowde: London. Reprinted by Oxford University Press: Oxford, 1981. (*EDD*)

Wright, J. (1892) *A Grammar of the Dialect of Windhill in the West Riding of Yorkshire*. Trübner: London.

Wright, J. (1905) *The English Dialect Grammar*. Henry Frowde: Oxford. (*EDG*)

Wright, J. and E. M. Wright (1924) *An Elementary Historical New English Grammar*: Oxford University Press: London.

Yamamoto, T. (1950, 2003) *Growth and System of the Language of Dickens: An Introduction to A Dickens Lexicon*. The third edition. Keisuisha: Hiroshima.

Pip's Point of View in *Great Expectations* in Terms of Humanisation and Dehumanisation

Saoko Tomita

1. Introduction

Dickens's techniques of description such as simile and metaphor play an important role in exhibiting the particular characteristics of human beings, non-human living beings and artificial objects seen in his literary works. Although we find a large variety of metaphoric expressions employed by various poets and authors (e.g. Chaucer, Spencer and Shakespeare), it is one of Dickens's peculiarities that he intends not only to combine two dissimilar qualities of the animate or the inanimate but also to suggest each character's inner thoughts and his own attitude towards the outer world by means of simile and metaphor. In *Great Expectations*, the total number of the two devices amounts to 794 examples, and thus various patterns of transference from one semantic component to another are found in each expression. Above all, the novel basically includes descriptions of particular characters transferred to other human beings, non-human living creatures or non-living objects, as Pip the narrator carefully observes the appearances of various people he meets, and intends to explain them concretely or humorously with his imagination. However, the transposition of their attributes is largely performed by *dehumanisation*, which is very effective in evoking an association between a human being and a non-human living being (or object) in the reader's mind. On the other hand, the transformation of an animal (or lifeless object) into a human being is also important for the hero in describing the scenes and the surroundings more vividly or dynamically. This type of transposition is called *humanisation*.

This paper, therefore, aims firstly to highlight the features of these technical devices considering the narrator's point of view, and secondly to see how Pip's surroundings profoundly influence his life and fortune, referring to the social and cultural background in the novel.

2. Humanisation and Dehumanisation

In Dickens's novels, a large variety of characters are described colourfully in terms of their appearances and behaviours by simile and metaphor, and above all, the author intends to accentuate the resemblance between a human being and a non-human living creature or lifeless object. Fawkner remarks on Dickens's technical use of the converse process involved in treating things as living creatures, or to the contrary describing living creatures as lifeless objects:

> Dickens frequently animates insentient objects in the inanimate background and deanimates living creatures in his novels. He constantly uses *animation* and *reification*–the tension between the human and the non-human–to analyse and describe man's imprisonment in a dehumanising society. (1977: 11-14)

Although Fawkner mentions the terms, *animation* and *reification*, he also uses the words *humanisation* and *dehumanisation* instead as their synonyms. However, in this paper I would like to use the latter two words, for Dickens uses these techniques not only to animate objects or deprive people of their animate quality, but also to illustrate the human or inhuman nature of particular characters in society by comparison with other living creatures or artificial objects. Besides, Kincaid (1971: 169) uses the term *dehumanisation* to refer to Dickens's method of emphasising the humanity of good people and the brutality of evil people by reference to harmless domestic animals and dangerous predatory beasts respectively. For this reason, we shall observe the process by which human beings are associated with "animals" or "objects" in terms of their dispositions. In this novel, the process mainly serves the function of attacking people or underlining their lifelessness and insentience. In contrast, the author describes an artefact or natural environment connected with a certain character as if it were a human being, which is effective in emphasising a unifying symbolic surface in the novel.

First, we shall direct our attention to the forms employed in *humanisation* and *dehumanisation*, and by so doing elucidate how the narrator's attitude or inner thoughts are reflected in each expression, referring to his point of view.

2.1. Forms

2.1.1. Simile

With regard to the converse process in simile, Dickens makes good use of the form of comparison with words such as *like*, *as* and *as if* by saying, for example, "you're ***as** dumb **as** one of your own keys*" (260), "I leaned down, and her calm face was ***like** a statue's*" (264), or "the great numbers on their backs, ***as if*** *they were street doors,* made them a most disagreeable and degraded spectacle" (225), and so on. However, in this novel, *dehumanisation* is more frequent than *humanisation* in simile, for the former includes 72 examples, whilst the latter has 27 examples. Besides, expressions with *like* are, above all, most frequent in *dehumanisation* (51 examples), as they are highly effective in portraying the appearances or behaviours of particular characters graphically and realistically in comparison with non-human living creatures or lifeless objects. On the other hand, expressions with *as* are less frequent than those with *like* (or *as if*), as only 5 examples are found in both techniques. Besides, fanciful comparison[1] using *as if* is most frequent in *humanisation* (17 examples), for the narrator tends humorously to delineate lifeless objects as if they were human beings.

2.1.2. Metaphor

Similarly, with regard to metaphor, *dehumanisation* is more frequent (136 examples) than *humanisation* (99 examples), as the former mainly plays a vital role in attacking or expressing contempt for evil people so that the narrator may show his indignation or animosity towards them. Although the hero occasionally despises himself, as in the phrase "*I* ***was*** *a brick in the house-wall!*" (457), the technique is fundamental to representing their lack of humanity. Regarding the forms of both devices, the following types are most frequent in the novel.

A. **Apposition with *as***
(1) She concluded by throwing me—*I often served her* ***as*** *a connubial missile*—at Joe, who, glad to get hold of me on any terms ... (9)

B. **Verb "To be"**
(2) He had said *I should* ***be*** *a fierce young hound* if I joined the hunt against him. (34)

C. **Verb**
(3) *I saw the cattle lifting their heads to* ***gaze*** *after him*, I wondered whether *they* ***thought*** *so too.* (7)

D. **Adjective Phrase**
(4) ... and that Drummle was rallied for coming up behind of a night *in that slow* ***amphibious*** *way of his.* (211)

E. **Noun Phrase**
(5) He gave me one other nod, *compressed* ***the post-office*** *exceedingly*, gave me one last nod, and ... (366)

To begin with, the instance (1) presents an expression in which the hero regards himself as a *missile* towards her sister Mrs. Joe. As

Brooke-Rose (1958: 97) says, this type of expression by apposition with *as* is effective in linking two nouns, as it evokes "to treat A as B," and therefore the reader may recognise how the hero treats himself as *a connubial missile*. Secondly, as shown in the example (2), the form "to be" is the most direct way of linking a metaphor (*a fierce young hound*) to its proper noun (*I* = Pip). Although this type of expression is less frequent than other methods in the novel, it is also useful in characterising various people colourfully. Besides, verbal metaphor as in (3) is a most frequent form in the novel, for the author tends to attribute human emotion and abilities to non-human living creatures or lifeless objects especially for *humanisation*. Next, the author also uses the form of an adjectival phrase particularly in order to dehumanise people into animals as in (4). Although this form is very rare in the novel, it is most effective for Pip in describing the behaviour or appearance of a repulsive or dislikeable character comically or realistically. Lastly, the form of a nominal phrase as in (5) is most frequent in *dehumanisation*, by which the narrator intends symbolically to represent various features or appearances of particular characters in this novel.

3. Characters' Points of View

So far we have analysed the forms of *humanisation* and *dehumanisation* in terms of simile and metaphor referring to some examples, and found that *dehumanisation* is more frequent than *humanisation* in *Great Expectations*. However, *humanisation* is also of great importance in the novel, for it may reflect the hero's/author's inner feelings or attitudes towards his surroundings in the world. In this section, we shall, therefore, direct our attention to the narrator's point of view and observe how the author delineates the appearances of his surroundings by means of both techniques, and attempts to convey his vision of the world.

3.1. Humanisation from Pip's Point of View

To start with, we shall consider Pip's childish point of view in terms of *humanisation*. It is a remarkable feature of Dickens's novels that imaginative and sensitive children abandoned in a life-denying society tend to humanise various inanimate objects in order to contrast their unspoiled humanity with the sterile inhumanity of the adult world. As Fawkner (1977: 29) remarks, "*Great Expectations* also deals with the neglected child Pip, who is surrounded by the cruel atmosphere of insensitivity," the narrator also tends to employ the method of humanising numerous lifeless objects with his careful observation and imagination. With regard to this novel, we may find some psychological factors in the child because of which his surroundings such as buildings or houses are animated as if they were human beings. As in the following instances (6) - (9), the narrator's *fear* or *sense of guilt* is symbolically reflected in each description.

(6) The man, after looking at me for a moment, turned me upside-down, and emptied my pockets. There was nothing in them but a piece of bread. When *the church* ***came to itself***—for he was so sudden and strong that he made it go head over heels before me, and I saw the steeple under my feet—when *the church* ***came to itself***, I say, I was seated on a high tombstone, trembling, while he ate the bread ravenously. (4)

(7) The gates and dykes and banks ***came bursting at me*** *through the mist, as if they* ***cried*** *as plainly as could be, "A boy with Somebody-else's pork pie! Stop him!"* (16-17)

(8) Cribbed and barred and moored by massive rusty chains, *the prison-ship seemed in my young eyes to* ***be ironed*** *like the prisoners*. (40)

(9) ... and in my sleep I saw *the file* ***coming at me*** *out of a door*, without seeing who held it, and I screamed myself awake. (77)

To begin with, the instance (6) explains the way in which Pip is turned upside-down and suspended heels over head by Abel Magwitch the escaped convict, who appears suddenly in a graveyard and assails him with threats. Because of the inversion of the natural order, the child comically humanises the church to explain the situation, and as Van Ghent (1967: 36) remarks, he gradually becomes aware of the identity of things and comes to acquire self-consciousness about guilt. Similarly, the next example (7) implies Pip's fear and sense of guilt after he was forced by the convict to bring stolen food for him. As Fawkner (1977. 32) observes, "Pip finds that guilt and terror causes every inanimate object to be animated with reproachful suspicion and alarming wakefulness," from his childish point of view the objects such as *gates*, *dykes* and *banks* appear to threaten and pursue him crying from behind.

In *Great Expectations*, these types of *humanisation* from Pip's childish point of view include 30 examples in both similes and metaphors. Observing the forms and vocabularies, we find that almost all of the artificial objects he describes are animated with verbs such as *come*, *jump*, *look*, *direct*, *shut*, *pursue*, *stare*, *glare*, *peep*, *arise*, *moan*, *address* and so forth. Particularly in metaphor, Pip's delicate sensitivity to inanimate objects is evident, as he is full of awareness of being pursued or threatened by his surroundings in the insentient world. Because of this, the hero is in the habit of describing the sudden appearances of inanimate objects by means of verbal metaphors, which serve to suggest his fear and sense of guilt towards the inhuman adult world. Besides, although less frequent than metaphor, the device using simile is also found in Pip's *humanisation*. The instance (8) describes the way in which the black Hulk lying out over the shore seems in his eye to be ironed like the prisoners, for his great sensitivity and imagination allows him to associate the prison-ship with leg-ironed prisoners. In addition, the use of the verb "iron" is most effective in exhibiting Pip's inner thoughts towards Abel Magwitch, as the child unconsciously associates the prison-ship with his leg-iron in his mind.

However, as Pip grows up in later chapters of the novel, he no longer sees lifeless objects appearing suddenly or rushing at him from behind. The reason for this is that the fear and sense of guilt in his childhood gradually disappear as he enters into a new life where he suddenly acquires a large fortune, and at the same time he comes to be obsessed with the idea of being a gentleman.

> (10) I whistled and made nothing of going. But the village was very peaceful and quiet, and *the light mists were solemnly rising as if to* ***show*** *me the world*, and I had been so innocent and little there, and all beyond was so unknown and great, that in a moment with a strong heave and sob I broke into tears. It was by the finger-post at the end of the village, and I laid my hand upon it, and said, "Good-by O my dear, dear friend!" (157)

> (11) For now, *the very* ***breath*** *of the beans and clover* ***whispered*** *to my heart* that the day must come when it would be well for my memory that others walking in the sunshine should be softened as they thought of me. (275)

Firstly, as in the example (10), the moment of the hero's breaking away from the vulgar past is symbolised by mists that gently rise into the sky and show him the world lying spread out before him. The mists are humanised in that the author imbues them with a human ability "to show" the narrator what the world he is about to enter is like, and at the same time the rising of the mists suggests the rising of Pip's expectations. Similarly, the next example illustrates the way in which the scent of the beans and clover whispers to him in order to express sympathy with his sorrow for his sister's death. In contrast with his childhood, the surrounding scenery in his adulthood no longer appears suddenly to threaten him or inspire fear in his heart. Instead, it is rather gentle and sympathetic, for natural phenomena such as mists and wind in this novel function as agents to mirror symbolically his life and his fortunes in the social world.

Furthermore, as Fawkner (1977: 39-41) remarks, "the mist functions as an introductory image of illusion in this novel," it can be said that the narrator comes to live in a world of false appearances, where the inheritance of great wealth only worsens things. Besides, as shown in Table 1, we can see how the author humanises non-human living creatures, natural phenomena and artificial objects, employing either stative verbs (which denote cognitive states) or non-stative verbs (which denote events or actions) from Pip's point of view. The nouns in round brackets denote a subject of verbal metaphor. However, as Meier (1982: 109) points out, the author does not merely intend to depict something in vivid colours, but also to reflect the narrator's inner feelings or attitudes towards the outer world that profoundly influences his life, and thus we can recognise Dickens's imagination and his creative energy in each rhetorical expression.

Table 1 Humanisation in Verb Metaphor (from Pip's Point of View)

	Stative Verb	Non-Stative Verb
Animal or Bird (3 exx.)	*think* (cattle), *think* (pigeon), *know* (fowl)	
Plant (2 exx.)	*want* (flower-seeds and bulbs)	*whisper* (beans and clover)
Nature (6 exx.)		*show* (mists), *disclose* (mists) *mutter* (wind), *assail* (wind), *tear* (wind), *freshen* (air, sunlight, river)
Artefact (23 exx.)	*stare* (grounds, dykes, sluices), *think* (tabacco)	*jump* (church), *direct* (wooden finger), *shake* (window), *die* (spark), *drown* (beer), *reappear* (file), *come* (file), *address* (rot), *moan* (rot), *absorb* (doorway), *lead* (church-clocks), *accompany* (church-clocks), *follow* (church-clocks), *whisper* (closet), *sigh* (fireplace), *tick* (washing-stand), *play* (guitar-string), *run*, *sympathise*, *animate*, *encourage* (road)

If we refer to the table, it can be said that Dickens makes good use of non-stative verbs in order to project human emotion and powers into lifeless objects, as Pip's feelings of "guilt and fear" towards the inhuman, insentient world are insinuated into his mind. Although not frequent in the novel, non-human living creatures such as animals, birds and plants are also humanised with emotional verbs such as *think*, *know* and *want*, as the hero relies on his own imagination in describing their appearances graphically. Besides, natural phenomena and artificial objects are frequently humanised with non-stative verbs such as *come*, *assail*, *mutter*, *follow*, *play* and *run*, which may give a symbolical delineation of his psychological state.

3.2. Dehumanisation from Pip's Point of View

Next, we shall observe the converse process, *dehumanisation*, by which human beings are treated as non-human living creatures or non-living objects. In the novel, this technical device is a most frequent means of description, as there are 136 examples in metaphor, while 72 examples are found in simile. Although some characters are associated with abstract qualities such as *natural depth* and *dreadful mystery* in the novel, we shall direct our attention to the descriptions of human beings dehumanised into other living creatures or lifeless objects, for it may effectively reflect the narrator's mental attitude towards the surroundings in society.

3.2.1. Transition from Human Beings to Animals

In the novel, Dickens most frequently uses the transformation of human beings into animals in order to evoke the hero's impression of particular characters he observes. It is one of his characteristics in animal-metaphor that the implications of the contexts are negative, rather than positive, for, as Fawkner (1977: 73) remarks, the people dehumanised in Dickens's novels tend to be deprecated as they usually seem dislikeable, or at least ridiculous. In *Great Expectations*, the narrator is inclined to dehumanise people such as Abel Magwitch, Mrs. Joe, Mr. Pumblechook, Dolge Orlick and Bentley Drummle, all of whom are, in Pip's eye, dislikeable or uncouth, and therefore, they are usually portrayed as dangerous predatory beasts by means of simile and metaphor. Although the description of animalised people is rich in humour and comedy, the function of the device, as Meier (1982: 9) remarks, ranges from mere embellishment of description to the expression of the novel's deepest concerns. We shall, therefore, focus on how some characters are animalised into various species from Pip's point of view.

Firstly, Magwitch is one of the characters most frequently animalised by the narrator with both simile and metaphor. At the very beginning of the novel, he meets the convict who rises up from the graves, threatens to kill him, holds him upside down, and ends by forcing the boy to steal food for him. The moment of this dramatic encounter causes the hero to become aware of the identity of things, and he comes to feel fear and criminal guilt. Because of this, he makes a habit of treating the fearful and dislikeable convict as *a dog* or *beast* as in (12) and (13):

Magwitch > dog; wild beast

(12) I had often watched a large dog of ours eating his food; and I now noticed a decided similarity between the dog's way of eating, and the man's. *The man took strong sharp sudden bites, just* ***like*** *the dog*. (19)

(13) The abhorrence in which I held the man, the dread I had of him, the repugnance with which I shrank from him, could not have been exceeded if *he had been some terrible beast*. (315)

The treatment of the convict as *a dog* or *wild beast* is effective in emphasising his aggressive way of eating and the dangerous quality inherent in him. However, as Stange (1995: 519-20) maintains, the hero attempts not only to achieve comfort in a fantasy life by attacking him as *a dog* but also gradually to accept him and come to love him as a true father. In this way, a bond between the two characters is established, for Magwitch was first arrested for stealing turnips, and the child's stealing of food duplicates the convict's act (Van Ghent 37). As he is projectively responsible for Magwitch's existence and for his brutalisation, the hero thenceforth identifies himself with *a young wolf* or *wild beast* when a hostile confrontation occurs between Pip and Orlick the villain in Chapter XI.

Pip > wolf; wild beast,

(14) He seemed so brave and innocent, that although I had not proposed the contest I felt but a gloomy satisfaction in my victory. Indeed, I go so far as to hope that *I regarded myself while dressing,* ***as*** *a species of savage young wolf, or other wild beast*. (90)

In this passage, the hero's treatment of himself as *a wolf* or *beast* is explained by means of metaphor, which takes the form of apposition with *as*, expressed by the verb *regard*. Although very rare in the novel, this type of apposition is effective in linking directly the two nouns, that is to say *myself* (= Pip) and *a species of savage young wolf* (or *other wild beast*). Besides, in Dickens's novels, *a dog* or *a beast* is one of the species that symbolises a person's dangerousness, brutality, aggressiveness or criminality, and therefore, other prisoners in this novel are also described by simile as *dogs* or *lower animals* from Pip's point of view.[2]

However, the author's intention in animalising people is not merely to suggest a close resemblance between a human being and an animal species, but also to emphasise the situation of a character who is humiliated by society and degraded to an animal-like state, which does not allow him to keep the slightest trace of dignity (Meier 63). As the hero also despises himself as "an unfortunate little bull in a Spanish arena" (25), this type of animalisation plays a role in representing a character who is repressed and tortured by established society.

In the novel, despicable and fearful characters are frequently dehumanised into dangerous, repulsive or predatory animals from Pip's point of view. For instance, Mr. Pumblechook's mouth is "like *a fish*" (24), Mrs. Joe pounces on Pip "like *an eagle*" (51-52), Drummle creeps "like *some uncomfortable amphibious creature*" (201), and Orlick's mouth snarls "like *a tiger's*" (420).[3] As these characters treat the hero in his childhood as if he were a felon, he becomes aware of the false society in which they are essentially involved. For this reason, the hero uses animal imagery in order to highlight the denial of their human nature brought about by society.

In contrast, the mild, good-natured Joe is treated by Pip as *a bird*, as in "the crown of his head stands up "like *a tuft of feathers*" (97), and "he takes his hat up carefully with both hands like *a bird's nest with eggs in it*" (217). Joe is the only character whom the hero speaks well of in the novel, for *a bird* symbolises his harmless, friendly and gentle comportment from Pip's point of view. In Dickens's novels, Little Emily and Mr. Chillip in *David Copperfield* and Poll Sweedlepipe in *Martin Chuzzlewit* are similarly compared to *birds* owing to their shy, timid but friendly or sweet-tempered character (Tomita, *ERA*: 46-47).

3.2.2. Transition from Human Beings to Artefacts

In addition to the device of dehumanising people into animals, there is yet another type of process by which human beings are described as if they were lifeless objects. This is one of the most frequent patterns in the novel, as 50 examples are found in both simile and metaphor. Among all the examples of this mechanisation, almost all of the characters are described from Pip's point of view, and above all, Mr. Wemmick is one of the characters who is most frequently referred to as an artificial object, for his wooden figure impresses the narrator so deeply. Because of this, he makes a habit of depicting the motions of his mouth as *a post-office* in order to emphasise his lack of animation (Tomita, *ERA*: 39-40).

Mr. Wemmick > post-office

(15) When *Mr. Wemmick had put all the biscuit into* ***the post***, and had paid me my money from a cash-box in a safe, *the key of which safe he kept somewhere down his back and produced from his coat-collar like an iron pigtail*, we went up-stairs. (197)

(16) By degrees, Wemmick got dryer and harder as we went along, and *his mouth tightened into* ***a post-office*** *again.* (207)

(17) His personal recognition of each successive client was comprised in a nod, and in his settling his hat a little easier on his head with both hands, and then *tightening* ***the post-office***, and putting his hands in his pockets. (258; vol.a!, c)

(18) "I have an impending engagement," said I, glancing at Wemmick, *who was putting fish into* ***the post-office***, "that renders me rather uncertain of my time. At Once, I think." (384)

As in the examples (15) - (18) above, the narrator comically portrays his wooden appearance by association with *a post-office* as it serves to emphasise his lack of expression. Although *dehumanisation* is most effective in attacking and lowering the quality of each character in Dickens's novels, the hero in this case does not use it in order to express contempt for or to attack Mr. Wemmick with hatred. Furthermore, as Fawkner (1977: 75) maintains, he is primarily wooden, but with his appearance of having an iron pigtail he also seems slightly metallic as in (15).

Similarly, Miss Murdstone in *David Copperfield* is recognised by metaphor as *a metallic lady*, for her belongings reflect her cold-heartedness and inhumanity as in the following instance:

cf. (19) She brought with her, *two uncompromising hard black boxes, with her initials on the lids in hard brass nails*. When she paid the coachman *she took her money out of a hard steel purse, and she kept the purse in* ***a very jail of a bag which hung upon her arm by heavy chains****, and shut up like a bite. I had never, at that time, seen such a metallic lady altogether as Miss Murdstone was.*

(*David Copperfield*, 45)

The first-person narrator David gives a symbolic representation of Miss Murdstone's purse as *a very jail of a bag which hung upon her arm by heavy chains*, which associates her with imprisonment. Whereas the metallisation of Miss Murdstone represents her cold-hearted inner hardness and inhumanity, Mr. Wemmick's mechanical appearance does not necessarily denote an image of his inhuman lifelessness or rigidity, but rather one of his comically lifeless appearance.

From Dickens's point of view, the dehumanisation of Mr. Wemmick suggests his queer and comical stiffness, while that of Miss Murdstone represents her complete lifelessness and insensitivity. However, the author's purpose in dehumanising these two characters is not merely to compare their lifeless appearances but to reflect social attitudes that restrict, suppress, and imprison the individual in the false liberty of self-sufficiency (Fawkner 80-81). For this reason, it can be said that the author makes good use of *dehumanisation* so that the reader may recognise not only its symbolic descriptive effect but also the hero's fearful attitude towards the insentient world that deprives him of human love, brotherhood and mutual interdependence. Although the mechanical appearance of Mr. Wemmick's mouth seems to be comical on the surface, his *post-office* has a symbolical effect that suggests the non-human artificiality in a civilised society. In addition, as the narrator often employs metaphors in dehumanising himself into objects such as *a model with a mechanical heart*, *brick* and *steel beam of a vast engine*, we can say that his mechanical figures also suggest the mechanical civilisation that Dickens considered a threat to natural human values.

4. Conclusion

We have analysed the forms of *humanisation* and *dehumanisation* by means of simile and metaphor in *Great Expectations*. Both devices are particularly employed from Pip's point of view, as the hero intends to vitalise various artefacts so that they can symbolically reflect his inner attitude towards the insentient world that attacks and threatens him in his childhood. On the other hand, *dehumanisation* is of great use in attacking people with evil qualities, so that the hero may feel comfort in his fantasy world. Although they are portrayed vividly or comically by means of his great imagination, the device is not merely used to embellish their artificial or animal-like qualities, for by so doing the hero/author attempts to suggest to the reader his fear of an inhuman society that oppresses him.

Notes

1 Brook (1970: 33) introduces Dickens's particular method of comparison called "fanciful *as if*," which takes the form of the invention of some improbable

but amusing explanation of the appearance or behaviour of one of the characters in a novel.

2 In *David Copperfield*, the narrator *David* considers himself *a dog* in his childhood when Mr. Murdstone severely educates and brutalises him as if he were less than human. As David gradually accepts his dog-like quality and feels a sense of guilt towards the man, he comes to think of his own behaviour as a criminal act. See my article in *PHOENIX* (2002): 16-17, for further details.

3 In Dickens's novels, dull, repulsive or dislikeable characters like Drummle, Mr. Pumblechook, and Uriah Heep are described by means of simile as wet or slimy creatures such as *amphibian*, *fish*, *snail* and *frog*. The villains such as Drummle and Heep are also metaphorically depicted as *a spider* and *a vulture* respectively, as their dangerous and aggressive qualities are embodied in their attitudes towards the two narrators, David and Pip.

Texts

Dickens, C. (1981) *David Copperfield*. Ed. Nina Burgis. The World's Classics. Oxford: Oxford University Press.

Dickens, C. (1993) *Great Expectations*. Ed. Margaret Cardwell. The World's Classics. Oxford: Oxford University Press.

References

Brook, G.L. (1970) *The Language of Dickens*. London: André Deutsch.

Brooke-Rose, C. (1958) *A Grammar of Metaphor*. London: Secker.

Fawkner, H. W. (1977) *Animation and Reification in Dickens's Vision of the Life-Denying Society*. Stockholm: Liber Tryck.

Hagan, J. H, Jr. (1990) "The Poor Labyrinth: The Theme of Social Injustice in Dickens's *Great Expectations*." *Critical Essays on Charles Dickens's* Great Expectations. Ed. Michael Cotsell. Boston: Hall, 56-63.

Kincaid, J. R. (1971) "Laughter and Point of View." *Dickens and the Rhetoric of Laughter*. Oxford: Clarendon Press, 162-91.

Meier, S. (1982) *Animation and Mechanization in the Novels of Charles Dickens*. Bern: Francke.

Moynahan, J. (1990) "The Hero's Guilt: The Case of *Great Expectations*." *Critical Essays on Charles Dickens's* Great Expectations. Ed. Michael Cotsell. Boston: Hall, 73-87.

Pearlman, E. (1995) "Inversion in *Great Expectations*." *Charles Dickens: Critical Assessments*. Ed. Michael Hollington. 4 vols. East Sussex: Helm, 549-61.

Quirk, R. (1974) "Charles Dickens, Linguist." *The Linguist and the English Language*. London: Arnold.

Stange, G. R. (1990) "Expectations Well Lost: Dickens's Fable for His Time." *Critical Essays on Charles Dickens's* Great Expectations. Ed. Michael Cotsell. Boston: Hall, 56-63.

Tanabe, Y. (2003) "Sam Weller no Hiyuhyougen: *The Pickwick Papers* ni okeru Igi to Kouka." *Ful of Hy Sentence: Eigogoironsyuu*. Ed. Masahiko Kanno. Tokyo: Eihousha, 55-65.

Tomita, S. (2002) "Similes in *Great Expectations.*" *PHOENIX*, 58, 1-22.
Tomita, S. (2003) "Metaphors in *Great Expectations.*" *ERA*, nos. 20, 1-2, 34-52.
Van Ghent, D. (1967) "The Dickens World: A View from Todgers's." *Dickens: A Collection of Critical Essays*. Ed. Martin Price. Englewood Cliffs: Prentice-Hall.

Katherine Mansfield's "The Fly" Revisited: With Special Reference to Its Expressions of <Desire>

KEN NAKAGAWA

1. Introduction

The purpose of this paper is to make an analysis of the verbal expressions realized in Katherine Mansfield's "The Fly." According to literary critics, F. W. Bateson and B. Shahevitch (39), "The Fly" is a densely structured work that allows an elaborate analysis.

I would like to pay special attention to the verbal expressions of <desire> and observe the dynamic yet subtle movements of the characters' psychology. As a conclusion, I want to point out Katherine Mansfield's aim to express the idea that 'life is not always what one likes.'

As is done by Bateson and Shahevitch (52), this fiction can be seen as a three-act play. In order to easily understand my argument, let me summarize the structure of "The Fly" for our convenience:

Act 1: Woodifield's episode (to l.15, p. 425)
Act 2: Boss's re-enactment of the son's death (to l.33, p. 426)
Act 3: Boss's murder of the fly

Now let us go into the details of the story.

2. Act One

At the very beginning of Act One, Old Mr. Woodifield, who came to see the boss at his office, speaks in a high voice, 'Y'are very snug in here.' His talk is over. Now it is time for him to go back home. But he did not want to go. Since his stroke, Old Woodifield is allowed to visit his friend once a week. He is boxed up by his family members except on Tuesdays. This 'boxed up' image at line 6 on page 422 is very important to understanding the meaning of this short story. Old Woodifield stares at the boss almost greedily.

At the start of the second paragraph, again old Woodifield's speech appears: 'It's snug in here, upon my word!' which is a variation of line 1: 'Y'are very snug in here.' What we must notice here is the connotation of the adverbs of manner: 'Wistfully, admiringly (422.17)' together with 'greedily,' which appeared four lines earlier.

What expresses <desire> is not only a verb but also an adverb. What does he desire? What does he admire? What is he greedy for? To put it bluntly, what he wants is freedom, freedom from confinement. People who are under constraints, bondage due to Fate and the realities of life, will certainly desire escape from those constraints. That is why I mentioned a little earlier the importance of the 'boxed up' image. The object of his envy is never 'a great, green-leather armchair,' nor 'new carpet,' nor 'new furniture,' nor 'electric heating.'

Old Woodifield uses the word 'snug' in the sense of 'feel spiritually comfortable, breaking away from the yoke of the wife and girls.' In contrast, the boss seems to use 'comfortable' in the sense of 'feel physically satisfied, surrounded by new and rich furnishings.'

With a paper-knife the boss flipped through pages of the prestigious *Financial Times*, which shows he is still working at the forefront of the business world. After the description, Mansfield inserts a phrase, 'As a matter of fact.' What he really has in mind is that he is proud of his office-room and that he <u>wants</u> old Woodifield to admire it as well.

The boss does not notice the true meaning of Woodifield's words, that is to say, 'it is spiritually comfortable coming here, because in here there is nothing to constrain.'

Incidentally, what someone does not try to do sometimes reflects his or her inner psychology. The boss enthusiastically shows off his newly furnished office-room, but there is one thing he dares not draw Woodifield's attention to. It is a photograph of his son killed in the war. This attitude of the boss may be called <desire to a negative direction>.

In spite of the boss's strong expectations, Old Woodifield does not respond to his explanation but ignores it. He tries to remember his own episode but in vain. The boss, 'feeling kindly (423.25),' gives his old friend a whisky, which warms him and creeps into his chilled old brain. He remembers. He tells the boss that the girls went to Belgium to have a look at poor Reggie's grave, and that they happened to come across that of the boss's son.

In a sentence: 'Old Woodifield paused (424.24),' <desire not expressed explicitly> is hidden. Woodifield pauses on purpose, expecting the boss to respond to his words. In other words, he wants the boss to react. But the boss makes no reply, or rather cannot possibly answer. Woodifield uses a tag question, 'You've not been across, have yer? (424.30-31)' in order to make it easier for the boss to respond. Mansfield hints at the boss's attention by his body movement, that is, a slight 'quiver in his eyelids (424.25).'

At last the old man's way of speaking comes to be expressed by 'quaver (424.32)' (=say in trembling tone *COD*). Why? How come? The thing is that the roads on the graves are nice and broad. 'Nice broad paths' out of Woodifield's mouth is repeated again in a narrative part: 'It was plain from his voice how much he liked a nice broad path (424.34-35).' The narrator, Mansfield, does emphasize old Woodifield's particular liking for 'a nice broad path.' Here we must remember the above-mentioned 'boxed up' image. Old Woodifield hates being placed under continual restraint, and therefore he loves a sense of liberation. It is because of this sense of unobstructed spaciousness that his voice trembles with joy when he mentions 'a nice broad path.'

Old Woodified pauses once again. He wants a quick and direct response from the boss. 'Then the old man brightened wonderfully (425.1-2).' Why? It is because he managed to remember what he wanted to say. Old Woodifield begins to talk about something trivial: his girls' being overcharged at a hotel restaurant. At this stage he gets elated by his own talk without reserve. He returns home without realizing at all what effect his words have had on the boss's emotions. Only here does Mansfield not put an epithet 'old' to Woodifield. Old Woodifield prevails elsewhere, though.

3. Act Two

After seeing the old fellow out, the boss returns to his desk in grave thought. It is because he could not avoid facing an old wound, that is, his only son's death in battle. Then, at line 25 on page 425, a series of problematic sentences appear. 'He wanted, he intended, he had arranged to weep...' Let us consider this by dividing it into three sentences:

(1) He wanted to weep.

(2) He intended to weep.

(3) He had arranged to weep.

As for the acceptability (Wales 3) of (1), there is no problem. Concerning sentence (2), there is something strange about the sentence. Usually a verb that should be supplied in 'intend to ~' is a self-controllable verb (Konishi 761, Ando 44), but in this case the verb is not self-controllable; 'weep' comes after the infinitive marker. Sentence (3) also seems strange to me for the same reason applicable to sentence (2). While sentences (1) and (2) are in the past tense, sentence (3) is in the past perfect tense. Why are they so structured?

The inclination of the boss to cry expressed in (1) would be genuine, just as everybody wants to cry at some time. When it comes to sentence (2), the genuine inclination of the boss to weep changes to distorted feelings. As mentioned before, 'intend to ~' should take a self-controllable verb. 'Weep' is not self-controllable. So sentence (2) seems to me unacceptable. But in a specific situation, sentence (2) becomes acceptable. Take an example of an actor on the stage. He or she can control their emotions irrespective of their natural feelings. Then, if we suppose that the boss is pretending to be an actor who is going to weep, are we not able to admit the acceptability of sentence (2)? Sentence (3) can be interpreted in this way: All the preliminaries for a performance have been arranged beforehand; namely, the actions of 'leaning forward' and 'covering his face with his hands' have been arranged before weeping. In other words, the preparatory stage of his weeping 'ritual (Bateson & Shahevitch 50)' has already been finished and 'arranged.'

Talking of 'arrangement,' there is a tendency for Mansfield to use verbal expressions with a semantic feature of <+by arrangement> for describing the boss's actions. Some examples include: 'Ever since his birth the boss had worked at building up this business for him (426.4-6),' or 'And he actually had the brilliant notion of breathing on it [the fly] to help the drying process (427.34-35).'

On the other hand, Woodifield's actions take on a semantic feature of <+by accident>. For example, in 'they *happen to come across* your boy's' there seems to be a crash of redundancy of <+by accident> coming from both 'happen to ~' and 'come across.' In a sentence, 'old Woodifield *sprang* that remark *upon* him about the boy's grave (425. 26-27)' as well, there seems to be a semantic feature of <+by accident>, as is clarified by its definition 'present suddenly or *unexpectedly* (*POD*).' The story of his girls' visit to their brother's grave in Belgium also develops accidentally into the one of the girls being overcharged at a hotel restaurant. It is not an intentional development at all. Table 1, below, based on the two distinctive features will help our understanding.

Table 1 <BYARRANGEMENT> vs. <BYACCIDENT>

	<BY ARRANGEMENT>	<BY ACCIDENT>
Boss's action	+	−
Woodifield's action	−	+

If we assume old Woodifield to be a person satisfied with the status quo, we can assume the boss to be a type trying aggressively to change the present circumstances. When people desire to do something on purpose, contrary to their expectations, they often fail to accomplish their purposes. This point has much to do with the conclusion of my argument.

What has become of the boss who 'wanted, intended,' who 'had arranged to weep...?' What old Woodifield talked about brought a terrible shock to the boss. The boss realized for the first time that his son lay under the ground infested with maggots. His son appeared to him for the first time as a dead person with the stench of a dead body (Nishidai 57). Till then he had been considered sacred and idealized. To use Mansfield's own words, 'the boss never thought of the boy except as lying unchanged, unblemished in his uniform, asleep for ever.' It was not until this time that the boss recognized the reality of the decomposition of his son's body. The boss groaned by saying 'My son!' but no tears came out. In the past months and even years after the boy's death he had only to say 'My son!' to be overcome by inconsolable grief. He used to cry loudly and weep bitterly. But this time no tears came.

By the way, performance is played on fiction. Now that the foundation of his idealized fiction crashes down, he discontinues giving a performance. The boss, who had shut his eyes to his son's death, has recognized the reality of his son's death. On page 426, there is a somewhat strange expression again:

> He wasn't feeling as he wanted to feel (426.29).

Usually 'want to ~' does not occur with 'feel,' because 'feel' is not a self-controllable verb. But in a particular situation, 'He wasn't feeling as he wanted to feel' does not sound strange. It is only on the stage that this sentence holds good.

At this point it occurs to me that the boss has lived in a world of drama where appearance prevails. The same impression, I think, might occur to Bateson and Shahevitch when they thought of "The Fly" as a three-act play.

The boss of Act One, indeed, is described as a strong character with a sense of superiority to his friend, and he appears to look down upon old Woodifield when he boasts of his refurbished office-room and provides him with a generous finger of whisky. But isn't he a man who is only concerned with keeping up appearances? The real figure of the boss is described as 'a broken man, with his life in ruins (426.25).' He is indeed neither more nor less than that.

4. Act Three

Let us here refer to Act Three very briefly. It is the ability of a small creature to survive that is expressed here. The vital force is at once the object of admiration and jealousy for the boss, who is keenly feeling the shadow of death approaching. The fly, which has been referred to as 'it,' abruptly changes to 'He' at line 25 on page 427. It is a reflection of the boss's sympathy to the fly. After throwing the body of the fly in the waste-paper basket, the boss is seized by 'such a grinding feeling of wretchedness.' He foresees his own death by looking at the fly's death. That is why 'he felt positively frightened (428.12).'

5. Data for Conclusion

So far we have followed characters' behavior and psychological movements by paying special attention to the expressions of <desire>. As a result, we can conclude that in this short story the idea that 'life is not always what one likes' is expressed. The data we go upon are as follows:

First, all the characters are placed in confinement in some way or other.

Seen from the point of Fate, old Woodifield, a supporting actor, has a stroke and is paralyzed on one side. He lost his son in the war. From a social point of view, he has no choice but to leave his job because of his illness and virtually lives in close imprisonment in his home. A metaphorical expression allotted to him is 'as a baby (422.3).' A baby is under constraint in diapers.

With regard to the boss's servant, Old Macey, he is in his 'cubby-hole (425.18),' in other words, in 'a small enclosed space (*LDOCE*).'

From an interpersonal point of view, he is a servant to the boss, and as such he has to obey his master's orders. A metaphorical expression allocated to him is 'like a dog (425.18).' A dog is chained up, that is, restrained by its owner. In this case, the dog is depicted as the one 'that expects to be taken for a run,' in other words, that wants to be released from constraint.

What about the fly? From the point of Fate, it happens to fall into an inkpot. Luckily it is helped out of the inkpot, but it is at the mercy of inkblots. It is under continuous restraint, and eventually dies.

The protagonist, boss seems to be under no constraint except for having lost his only son in the war. But when his son was alive, the boss had devoted his whole time and efforts to his son's stepping into his shoes. His only hope was his son's carrying on where he left off. The boss's attitude to life appears active and positive at first sight, but to look at it from a different angle, he is said to be bound hand and foot without doing what he likes, and now he is obsessed with the fear of death.

His only son himself was 'in his uniform,' which is associative of a strict military life restrained by military rules.

In this way all the characters are under some sort of constraint resulting from Fate and the real world.

Viewed from social and economic standpoints, the boss seems to be favored most. But even to him there are things that he cannot do as he wishes. Let us take notice of the expressions of <desire> once again.

Table 2 Expressions including 'want to ~'

SUBJECT	EXPRESSION	<FULFILLMENT>
Boss	He ***wanted,***...***to*** weep... 425.24-25	–
Boss	He wasn't feeling as he ***wanted to*** feel. 426.29	–
Woodifield	He did not ***want to*** go. 422.4-5	+
Woodifield	"There was something I ***wanted to*** tell you." 423.19	+

There are two 'want to ~' structures with the boss as their grammatical subjects. 'He *wanted,* [...] *to weep....*' but he was not able to weep. He was not able to feel 'as he *wanted to feel,*' either. Both of these result in <-fulfillment>. Interestingly enough, the same 'want to ~'

structures appear two times as well in describing the old Woodifield's desires. Ironically, these are fulfilled. To be concrete, 'he did not *want to go*,' and he was able to stay a little longer because he talked about his girls' visit to Reggie's grave. And once again 'There was something I *wanted to tell* you,' and though he had difficulty remembering, thanks to the whisky he finally managed to remember what he wanted to say.

Table 3 Three variants of 'remember'

SUBJECT	EXPRESSION	<FULFILLMENT>
Woodifield	his eyes grew dim ***remember***ing. 423.19-20	+
Woodifield	He **remember**ed. 424.17-18	+
Boss	For the life of him he could not ***remember***. 428.18-19	–

The word 'remember' leads me to look into its immediate context. There are three occurrences of 'remember' found in this story. Those relating to Woodifield are two: '"There was something I wanted to tell you," said old Woodifield, and his eyes grew dim *remembering*.' and 'But it warmed him; it crept into his chill old brain—he *remembered*.' Viewed in the light of <fulfillment>, the former 'remembering' is not relevant to <fulfillment> at least for the time being, but finally it leads to <+fulfillment>. The latter 'remembered' of course entails <+fulfillment>.

The 'remember' relating to the boss presents itself in the very last sentence of this work: 'For the life of him he could not *remember*.' 'Remember' in this case is strongly negated by using an adverbial phrase and, despite the boss's desperate efforts, the action is not in the least fulfilled.

On reflection, the verb 'fulfill' is closely connected with <desire>. Whenever we desire something in our daily life, the desire ultimately results in either <+fulfillment> or <–fulfillment>, regrettably with <–fulfillment> predominating.

Actually the very verb 'fulfill' has been used in "The Fly": 'And that promise had been so near being *fulfilled* (426.11).' This sentence well expresses the resentment of the boss. His attempt to have his son step into his shoes was only a step short of completion. After all, his effort is not 'fulfilled.'

6. Conclusion

Thus far we have observed the verbal expressions of <desire> in "The Fly" and found noticeable discrepancies in their acceptability. As a result, we can conclude the idea that 'life is not always what one likes' is expressed in "The Fly." Several desires ascending from the recess of mortal human existence, and irresistible impulse to make things go smoothly as we wish are frequently obstructed by something beyond human understanding. Might this also be the resignation of Katherine Mansfield who died of illness at the young age of thirty-four?

Note

This is a revised and abridged English version of my article that first appeared in Japanese in *The Journal of Yasuda Women's University* 13, (1985).

References

All quotations are taken from the *Collected Short Stories of Katherine Mansfield* (1945, 1984) Constable: London. The figures after each quotation indicate page and line respectively. All italics and underlines are mine except the *Financial Times*.

Ando, S. (1983) *Eigokyoshi no Bunpou Kenkyu*. Taishukan shoten: Tokyo.

Bateson F.W. & B. Shahevitch. (Jan. 1962) 'Katherine Mansfield's "The Fly": A Critical Exercise,' *Essays in Criticism*. Stephen Wall: Oxford.

Biber, D., S. Johansson, G. Leech, S. Conrad, E. Finegan. (1999) *Longman Grammar of Spoken and Written English*. Longman: London.

Carter, R. ed. (1981) *Language and Literature*. Unwin Hyman/Routledge: London.

Chatman, S. ed. (1972) *Literary Style: A Symposium*. Oxford University Press: London and New York.

Freeman, D.C. (1970) *Linguistics and Literary Style*. Holt, Rinehart & Winston: New York.

Konishi, T. ed. (1980) *A Dictionary of English Word Grammar on Verbs*. Kenkyusha Printing Co.: Tokyo.

Leech, G. & M. Short (1981) *Style in Fiction: A Linguistic Introduction to the English Fictional Prose*. Longman: London, esp. Ch. 3: 'A method of analysis and some examples.'

Nakatani, K. (1981) 'Retrieved life–The Structure and Meaning of Katherine Mansfield's "The Fly"' (in Japanese) *The Journal of Faculty of School Education* Part 2, Vol. 4. Hiroshima University: Hiroshima.

Nishidai, M. (1972) 'The end of Katherine Mansfield–"The Fly" and "The Canary"' (in Japanese) *Albion* 18. Kyoto University: Kyoto.

Short, M. (1996) *Exploring the Language of Poems, Plays and Prose*. Longman: London.

Toolan, M (1998) *Language in Literature An Introduction to Stylistics*. Arnold:

London.
Wales, K. (1989, 2001) *A Dictionary of Stylistics*. Longman: London.

Centering and Dialogue: A Preliminary Analysis of Referring Expressions in a Parallel Corpus of English and Japanese Map Task Dialogues

Etsuko Yoshida

1. Introduction

Centering theory is one of the most influential models in computational linguistics, and it provides a framework in which a speaker's local focus of attention can be described in more coherent referring expressions. This paper discusses the results of applying the centering framework to a parallel corpus of English and Japanese Map Task Dialogues. The main aim of the analysis is to show that discourse coherence can be associated with a more interactional use of referring expressions in both English and Japanese data. My current question is how the form of referring expressions in a discourse interact with centering constraints such as the transition states of utterances. I investigate the transition states of centers of the utterances in both English and Japanese spontaneous dialogue data. Then I suggest that such transition states tend to be affected by intentional states of participants and global discourse structure rather than purely grammatical Cf-ranking realized as a local focus.

After giving an overview of centering theory in section 2, I will describe the data and coding system I adopt for a statistical analysis of the data in section 3. In section 4, I present problematic issues in applying centering theory to the dialogue data. Section 5 presents the results of a preliminary analysis of the distribution of transition states and comments on the extracts from each transition. I also discuss the correlations between referring expressions and center transitions in the centering framework. Finally, in section 6, I will suggest ways in which the choice and distribution of referring expressions in English and their Japanese counterparts can be explained in an interactive discourse model integrated into global discourse structure.

2. Centering Theory

Centering is a model of the conversant's center of attention in discourse that is concerned with the relationship of attentional state, inferential complexity, and the form of referring expressions (Walker, Joshi, and Prince 1998). What they call 'center' is distinguished into three different types: Cf (U_i, D), Cb (U_i, D), and Cp. The Cf (U_i, D) indicates the FORWARD-LOOKING CENTER, representing discourse entities evoked by an utterance U_i in a discourse segment D (Webber 1988; Prince 1981). The Cb (U_i, D) indicates the BACKWARD-LOOKING CENTER, which is a special member of Cf representing the discourse entity that the utterance U_i most centrally concerns. The Cb is the entity that can commonly correspond to what is called 'topic' in Givon's sense, i.e. the current focus of attention in the utterance. In other words, the Cb is presumed to be the most salient entity in the current utterance, and is thought of as 'a local topic by both the speaker and the addressee' (Brennan 1995). The Cp is the PREFERRED CENTER representing a prediction about the Cb of the following utterance.

These three centers structure three constraints, two rules and the typology of transition states (i.e. CONTINUE, RETAIN, SMOOTH-SHIFT and ROUGH-SHIFT) as presented and interpreted by Walker, Joshi, and Prince (1998: 3). Three constraints of centering are as follows:

1. There is precisely one backward-looking center Cb (U_i, , D).
2. Every element of the forward centers list, Cf (U_i, D), must be realized in U_i.
3. The center, Cb (U_i, D), is the highest-ranked element of Cf (U_{i-1}, D) that is realized in U_i.

Centering also includes two rules:

For each U_i in a discourse segment D consisting of utterances U_1..., Um:

Rule 1: If some element of Cf (U_{i+1}, D) is realized as a pronoun in U_i, then so is Cb (U_i, D)

Rule 2: Transition states are ordered. The CONTINUE transition is preferred to the RETAIN transition, which is preferred to the SMOOTH-SHIFT transition, which is preferred to the ROUGH-SHIFT transition.

Rule 1 captures the intuition that pronominalization is one way to indicate discourse salience, and that Cbs are often pronominalized or deleted. According to Kameyama (1985), zero pronouns in Japanese correspond to unaccented pronouns in English, and Rule 1 was extended directly to zero pronouns (Walker, Joshi, and Prince, 1998). The definition of transition states in Rule 2 is summarized in Table 1. Following Walker, Joshi, and Prince (1998: 6) I use the notation Cb (U_{i-1}) = [?] for the utterance where there is no Cb (U_{i-1}):

Table 1 Centering transition states, Rule 2 (Walker, Joshi and Prince 1998)

	Cb (U_i) = Cb (U_{i-1}) OR Cb (U_{i-1}) = [?]	Cb (U_i) ≠ Cb (U_{i-1})
Cb (U_i) = Cp (U_i)	CONTINUE	SMOOTH-SHIFT
Cb (U_i) ≠ Cp (U_i)	RETAIN	ROUGH-SHIFT

Thus, based on Rule 2, this distribution of transition states is related to a coherence link between two utterances, from more coherent to less coherent, which, Walker, Joshi and Prince (1998) suggest, should be schematized as follows:

CONTINUE > RETAIN > SMOOTH-SHIFT > ROUGH-SHIFT

As seen above, Walker, Joshi, and Prince (1998: 6) assume that 'the combination of the constraints, rules, and transition states makes a set of testable predictions about which interpretation of an utterance hearers will prefer because they require less processing'. Basically, I will analyze the way these two rules can hold in dialogic discourse and evaluate how much these rules can predict centers to maintain coherent referring expressions within the discourse segment and over the discourse segment boundaries. I will address several specific questions:

i) While Rule 1 predicts that speakers can use 'underspecified pronouns' such as definite pronouns (Passonneau 1996: 247), a full NP rather than pronouns is frequently used to continue the current Cb in real text (Walker 1998). Why does this occur?

ii) In the application of Rule 2, are pronouns really preferred more in CONTINUE transitions than in other transitions?

iii) In what type of transition are full NPs used?

iv) In what type of transition are deictic NPs used?

v) How do deictic expressions contribute to the discourse organisation from the view of transition states?

vi) Are there any typical patterns of transition shifting for the center to be carried over the discourse segment boundaries?

Based on transition states of the utterances in spontaneous dialogue data, a statistical analysis of centering transition will show that discourse coherence can be associated with more interactional use of referring expressions in both English and Japanese by using centering as a tool to track the flow of salience across the discourse segment.

3. Data

The findings reported in section 5 are based on a quantitative analysis of two corpora, one English and the other Japanese. The English corpus is a spontaneous dialogue called the Map Task Corpus (MTC) compiled by the Human Communication Research Center (HCRC), Edinburgh, UK. MTC is based on maps with landmarks. The total number of landmarks is eleven or twelve, and each landmark is labeled. Two participants had maps with various landmarks that were in some cases labeled differently on the two maps. One speaker played the role of instruction-giver describing a route to the instruction-follower, who then had to reproduce this route on his own map. The original corpus consists of recordings and transcriptions of 128 dialogues produced by speakers of Scottish English. Informants were 64 undergraduates of University of Glasgow, with a mean age of 20, both males and females. (See Anderson et al. 1991; Carletta et al. 1993; Deverell 1994; Miller and Weinert 1998) For the present study, I selected eight experimentally-collected dialogues based on maps that did not have written labels to identify the landmarks. This is a small set of data experimentally collected after completing the original MTC. One of the predictions is that the speakers in the labelless MTC, especially the giver, tend to use deictic pointers more frequently to describe the landmarks and explaining the routes between landmarks than the speakers in the labeled MTC.

The Japanese MTC has been conducted as a project at Chiba University (henceforth Chiba Corpus), Japan, since 1993, based on the Edinburgh MTC with respect to map and route designs and situational parameters such as familiarity and eye contact. As in the HCRC study, 128 dialogues have been collected (See Horiuchi et al. 1999). Following the specification and transcription policy of the Chiba Corpus, the small set of 8 dialogues based on the Japanese labelless MTC were collected at Mie University, Japan, using the same labelless maps as MTC and the same experimental design: familiar and unfamiliar pair of speakers; each participant plays a role as giver twice on the same map with different followers, and then as follower twice with different givers and different maps (See Yoshida 2002). In the Japanese data, I also predicted that there would be a number of deictic expressions that could be considered parallel in discourse function to the ones I assume in the English labelless MTC.

4. Centering and Dialogue Data

Most of the centering work targets naturally occurring utterances. The original research by Grosz and Sidner's (1986) stack model was based on task-oriented dialogue and discussed attentional states in discourse consisting of two levels of focusing: global and local, by introducing the notion of 'push' and 'pop'. However, their dialogue data is rather unnatural and their model of global focus cannot predict some phenomena that Walker (1998) points out. There are more studies on centering based on narratives (Passonneau 1996, 1998; Walker 1998), but there are few studies that have attempted to extend the model to multi-party discourse (Brennan 1998; Walker 1998; Byron and Stent 1998). Obviously, dialogue needs special treatment in applying to the data in the sense that the conversant's center of attention is affected more directly by the other participants, and the discourse segment can be controlled by the speaker's turn and contextual information shared with the discourse participant. For example, the speaker boundary can be a potential candidate to decide the discourse segment boundary in the light of center-transition, but this is not always the case.

First of all, there are several issues to be considered in applying centering to the dialogue data. Byron and Stent (1998) mainly discuss the following problems:

1. 'Utterace boundaries are difficult to pin down in spoken dialogue, and their determination affects the Cf lists.'
2. 'Whether the dialogue participants, referred to via first and second person pronouns (1/2PPs), should be considered as 'discourse entities' and included in Cf.'
3. This may be related with the issue 1: 'Which utterance should be considered 'previous' for locating Cfn-1: the same speaker's previous utterance or the immediately preceding utterance, regardless of its speaker?'
4. 'What should be done with abandoned or partial utterances and those with no discourse entities?'

As a starting point, let us consider these issues and attempt to provide the preliminary base line in applying the centering framework to the Map Task dialogue.

Issue 1. Utterance boundaries

In both English and Japanese data, utterance boundaries can be defined as a finite clause, including at least the subject (whether explicit or implicit in form) and the verb regardless of whether the clause is subordinate or non-subordinate. Any partial utterance without any discourse entity, such as minor clauses, discourse markers, ellipsed items, and various cue phrases such as back channels are excluded. Utterance boundaries are not normally extended across the speaker boundary, though there are cases that appear to be one single utterance by more than one participant. For example, in the following extract, utterances TA3 and TA5 by the giver are two utterances rather than just one utterance broken by the follower's utterance TB4:

(1) English: Lleq4c8

*TA 3
if you go down to the bottom left hand corner of your page, >
*TB 4
Aha.
*TA 5
do you have a van?

TA3's utterance is syntactically a conditional clause followed by TA5's non-subordinate interrogative, but, functionally, TA3 is performed as an imperative implying the follower's acceptance *Aha*. In the following exchange, the follower's utterance of checking a specific entity *kuruma* appears to be completed by the giver's prompt utterance with topic marker and finite verbs. Is this exchange separate utterance or combined complete clause?

(2) Japanese: ab

G: kuruma no tokoro made ø nankashite kudasai
van GEN place to SUBJ go down south please
'(You) go down south to the place of a/the van, please.'
F: eto kuruma
eh van
'eh, a/the van.'
G: ø wa minami ni miemasu ka
SUBJ TOP south in see Q
'Do (you) see (a van) in the south?'

I regard this exchange as two complete utterances, because the follower's remention of the entity *kuruma* functions as a checking device, and this may cause the change of grammatical mood in giver's utterance perspective from imperative *kudasai* to interrogative *ka*.

Issue 2. Selection of items for Cf

In both English and Japanese data, I include all discourse entities of 'objects' that are referred to in the utterance for Cf. The determined elements of Cf are commonly ranked as Cf ordering. Based on Walker, Joshi and Prince (1998), I adopt this ranking in analyzing both English and Japanese data. Cf ranking for English is simply ordered by canonical word order:

Subject > Object (s) > Other

According to Kameyama's original proposal that zero pronouns in Japanese correspond to unaccented pronouns in English (Kameyama 1985), Rule 1 is extended directly to zero pronouns: 'If some element of Cf (U_{i+1}, D) is realized as a pronoun in U_i, then so is Cb (U_i, D)'. Cf ranking for Japanese is ordered by discourse function as follows (Walker, Iida and Cote 1994; Iida 1998):

(GRAMMATICAL OR ZERO) TOPIC > EMPATHY > SUBJECT > OBJECT2 > OBJECT > OTHERS

Regarding English data, I exclude discourse participants referred to by the first and second person pronouns as discourse entities for Cf, because those are considered to be outside the purview of the original centering framework. In Japanese data, on the other hand, since most of the first and second person pronouns are realized in subject position in either implicit forms or zero topic, I do not intend to retrieve them in the Cf lists. Hurewitz (1998) and Di Eugenio (1998) also touched upon the problem of how to deal with situational deictics such as *I* and *you* in terms of the Cf list, and Hurewitz concludes that *I* and *you* are always categorized as 'activated' in the sense of Gundel, Hedberg and Zacharski (1993), and do not match the real topic of utterances even if they are realized in the grammatical subject (1998: 279).

Issue 3. Previous utterances

I consider only the immediately preceding utterance as 'previous utterances', regardless of its speaker. Empty utterances containing no discourse entities are skipped in determining Cf. These empty utterances include acknowledgements such as *OK* and *Yes*, Japanese hesitations such as *etto* and *ano*, and utterances of explaining location such as *Three centimeters ... above the bottom of the page?*

Issue 4. Utterances without discourse entities

As I discussed in Issue 1 and Issue 3, I exclude any partial utterance and utterances with no discourse entities (i.e. empty utterances). However, discourse entities often occurring more spontaneously reflect the communicative interaction of the participants. Let us consider the following example:

(3) English: Lleq4c8

*TA 9
is, do you have a building directly below that? >
*TB 10
< Sort of like or something,
*TA 11
Yes.
*TB 12
cameras or something, /

Given that the utterance boundary is defined as a finite clause, the noun phrases TB 10 and TB 12 in example (3) will be excluded despite the assumption that they may be 'expanding' the giver's initial noun (Clark 1992) by adding more information to the first mentioned discourse entity *a building*. This shows, however, how the giver and the follower contribute to the discourse representation in establishing understanding where 'the speaker and addressee put in extra effort, generally together, to make sure the reference has been understood' (Clark, 1992). When these noun phrases are included as the Cf lists, the transition states will be SMOOTH-SHIFTs, because $Cb\ (U_i) = Cp\ (U_i)$ and $Cb\ (U_i) \subset Cb\ (U_{i-1})$. Incidentally, as seen in example (8) afterward, the Japanese subjectless clause including a zero pronoun with no topic marker will be regarded as an utterance unit regardless of whether the rest of the clause contains a finite verb or not.

5. Results and Analysis

This section discusses the findings. Out of 16 dialogues from English and Japanese MTC, Table 2 and 3 summarize the distribution of transition states in each dialogue data.

Table 2 English Map Task Dialogue (%)

Data no.	No Cb	CON-TINUE	RETAIN	SMOOTH-SHIFT	ROUGH-SHIFT	Total
Lleq4c2	39(41.9)	45(48.4)	1(1.1)	8(8.6)	0	93(100)
Lleq4c8	35(44.9)	36(46.2)	2(2.6)	5(6.4)	0	78(100)
Lleq4c1	16(19.3)	40(48.2)	0(0)	27(32.5)	0	83(100)
Lleq4c9	12(34.3)	16(45.7)	2(5.7)	5(14.3)	0	35(100)
Lleq4c3	19(41.3)	20(43.5)	1(2.2)	6(13.0)	0	46(100)
Lleq4c5	22(40.7)	28(51.9)	0	4(7.4)	0	54(100)
Lleq4c4	40(34.2)	46(39.3)	0	31(26.5)	0	117(100)
Lleq4c6	16(24.2)	37(56.1)	2(3.0)	11(16.7)	0	66(100)
Average	(35.1)	(47.4)	(1.8)	(15.7)	(0)	(100)

Table 3 Japanese Map Task Dialogue (%)

Data no.	No Cb	CON-TINUE	RETAIN	SMOOTH-SHIFT	ROUGH-SHIFT	Total
ab	26(32.1)	49(60.5)	4(4.9)	2(2.5)	0	81(100)
ac	14(29.2)	27(56.3)	3(6.3)	3(6.3)	1(2.1)	48(100)
cd	29(31.5)	56(60.9)	4(4.4)	3(3.3)	0	92(100)
cb	15(28.3)	33(62.3)	2(3.8)	3(5.7)	0	53(100)
ba	36(41.9)	33(38.4)	7(8.1)	10(11.6)	0	86(100)
bd	25(32.1)	33(42.3)	9(11.5)	8(10.3)	3(3.8)	78(100)
da	32(34.4)	53(57.0)	3(3.2)	5(5.4)	0	93(100)
dc	19(25.7)	34(45.9)	8(10.8)	12(16.2)	1(1.4)	74(100)
Average	(31.9)	(53.0)	(6.6)	(7.7)	(0.9)	(100)

As can be seen from the data in Table 2 and 3, a large percentage of transitions are CONTINUEs and NO Cbs in both English and Japanese: nearly half of the transitions are CONTINUEs (47.4% in English and 53.0% in Japanese on average) and at least 30 % on average of the utterances are found in NO Cbs. This also shows that RETAIN, SMOOTH-SHIFT, and ROUGH-SHIFT transitions occur infrequently. As is predicted, ROUGH-SHIFTs are very rare (less than 1 % in both data), but SMOOTH-SHIFTs are used more frequently than RETAINs and ROUGH-SHIFTs, especially in English data. This result is measured by the χ^2 test. Null hypothesis H_0 states that there is no difference between these two samples other than that due to random sampling variations. Using the 0.01 and 0.05 significance level, the test statistic does not exceed the critical values, and H_0 is not rejected. Therefore, English and Japanese are not deemed to indicate different distribution.

Let us consider typical uses of referring expressions occurring in the three main transition states.

5.1. No Cb

NO Cbs (U_{i-1}), which mainly results from abrupt topic shifts, are usually used to refer to the entity as the first mention in the utterance as follows:

(4) English: Lleq4c8

*TA 168
{m Erm}... So where are {a y}... You've just finished at the top right /
*TB 169
Yeah, yeah.
*TA 170
right hand corner of the telephone box? >
*TA 171
< If you ... /
*TB 172
I've got a level crossing,

Here, the utterances *You've just finished at the top right/ right hand corner of the telephone box?* (TA168/170) and *I've got a level crossing* (TB 172) show a shift of real topic entities from *the telephone box* to *a level crossing*. One of the problems of NO Cbs is that centers are often continued over discourse segment boundaries with a full noun instead of pronouns occurring frequently after a brief interruption. The entities in the following example are highly coherent in the context of the utterance, but centering analyzes the second mention of an entity as no Cb:

(5) Lleq4c9

*TB 19
you got... Have you got a $bridge_i$? /
*TA 20
A $bridge_i$.
*TB 21
No? >
*TA 22
Yeah, but the $bridge_i$ is...
*TB 23
Above?
*TA 24
Is above. Do you have {a a} little $houses_j$ in the bottom?
*TB 25
No.
*TA 26
You don't. Okay then, maybe your explorer forgot to draw $that_j$ then.

{n laugh}. {m Erm} Well the safest thing is just go along the bottom of the page to the left hand corner, and then go up the page... Up the left hand side of the page until you're level with the bridge$_i$. And then you cross the bridge$_i$, moving over to the right.

In the utterances from TB 19 to TB 23, *the bridge* realizes a CONTINUE transition. After the introduction of initiating entity *little houses* in utterances TA 24 and TB 25, their center returns to *the bridge* in TA 26, which the hearer can easily recover because this is 'activated' in the sense of Gundel, Hedberg and Zacharski (1993). However, the centering fails to predict this. Similarly, in Japanese, the Cb of an utterance in a prior discourse segment is more likely to be rementioned by repeating the same full NP or by a deictic *sono* 'that' NP in the initial utterance of a return.

5.2. CONTINUE

Most common type of discourse entity realized in CONTINUE transitions is the landmark of the map in the context where the speakers confirm its existence or non-existence and describe its shape, its location, and the route to a target landmark. It is common that centers are often continued within a discourse segment with pronouns or zero pronouns, usually in subject position. Consider examples (6) and (7) below:

(6) English: Lleq4c8

*TA 42
Do you have anything in between the field$_i$ and that?
*TB 43
The field$_i$?
*TA 44
Well, the...
*TB 45
< Like hummocky grass type stuff. Hummocky
*TA 46
Directly below the derelict building?
*TB 47
ground like grass.>
*TB 48
< No. /
*TA 49
Where is it$_i$?
*TB 50
sort of... It's$_i$ {m um} the north westerly direction from there. >
*TA 51
[Above it?
*TB 52

{m Mm} above it.

The intended topic here is *anything* introduced by TA 42, but the hearer's attention turned to *the field* in TB 43, which is replaced with the pronoun *it* in TA 49 and TB 50, and then the subject is eliminated and the prepositional phrase *above it* is raised into topic position in TA 51 and TB 52. All the utterances from TA 46 to TB 52 are realized as CONTINUE transitions, with the exception of utterances TB 45 and 47, where the semantic meaning of *the field* is expanded: these can be analyzed as SMOOTH-SHIFTs.

(7) English: Lleq4c8

*TB 56
Yeah. there's {m erm} a building$_i$, has {c entrance} written on it.
*TA 57
Right, and where's that$_i$?
*TB 58
That$_i$ is...
*TA 59
Directly below the derelict building?

Here again the entity *the building* in TB 56 is replaced with the demonstrative pronoun *that* in TA 57 and TB 58 and then is shifted to the zero topic followed by prepositional phrase in TA 59. All the utterances from TA 57 to TA 59 realize a series of CONTINUE transitions. In the following example from Japanese data, on the other hand, the topic entity *a field* is replaced with a zero pronoun with no topic marker (i.e. zero topic) and the transition state remains as a CONTINUE by applying the rule of Zero Topic Assignment (Walker, Iida, and Cote, 1994).

(8) G: jaa to sono tatemono to kuruma no chikaku ni wa
so DEM (M) building and the van near TOPIC
'so near that building and the van'
hatake wa miemasu ka
fields TOPIC see Q
'So, near that building and the van do you see a field?'
F: to ø arimasu
SUBJ is
'There is (a field).'
G: ø arimasu ka
SUBJ is Q
'Is there a field?'
F: hai hai
yes yes

'yes, yes.'

In Japanese data, however, it is also common for centers to be continued by a bare NP within a discourse segment, usually at the subject position:

(9) G: kuruma wa dottchihoukou ni arimasu ka
a van TOPIC/SUBJ which direction to is Q
'To which direction is there a van?'
F: kuruma wa kita ni arimasu
the van TOPIC/SUBJ the north in is
'The van is in the north.'

5.3. SMOOTH-SHIFT

There are more utterances realized in SMOOTH-SHIFTs in English than those in Japanese data. Here may be a typical example from English data:

(10) English: Lleq4c9

*TA 28
And then... You go down towards the bottom of the page for about two centimetres... down your page... then along to the right, just for, maybe four centimetres. Then, do you have a little bit of broken fencing$_i$?
*TB 29
No.
Near the right hand side of the page?
*TB 31
Might, might be. {n laugh}
*TA 32
Well, something like that$_i$. Anyway, before you get there$_i$, you've got to like, go up towards the top of the page. Till you're about half way up the page.

As Clark (1992:123) categorizes the first full noun phrase into six distinct types, the initial mention of entities takes various forms of referring expressions. The entities being referred to in vague expressions, *a little bit of broken fencing* (TA28), *something like that* (TA32), and the deictic *there* (TA32) are analyzed as SMOOTH SHIFTs. Japanese data also contains these vague expressions, deictic NPs and deictic pronouns. There may be other types of expressions realized as SMOOTH-SHIFTs in Japanese, but an examination of every type will be discussed in later study.

6. Conclusion

In this paper, I have presented a corpus-based analysis of the distribution of discourse entities, and have found out that a large percentage of transitions are CONTINUEs and NO Cbs in both English and Japanese, and that RETAIN and SMOOTH- or ROUGH-SHIFT centering transitions are rather infrequent in both sets of data. This result indicates that centering behavior in dialogue data is basically consistent with that found in naturally occurring narrative discourse despite a number of grammatical differences between English and Japanese. Given this result, it appears that the transition states of utterances tend to be affected by intentional states of the participants and global discourse structure rather than purely grammatical Cf-ranking realized as a local focus. In dialogue, more specifically, discourse entities are more likely to have the CONTINUE transition than in narratives over the segment boundaries, and entities in the SMOOTH-SHIFT transition occur in highly coherent structures that often continue with the same local topic as the previous utterance.

However, the issues related to dialogue data in applying centering theory have not been completely solved yet. Particularly, the questions raised in section 2 remain open. Further investigation should reveal what kind of transitional states can indeed affect the interpretation of discourse entities in the form of coherent referring expressions, and to what extent other discourse factors such as connectives and cue phrases can affect the discourse organization in structuring and focusing the discourse segment.

References

Anderson, A. H., M. Bader, E. G. Bard, E. Boyle, G. Doherty, S. Garrod, S. Isard, Kowtdo, J. McAllister, J. Miller, C. Sotillo, H. Thompson, and R. Weinert (1991) "The HCRC Map Task Corpus." *Language and Speech*, 23 (3): 351-66.

Brennan, S. E. (1995) "Centering attention in discourse." *Language and Cognitive Processes,* 10: 137-167.

Brennan, S. E. (1998) "Centering as a Psychological Resource for Achieving Joint Reference in Spontaneous Discourse." In M. A. Walker, A. K. Joshi & E. F. Prince (eds.), *Centering Theory in Discourse*. Oxford: Clarendon Press. 227-249.

Byron, D and A. Stent (1998) "A Preliminary Model of Centering in Dialog." Technical Report 687, The University of Rochester CS Department. http://www.cs.rochester.edu/trs/ao-trs.html

Carletta, J., R. Caley, and S. Isard. (1993) "A collection of self-repairs from the Map Task Corpus." *Research Paper HCRC/TR*-47. Edinburgh: University of Edinburgh. (HCRC Publications)

Clark, H. H. (1992) *Arenas of Language Use*. Chicago: University of Chicago

Press.
Deverell, J. (1994) "Referring expressions in the Map Task Corpus." *Unpublished paper* (Center for Cognitive Science, University of Edinburgh)
Di Eugenio, B. (1998) "Centering in Italian." In M.A. Walker, A.K. Joshi & E.F. Prince (eds.), *Centering Theory in Discourse*. Oxford: Clarendon Press. 115-137
Grosz, B. J. and C. L. Sidner (1986) "Attentions, Intensions and the Structure of Discourse." *Computational Linguistics*, 12: 175-204.
Gundel, J. K., N. Hedberg and R. Zacharski. (1993) "Cognitive status and the form of referring expressions in discourse." *Language*, 69 (2): 274-307.
Horiuchi, Y., Y. Nakano, H. Koiso, M. Ishizaki, H. Suzuki, M. Okada, M. Naka, S. Tutiya, A. Ichikawa (1999) "Nihongo Chizu Kadai Corpus no Sekkei to Tokuchou." (The Design and Statistical Characterization of the Japanese Map Task Dialogue Corpus) *Jinkouchinou Gakkaishi (Journal of Artificial Intelligence Society)*, 14 (2): 261-271.
Hurewitz, F (1998) "A quantitative look at discourse coherence." In Walker M. A., A. K. Joshi and E. F. Prince (eds.), *Centering Theory in Discourse*. Oxford: Clarendon Press. 273-291.
Iida, M. (1998) "Discourse coherence and shifting centers in Japanese texts." In M. A. Walker, A. K. Joshi and E. F. Prince (eds.), *Centering Theory in Discourse*. Oxford: Clarendon Press. 161-180.
Kameyama, M. (1985) *Zero Anaphora: The Case of Japanese*. Ph.D. thesis, Stanford University.
Miller, J. and R. Weinert. (1998) *Spontaneous Spoken Language*. Oxford: Clarendon Press.
Passonneau, R. J. (1996) "Using Centering to Relax Gricean Informational Constraints on Discourse Anaphoric Noun Phrases." *Language and Speech*, 39, Special Double Issue on Discourse and Syntax, J. Delin and J. Oberlander (eds.), pts. I and 2: 229-65.
Passonneau, R. J. (1998) "Interaction of Discourse Structure with Explicitness of Discourse Anaphoric Noun Phrases." In M.A. Walker, A.K. Joshi and E.F. Prince (eds.), *Centering Theory in Discourse*. Oxford: Clarendon Press. 227-249
Prince, E. (1981) "Toward a taxonomy of given-new information." In P. Cole (ed.), *Radical Pragmatics*. New York: Academic Press. 223-56.
Walker, M. A. (1998) "Centering, anaphora resolution, and discourse structure." In M. A. Walker, A. K. Joshi and E. F. Prince (eds.), *Centering Theor in Discourse*. Oxford: Clarendon Press. 401-435
Walker, M. A., M. Iida and S. Cote (1994) "Japanese discourse and the process of centering." *Computational Linguistics*, 20: 193-232.
Walker, M. A., A. K. Joshi and E. F. Prince (eds.) (1998) *Centering Theory in Discourse*. Oxford: Clarendon Press.
Webber, B.L. (1988) 'Discourse deixis: reference to discourse segments,' *The 26th Annual Meeting of the Association for Computational Linguistics, Proceedings of the Conference*. 113-122.
Yoshida, E. (2002) "Nihongo Meishonashi Chizukadai Taiwa Corpus no Gaiyou

to Tenki Text no Sakusei: Houkoku." (An Outline and Transcription Text of Japanese Unlabelled Map Task Dialogue Corpus : A Report) *Jinbun Ronso* (*Bulletin of the Faculty of Humanities and Social Sciences, Mie University*, 19: 241-249)

Critical Linguistic Approaches to the British Press Reports on a Criminal Trial

HIROYUKI SAKAUCHI

1. Introduction

This paper presents some linguistic contributions to interpreting British press reports more closely and critically than a so-called 'normal' reader would do. The contents are as follows:

Section 2	Sources of the data
Section 3	Shifting patterns in modes of speech presentation
Section 4	Speech within speech: the embedded quotation
Section 5	To what extent is the press DS presentation faithful to the original utterance in the court?
Section 6	Reporters' social attitudes to the participants in the criminal case

2. Sources of the data

I shall refer to eight articles which appeared in the following newspapers on 27 April 2001, with the writer of each article in parentheses[1]:

National broadsheets	
- *The Daily Telegraph*	(Maurice Weaver)
- *The Independent*	(Jason Bennetto)
- *The Times*	(Oliver Wright)
Local broadsheet	
- *The Birmingham Post*	(Ross McCarthy)
National tabloids	
- *The Daily Express*	(Martin Stote)
- *The Evening Mail* <the early edition>	(Ross McCarthy)
- *The Evening Mail* <the late night final edition>	(Ross McCarthy)
- *The Sun*	(John Scott)

All of the articles were written about a criminal trial held at Birmingham Crown Court on 26 April 2001. In what follows, paragraph and sentence numbers are given to each passage cited from these texts. Thus, 'P1' and 'S7.2' mean 'the first paragraph' and 'the second sentence of the seventh paragraph' respectively. Due to limited space, here I quote only one text in full, the *Daily Express* article, in order to offer background information on the criminal trial to those who have no previous acquaintance with it:

The *Daily Express* article by Martin Stote

P1	ATHLETE Ashia Hansen told yesterday how a fake racist campaign allegedly planned by her former boyfriend disrupted her training for the Sydney Olympics.
P2	She flew to America two weeks after Chris Cotter, 29, and two other men are said to have staged a knife attack on him, partly in an attempt to rekindle his fading relationship with the triple jumper, a court heard.
P3	But during her stay in Florida with Cotter, where she was preparing for the Games, she was often reduced to tears, she told the jury yesterday.
P4	Miss Hansen said she was "shocked and upset" when she found that Cotter, who had suffered four wounds, was bleeding quite heavily from a cut to his forehead when he arrived at her home one night in an attempt at a reconciliation.
P5	The prosecution claim that Cotter, Surjit Singh Clair, 32, and Craig Wynn, 30, staged the attack and sent Miss Hansen and four other black athletes race hate mail.
P6	Miss Hansen, 30, who had earlier told the jury that she had been regarded as a "serious prospect" for a medal in the Sydney games, was asked by Tim Raggatt, QC, prosecuting at Birmingham Crown Court, if the events had disrupted her training.
P7 S7.1 S7.2 S7.3 S7.4	She replied: "I couldn't concentrate properly for part of my training. I was upset a lot. I would come to training in tears and things like that." The court heard how three weeks after allegedly staging the knife attack, Cotter had asked Miss Hansen to marry him while they were in Florida together.
P8 S8.1 S8.2 S8.3	She told the jury that she had declined, and he had then stopped talking to her. "I got upset. I went out of the room and went for a walk," she said.
P9	Mr Raggatt said that by the time of the trip to America, the police were already investigating apparent discrepancies in Cotter's story, and Miss Hansen may also have started to question the events.
P10 S10.1 S10.2	"By now, you may think the dawning of a suspicion was there in her mind," he told the jury. There had been conversations in which the question of whether Mr Cotter had been involved in some way

other than as a victim had cropped up."

P11 The prosecution claim that the three men hatched a confidence trick motivated by greed, in which they intended to sell the story about Cotter and Miss Hansen to the press.

P12 The Daily Express had been poised to pay for the story, but withdrew after demands were made for the money to be issued in cash.

P13 The day before Cotter flew to America, he and the other two men
S13.1 had been observed by plain-clothed policemen on a surveillance
S13.2 operation, meeting together for two hours in a pub in Walsall, West
Midlands. Miss Hansen, who the jury was told had known nothing of the alleged deception, and her ex-boyfriend were questioned by police about the press coverage of the story on their return from America.

P14 "He said he had been hounded by the Press, and chased through Birmingham like an episode from a TV programme, Starsky and Hutch," said Mr Raggatt.

P15 The three men are alleged to have colluded to market the story and organised a meeting in a hotel in Birmingham to do so, the court was told.

P16 Cotter, from Bromford in Birmingham, Clair, from Walsall, West Midlands and Wynn from Kingstanley, Birmingham all deny conspiracy to pervert the course of justice and attempting to obtain property by deception.

P17 Mr Raggatt said their plot had been motivated by an attempt to make money, possibly notoriety and to dupe Miss Hansen.

P18 But he added: "It was a failure. It had very serious overtones of
S18.1 using as the means of deception the manipulation and misuse of
S18.2 what some people call the race card. That's a scandalous thing to do,
S18.3 if it's what happened.

P19 "It prays upon deeply-held sensitivities, and causes great distress in many quarters and causes people to take things extremely seriously and to investigate them with great care."

P20 The trial continues.

3. Shifting patterns in modes of speech presentation

The largest component of a newspaper article about a trial is, by its nature, reports of speech by the people concerned such as the defendant, the prosecutor, etc. This suggests that a speech-presentation analysis of such an article is one of the ways in which linguistics can contribute to our better understanding of it.

This section explores the linguistic and textual properties of the above-quoted *Daily Express* report, with special focus on the shifting patterns in modes of speech rendering, and suggests how these properties accord with the writer's intention to control the reader's process of decoding messages from the report.

3.1. Framework

This analysis adopts the categories of speech presentation in Semino *et al.* (1997) which itself draws heavily on the categories proposed in Leech and Short (1981: 318-51), though adding two: Narrator's Report of Voice (NV) and Narrator's Representation of Speech Act with Topic (NRSAT) as follows[2]:

> Narrator's Report of Voice (NV)
> Narrator's Representation of Speech Act (NRSA)
> Narrator's Representation of Speech Act with Topic (NRSAT)
> Indirect Speech (IS)
> Free Indirect Speech (FIS)
> Direct Speech (DS)
> Free Direct Speech (FDS)
>
> A '**Q**' which may be added to any of the above abbreviations (except DS and FDS) shows the presence of a direct quotation embedded inside the relevant category.

Here I briefly explain NV, NRSAT and 'Q' phenomenon, borrowing examples from Semino *et al.* (1997), with the parts of speech presentation in bold type:

(i) **We spoke to vice madam Michaela Hamilton from Bullwell, Notts,** who arranged girls for a Hudson orgy at the Sanam curry house in Stoke. (*The News of the World* <NV>)

(ii) **Mr Major warned yesterday of the dangers of Britain being left behind if a group of European Union members pushed ahead with a single currency.** (*The Independent on Sunday* <NRSAT>)

As in (i), NV serves to capture 'references to the fact that a particular character/person engaged in some form of verbal activity' or 'general references to speech events that involved a large number of participants' (Semino *et al.*: §4.1). NRSAT, the sub-category of NRSA, is employed to capture 'all those cases where there is no reported clause but where the report of the speech act is accompanied by an explicit indication of the subject-matter of the utterance or utterances in question' (Semino *et al.*: §5.1). In (ii), the speech act verb *warned* is followed by the details of the content of the utterance in the form of complex noun phrases.

The primary reason why I employ this framework is that it enables the analyst to capture 'embedded quotation phenomena ('Q')' (Semino *et al.*: §5.2). Two illustrations will suffice:

(iii) He said the decision to discipline the rebels was "certainly not a mistake," (*The News of the World* <ISQ>)
(iv) The President of the Board of Trade accused Labour of "undermining the very fabric of our political constitution." (*The Independent* <NRSATQ>)

Example (iii) is ISQ where a quotation is embedded in IS. (iv) is NRSATQ in which a quotation is incorporated into NRSAT. I will study this intriguing 'Q' phenomenon closely in Section 4, but not in this section where the central focus is placed on the transitional patterns in modes of speech presentation.

3.2. Analysis and discussion

This section provides a descriptive analysis of only the first eight paragraphs of the *Daily Express* article due to limits of space. The result is shown in the table as below:

Posi-tion	Text	Speech presen-tation	Textual function
P1	ATHLETE Ashia Hansen told yesterday how a fake racist campaign allegedly planned by her former boyfriend disrupted her training for the Sydney Olympics.	NRSAT	Introductory summary of a topic
P2	She flew to America two weeks after Chris Cotter, 29, and two other men are said to have staged a knife attack on him, partly in an attempt to rekindle his fading relationship with the triple jumper, a court heard	NRSA	Specification of the topic
P3	But during her stay in Florida with Cotter, where she was preparing for the Games, she was often reduced to tears, she told the jury yesterday.	IS	Specification of the topic
P4	Miss Hansen said she was "shocked and upset" when she found that Cotter, who had suffered four wounds, was bleeding quite heavily from a cut to his forehead when he arrived at her home one night in an attempt at a reconciliation.	ISQ	Specification of the topic

P5	The prosecution claim that Cotter, Surjit Singh Clair, 32, and Craig Wynn, 30, staged the attack and sent Miss Hansen and four other black athletes race hate mail.	IS	Specification of the topic
P6	Miss Hansen, 30, who had earlier told the jury that she had been regarded as a "serious prospect" for a medal in the Sydney games, was asked by Tim Raggatt, QC, prosecuting at Birmingham Crown Court, if the events had disrupted her training.	IS (with the relative clause in ISQ)	Specification of the topic
S7.1, 7.2, 7.3	She replied: "I couldn't concentrate properly for part of my training. I was upset a lot. I would come to training in tears and things like that."	DS	Conclusion of the topic with DS
S7.4	The court heard how three weeks after allegedly staging the knife attack, Cotter had asked Miss Hansen to marry him while they were in Florida together.	NRSAT	Introductory summary of another sub-topic
S8.1	She told the jury that she had declined, and he had then stopped talking to her.	IS	Specification of the topic
S8.2, 8.3	"I got upset. I went out of the room and went out and went for a walk," she said.	DS	Conclusion of the topic with DS

As this table reveals, this report opens with an NRSAT paragraph (the summary of a participant's speech on a topic), continues with another NRSA paragraph and then slips into four IS paragraphs for the progressive specification of the topic and concludes with three DS sentences that give the reader an impression of being a faithful report of the original speech.

The reason for the use of this kind of transitional pattern is perhaps partly the writer's aim of prolonging the reader's curiosity about the topic as much as possible, by shifting from the least definite and the least direct mode to the most definite and the most direct one. Furthermore, the writer may also wish to add variety to the modes of speech presentation in order to avoid the monotony which would result from repeating the same propositional content of the same speech.

To conclude this section, I would like to admit that the *Daily Express* text has been selected for analysis because it is the only one among all the articles collected that manifests a straightforward shifting pattern in the modes of speech presentation. The other articles exhibit more complicated patterns in the shifts of the modes. Nonetheless, my analysis has proved that to read newspaper reports in speech-presentational terms is one of the useful ways of interpreting them with a critical linguistic awareness.

4. Speech within speech: the embedded quotation

Semino *et al.* account for the effects of the embedded quotation ('Q') phenomena in the press as follows:

> [The 'Q' forms of speech presentation] allow the reporter to foreground selected parts of the original utterance without having to provide a lengthy quotation. They achieve vividness and precision without sacrificing the need for brevity. (1997:§5.2)

There are some embedded quotations in the data I collected:

[NRSATQ = Quotation embedded in NRSAT]:

(1) Birmingham Olympic triple jumper Ashia Hansen told a court yesterday of her disgust at discovering that a story about a "racist attack" on her former boyfriend had been leaked to a newspaper. (*The Birmingham Post* P1)

[ISQ = Quotation embedded in IS]:

(2) Miss Hansen said she was "shocked and upset" when she found that Cotter, who had suffered four wounds, was bleeding quite heavily from a cut to his forehead when he arrived at her home one night in an attempt at a reconciliation. (*The Daily Express* P4)

(3) Ashia, 29, told Birmingham Crown Court she DID start sleeping with him again because "I suppose I felt sorry for him". (*The Sun* P3)

(4) But the prosecution said she turned down his proposal as the "dawning of suspicion" was in her mind. (*The Sun* P4)

(5) It is claimed the debt-ridden financial adviser and two pals invented a race-hate gang which they said "targeted" Cotter as a famous black girl's white boyfriend. (*The Sun* P6)

[IS with a relative clause in ISQ]:

(6) Miss Hansen, 30, who had earlier told the jury that she had been regarded as a "serious prospect" for a medal in the Sydney games, was asked by Tim Raggatt, QC, prosecuting at Birmingham Crown Court, if the events had disrupted her training. (*The Daily Express* P6)

According to the corpus study of speech presentation by Semino *et al.*

(1997:§5.2), the 'Q' feature may be found within all of the categories except DS and FDS. However, there occur clear though marginal instances of this feature within DS in my data. Note the embedded quotations 'yes' in (7) and 'Yeah' in (8):

[DSQ = Quotation embedded in DS]:

(7) Ms Hansen described the aftermath of the attack in March last year: "He was coming up my drive. He was bent over double holding his head.

"I could see he was bleeding and asked what had happened. I asked if he had been mugged and he said 'yes'. That night when Chris went up to the ward he told me that he did not want me to go home. That's when he told me it was a racist attack because he was going out with me." (*The Times* P6-7)

(8) She [Ashia Hansen] said: "I asked if he had been mugged and he said, 'Yeah' but didn't give any details." (*The Sun* P9)

In formal terms, both the words 'yes' and "Yeah" are considered to be reported by Hansen since they are embedded in her DS. However, it is not impossible to imagine that either the *Times* writer or the *Sun* writer has changed the word 'yes' into 'Yeah' or the other way around, thus manipulating her DS.

My data further shows that this embedded feature itself is not restricted to direct quotations. In other words, pieces of speech cast in other modes of speech presentation are also incorporated into different speeches cast in different modes. Here are examples of this kind, with the embedded speeches in boldface:

[NRSA embedded in DS]:

(9) Asked how he had appeared that night she said: "He was calm. He was not panicking or anything like that. **He just asked me to call an ambulance**. ..." (The late night final edition of *The Evening Mail* P6)

[NRSA embedded in IS]:

(10) Ms Hansen said **Cotter had not told her what had happened initially**... . (*The Birmingham Post* P12)

[IS embedded in DS]:

(11) "**Clair said that the police were going to leak the story to the newspaper and that we should leak it first**," she said. (*The Birmingham Post* P16)

(12) "**He said he had been hounded by the Press, and chased through Birmingham like an episode from a TV programme, Starsky and Hutch**," said Mr Raggatt. (*The Daily Express* P14)

[IS embedded in IS]:

> (13) Ms Hansen said **Cotter initially maintained that the incident had nothing to do with her and their relationship** and asked her to contact Clair. (*The Birmingham Post* P14)

[ISQ embedded in IS]:

> (14) She agreed that both her [*sic*] and Cotter had an extremely strong physical attraction for one another and that when **her former boyfriend told her the "attack" on him had been racially motivated** both of them had cried. (The late night final edition of *The Evening Mail* P11)

As regards (13), in formal terms the verb *maintain* shows Hansen's doubt about the report that **the incident had nothing to do with her and their relationship**, thus expressing her evaluation of the report (Thompson 1994: §2.40 ff.). It is, however, unclear whether the use of this evaluative reporting verb is her own choice or the writer's[3].

The reason why the type of embedded phenomenon I have pointed out in the examples from (9) to (14) arises in media reports is easy to appreciate. In essence, a news report on a trial is a story told by a reporter on the trial which itself consists of stories by the parties concerned. It is in this double-decker narrative situation (i.e. the press narrative layered onto the court narrative) that the embedded feature tends to occur.

To sum up the main point, this section has demonstrated that every kind of embedded phenomenon in speech presentation inserts narrative screens between the reader and the original speech, thus increasing the distance between them. Therefore, in reading passages of embedded speeches in a news story on a trial, it is important to be careful about whose point of view we are dealing with: here, the defendant's or the plaintiff's or the reporter's, etc.

5. To what extent is the press DS presentation faithful to the original utterance in the court?

In this section I investigate the press DS presentation and the conditions of its faithfulness to the original utterance in the court. As Semino *et al.* comment, with DS, it is conventionally assumed that a reporter faithfully represents the original utterance. However, they further point out:

> [I]t is well-known that not all instances of DS are accurate word-by-word representations of the original utterance. In essence, pragmatic

> criteria affect how accurate such quotations are. Obvious factors would be distance in time from the original speech situation, the size of the original utterance and how important it is to get the representation exactly right (for example, it is important to be accurate in public pronouncements and matters which might offend or even induce legislation, but such exactness is not usually important in casual private conversation). (1997: §3)

Since the utterances in the court are of crucial importance and sharply different from casual conversation, one may expect a DS presentation of such utterances in the press to be achieved accurately on a word-by-word basis. In order to test this view, here are three DS (or FDS) instances of what is supposedly the same original utterance given by Ashia Hansen:

(15) "He was bent double, holding his head. I thought he was messing about because he was bent double and because he carried on still bent double," she said. "I panicked **then** because I **knew** something was wrong, so I ran to the front door. He was on the drive and he was bleeding. I asked what had happened." (*The Independent* S6.3-6.7; written by Jason Bennetto)

(16) "He was bent double, holding his head. I though [*sic*] he was messing about because he was bent double and because he carried on still bent double.

"I panicked **then** because I **knew** something was wrong, so I ran to the front door. He was on the drive and he was bleeding. I asked what had happened." (*The Birmingham Post* P10-11; written by Ross McCarthy)

(17) Miss Hansen said she knew nothing of the incident until Cotter arrived bleeding from his wounds.

"He was bent **over** double, holding his head. I thought he was messing about. **Then** I panicked because I **could see** something was wrong." (*The Daily Telegraph* S7.2-P8; written by Maurice Weaver)

The instances of DS in (15) and (16) are quite similar. But there are certain differences between these two cases and (17). For example, we notice a few lexical differences (**knew**, **could see**, **over**). There are differences in their propositional contents as well. Notably, the DS stretch in (17) is much shorter than in the other two. The analysis so far might incline the reader to think that examples (15) and (16) are more faithful to the original utterance than (17) is.

However, compare the positional differences of the adverb **then** in the three examples:

(15)′ "I panicked **then** ..." (*The Independent*)
(16)′ "I panicked **then** ..." (*The Birmingham Post*)

(17)′ "… **Then** I panicked …" (*The Daily Telegraph*)

Since this adverb signals the textual cohesion between the foregoing sentence and the current one, it is natural for this adverb to stand at the beginning of the sentence as in (17) and not at the medial position as in (15) and (16)[4]. Analysing in this way, now the principle of linguistic naturalness might tempt the reader to consider (17) to be more faithful to the original utterance than the other two. However, it is still possible that Hansen may have used this adverb medially as in (15) and (16) if she had slowly and carefully chosen her words and sentence structures. In (15) the foregoing sentence and the sentence including the adverb **then** are split into two quotations. In (16) the preceding sentence and the sentence including the adverb **then** are separated into two paragraphs. This may imply that Hansen had a short moment of pause between the two sentences. On the other hand, in (17) it could be imagined that when for some reason or other the writer decided to truncate her spoken sentences and put them into one quotation, he was forced to transpose this adverb to the initial position for the sake of natural cohesion. Having considered these various factors, perhaps DS instances in (15) and (16) are more faithful representations of Hansen's original utterance than (17). But who knows except for the people who attended the trial?

It is sufficient in this section to point out that even DS presentation (or preferably *re*presentation) of an important participant's important utterance in an important criminal trial is not always faithful to the original utterance.

6. Reporters' social attitudes to the participants in the criminal case

In order to investigate the reporters' social attitudes to the parties in the criminal case, this final section takes a rather selective approach to the way in which the proper names **Ashia Hansen** and **Christopher Cotter** are titled by the reporters. The findings are tabulated as below:

The press type	Newspaper article	Article writer	Hansen's title	Cotter's title
National broadsheets	*The Independent* *The Times* *The Daily Telegraph*	J. Bennetto O. Wright M. Weaver	Ms Ms Miss	Mr Mr No title

Local broadsheets	*The Birmingham Post*	R. McCarthy	Ms	No title
National tabloids	*The Evening Mail* (Early edition)	R. McCarthy	Miss	No title
	The Evening Mail (Late night final edition)	R. McCarthy	Miss	No title
	The Daily Express	M. Stote	Miss	No title
	The Sun	J. Scott	No title	No title

In the national and local broadsheets, Hansen is always given the title **Ms** except in *The Daily Telegraph* where she is titled **Miss**. In the national tabloids, she is always granted the prefix **Miss** except in *The Sun* in which she is given no title and nearly always called by her first name **Ashia** only.

It is noteworthy that Hansen is titled **Ms** in *The Birmingham Post* and **Miss** in the early and the late night final editions of *The Evening Mail* all of which were written by Ross McCarthy. Notably, the two articles in *The Birmingham Post* and *The Evening Mail* (early edition) are quite similar except in the writer's titling practice. This difference in the title given to a single woman might reflect the house styles of the two newspapers rather than those of individual writers because both of them were written by the same reporter.

As regards Christopher Cotter, this accused person is granted the honorific title **Mr** only by two national broadsheets, *The Independent* and *The Times*.

This section suggests that newspaper reports are not only filtered through the writer's viewpoint but also influenced by the individual house ideologies in a broad sense.

7. Conclusion

This paper has pointed out the validity of certain critical linguistic approaches to and interpretations of some aspects of the British press reports on a criminal court case. The findings of the small-scale investigations made in the preceding sections have illuminated the double-or even multi-layered narrative situation in which the press stories were created.

Notes

* This paper is a revised version of my narrative analysis essay submitted

to the Postgraduate School of English at the University of Birmingham in 2001.

1 Since both articles, one from *The Birmingham Post* and the other from the early edition of *The Daily Mail*, were written by the same reporter and are similar in most respects, I will not deal with the latter in any sections except in Section 6 which includes a comparative discussion of these articles.

2 Here it would be also possible to employ more comprehensive frameworks of discourse presentation invented by Whynne *et al.* (1998) or by Short *et al.* (2002). However, in a small-scale study such as this section, the model in Semino *et al.* (1997) is the one I can work with most comfortably.

3 For a corpus-driven study of evaluative reporting verbs in British newspaper and magazine articles, see Sakauchi (2003).

4 According to M. Coulthard's seminal paper (1994) on forensic linguistics, the sequence *Then I* occurs ten times as often in the Bank of English spoken corpus as the sequence *I then* does. See also Hunston (2002:130-32), which summarises and supports his analysis.

References

Biber, D., *et al.* (1999) *Longman Grammar of Spoken and Written English.* London: Longman.

Caldas-Coulthard, C. R. (1994) "On reporting reporting" in M. Coulthard (ed.) *Advances in Written Text Analysis.* London: Routledge, 295-308.

Coulthard, M. (1994) "On the use of corpora in the analysis of forensic texts" *Forensic Linguistics* 1: 27-44.

Fairclough, N. (1995) *Media Discourse.* London: Arnold.

Fairclough, N. (1995) *Critical Discourse Analysis.* London: Longman.

Fairclough, N. (2001) *Language and Power.* 2nd ed. London: Pearson Education.

Fowler, R. (1991) *Language in the News.* London: Routledge.

Hunston, S. (2000) "Evaluation and the Planes of Discourse" in S. Hunston and G. Thompson (eds.) *Evaluation in Text.* Oxford: Oxford UP, 176-207.

Hunston, S. (2002) *Corpora in Applied Linguistics.* Cambridge: Cambridge UP.

Leech, G. N. and M. H. Short. (1981) *Style in Fiction.* London: Longman.

Lodge, D. (1996) *The Practice of Writing.* London: Secker and Warburg.

Montgomery, M., *et al.* (2000) *Ways of Reading.* 2nd ed. London: Routledge.

Reah, D. (1998) *The Language of Newspapers.* London: Routledge.

Sakauchi, H. (2003) "Averral and the Verbs of Attribution in Written Text" *ERA* New Series 20 (1&2): 1-17.

Semino, E., *et al.* (1997) "Using a Computer Corpus to Test a Model of Speech and Thought Presentation" *Poetics* 25: 17-43. Online on 27 Feb. 2001 at [http://www.comp.lancs.ac.uk/computing/users/eiamjw/stop/papers/index.html]

Short, M., *et al.* (1996) "Using a Corpus for Stylistics Research" in J. Thomas and M. Short (eds.) *Using Corpora for Language Research.* London: Longman, 110-31.

Short, M., *et al.* (2002) "Revisiting the notion of faithfulness in discourse presentation using a corpus approach" *Language and Literature* 11 (4):325-55.

Simpson, P. (1993) *Language, Ideology and Point of View*. London: Routledge.

Thompson, G. (1994) *Collins Cobuild English Guides 5: Reporting*. London: HarperCollins.

Toolan, M. (2001) *Narrative*. 2nd ed. London: Routledge.

Wynne, M., *et al.* (1998) "A Corpus-based Investigation of Speech, Thought and Writing Presentation in English Narrative Texts" in A. Renouf (ed.) *Explorations in Corpus Linguistics*. Amsterdam: Rodopi, 231-45.